AF473953

Americana

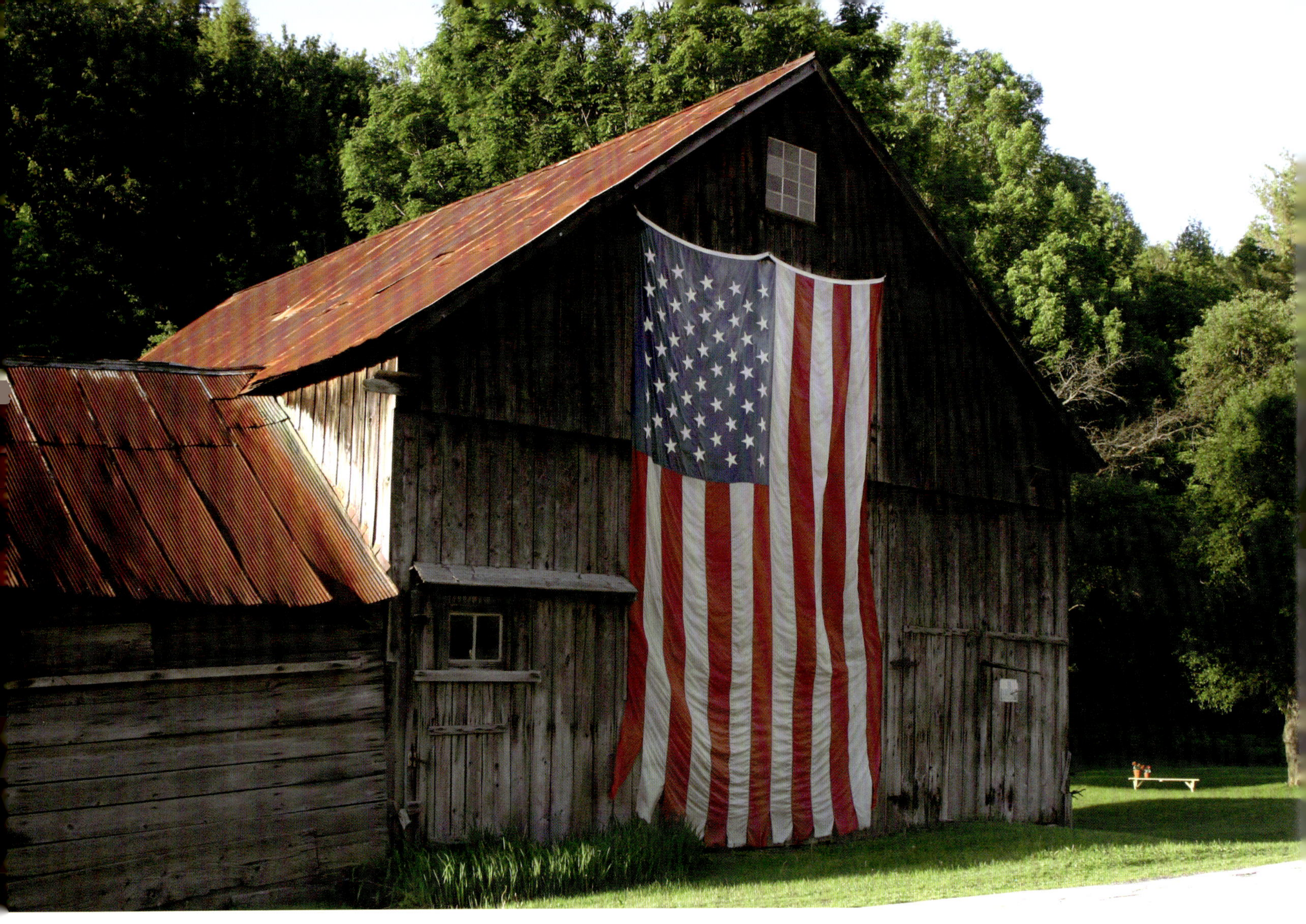

BARN WITH AMERICAN FLAG, Stockbridge, Vermont, 6/13/09

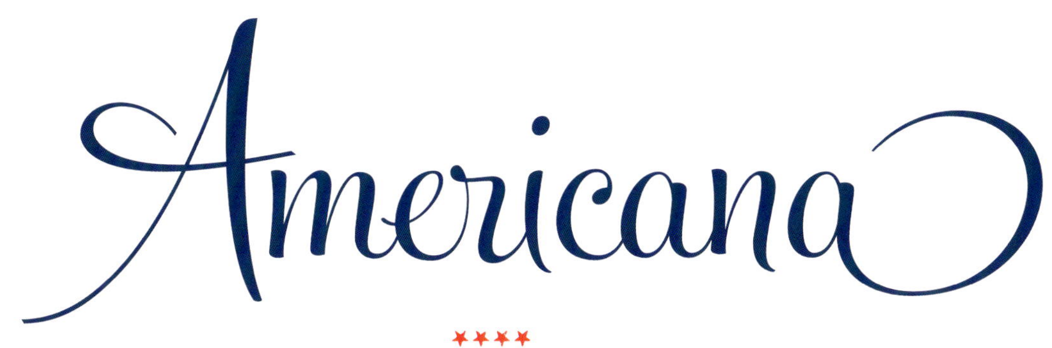

MATHEW TEKULSKY

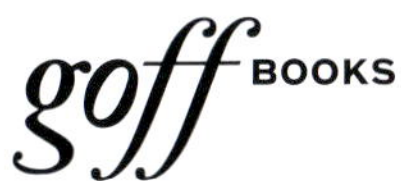

To my mother,

Patience Fish Tekulsky,

who accompanied me when

I took many of the photographs

that are in this book.

"*Americana* is any collection of materials and things concerning or characteristic of the United States or of the American people, and is representative or even stereotypical of American culture as a whole."

—*Wikipedia*

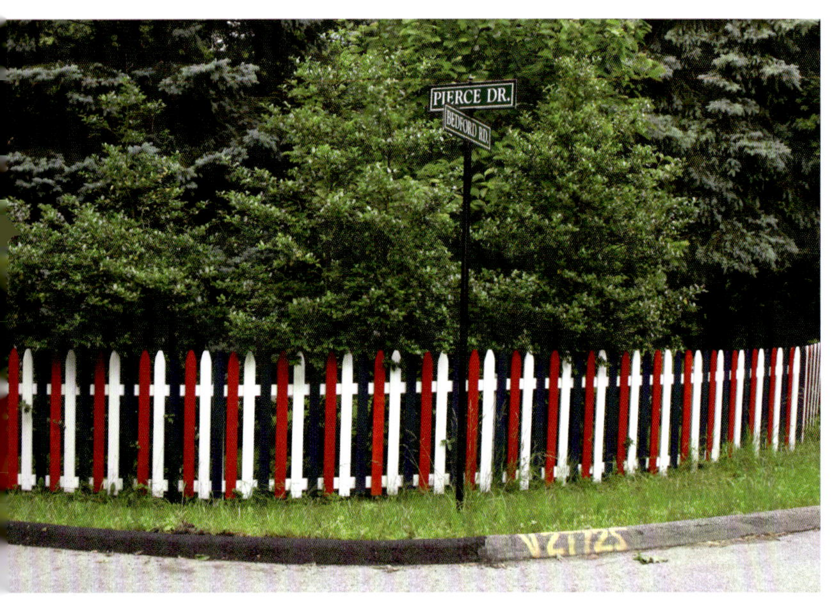
PIERCE DR.
BEDFORD RD.

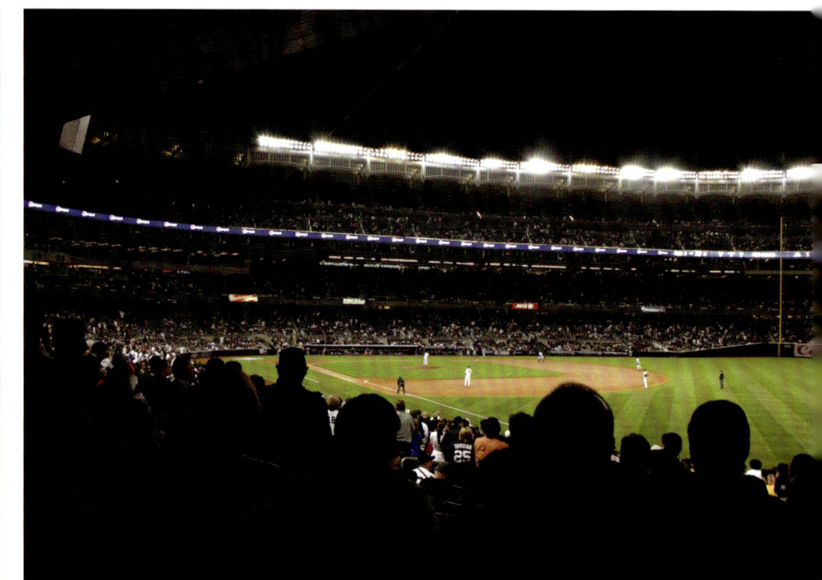

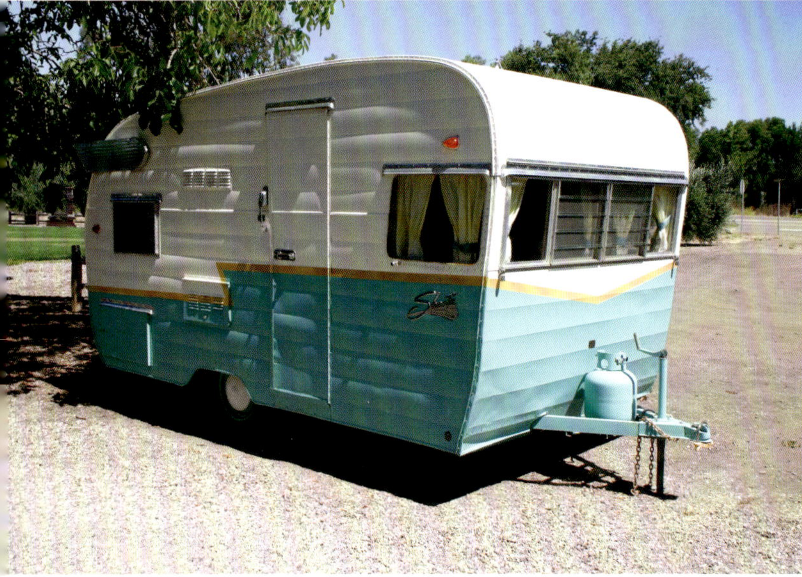

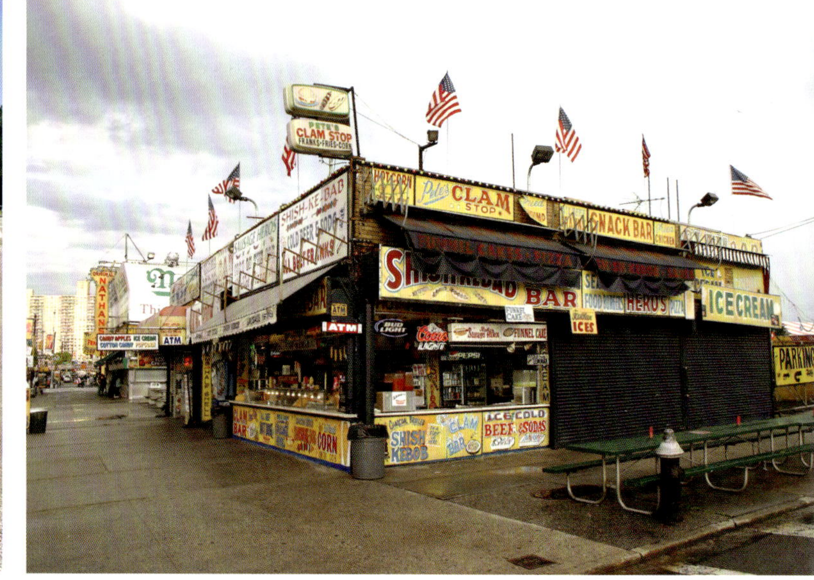
PETE'S
CLAM STOP
Pete's CLAM STOP
SHISH-KE-BAB
SNACK BAR
BAR
HERO'S
ICECREAM
ICES
ATM
SHISH KEBOB
CLAM BAR
CORN
ICE COLD BEER & SODAS
PARKING

Contents

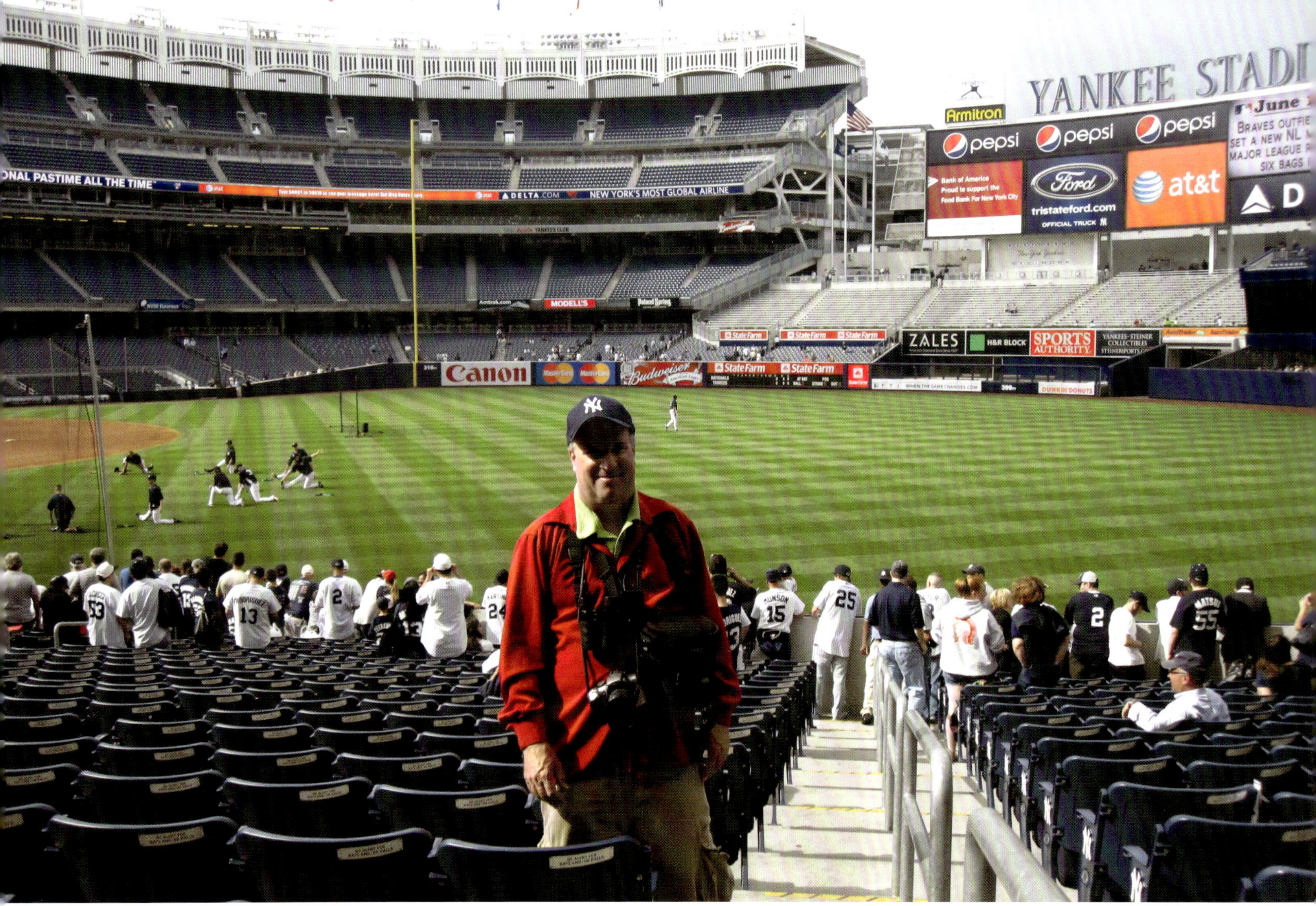

MATHEW TEKULSKY, Yankee Stadium, New York City, 6/16/09. Photograph courtesy of the author.

Introduction

★★★★

The history of American photography is highlighted by Robert Frank's iconic book *The Americans*, which was first published in the United States in 1959. This book included 83 photographs of quintessential American people and places, taken while Frank traveled around the country on a Guggenheim Fellowship.

In Americana: A Photographic Journey, I present 83 of my own photographs of American people and places. Each of these images is a moment in time in the American landscape, from Vermont and New York City to Los Angeles and Hawaii.

But what is Americana? To me, Americana involves anything that captures the true spirit of our nation, which was founded on individuality and has been developed through the hard work and persistence of its people. Americana can include the American flag and baseball, but it is also seen in buildings, cars, trucks, signs, fashion, politics, and even surfing. Examples of all of this are presented in these photographs, from a burger truck at Diamond Head in Honolulu to John Lennon's *Imagine* mosaic in New York City.

In Frank's book, the American flag is featured at certain points, and I have included a number of American flags in this book as well. There is something about that red, white, and blue (even if it is painted on a fence) that represents what America is all about. But a good Americana photograph cannot rely solely on an American flag.

In Brooklyn, for instance, two young girls purchase ice cream from a Van Leeuwen truck; in Coney Island, we see the Cyclone roller coaster; in Manhattan, we look out from the entrance of the Time Warner Center at the majesty of Columbus Circle; and no trip to New York City would be complete without taking in a New York Yankee baseball game, in this case with Mariano Rivera pitching his team to victory with yet another save.

In Fort Ann, New York, I photographed a rusty International Harvester truck and a 1962 Ford Falcon, both of which were sitting in a field; and in Fultonham, an inflatable Uncle Sam greeted me from the front yard of a white clapboard house that was festooned with red, white, and blue buntings along with an American flag.

In Stockbridge, Vermont, I saw an enormous American flag on the side of a barn along the roadway. Vermont, of course, has numerous barns and country stores, as well as roadside food vendors, maple syrup makers, and covered bridges. All of these subjects are presented here, including a restaurant named Thelma & Louise and another called the Farmers Diner. Antique cars, woodpiles, and peaches in a co-op also exemplify the rural aspect of Americana, not to mention golf clubs for sale and pumpkins on display.

In honor of America's greatest nature writer, John Burroughs, I have included two photographs: one of a small house on his family's dairy farm in Roxbury, New York, which he called Woodchuck Lodge; and another of his Slabsides cabin, in West Park, New York, where he wrote, explored the natural history of his surroundings, and entertained growing legions of nature enthusiasts.

Out West, we visit a Mormon homestead and a pioneer cabin, both of which are located in Grand Teton National Park. Then, in Southern California, we have an assortment of images, including a roller coaster at twilight on the Santa Monica Pier; the Beverly Hills Hotel; a "God Bless the Gipper" memorial to President Ronald Reagan; a French crepe stand at the Farmers Market; a brown tile with Clint Eastwood's name on it; and a Chevy Nova station wagon.

American flags abound in a display at Pepperdine University in Malibu; with the Jewish war veterans at the Los Angeles National Cemetery on Memorial Day; and on the exterior wall of an abandoned Ford dealership. The day before Senator John McCain lost his bid to become President of the United States, I captured an image of a sign on the garden wall of a house in Santa Monica that proclaimed him to be a "True American Hero."

In other areas of Southern California, we see the Queen Mary in Long Beach; a vendor at Angel Stadium in Anaheim; cowboy boots and a turquoise trailer in the tiny hamlet of Los Olivos; and a roadside stand with persimmons in Gaviota.

Venturing north into the Sierra Nevada Mountains, a tourist reaches out her hand with a camera at Tunnel View in Yosemite National Park; a giant fiberglass bull that served as a barbeque stand sits on a trailer in Three Rivers; and nearby, an abandoned Richfield gas station looks forlorn in the foothills of Sequoia National Park.

In Northern California, vintage flight attendant uniforms are featured in a museum display in San Francisco; a fruit and nut vendor offers his wares on the road to Mount Tamalpais; and a rooftop in Ukiah urges travelers to "Wake Up and Smell the Coffee!"

In Hawaii, we have three girls being photographed at the USS Arizona Memorial at Pearl Harbor; a hygienic store on the road to the north shore of Oahu; and a row of surfboards attached to a fence.

There is a great variety of scenes and subjects in this book, and yet, all of it is American to the core. However, in contrast to Robert Frank's pessimistic and cynical view of America, I choose to make photographs that show the optimism and generous spirit of our people. Each of these images has a story to tell, and I hope you enjoy experiencing through these photographs the spirit of America as much as I enjoyed taking the pictures.

Los Angeles, 2021

Photographic Journey

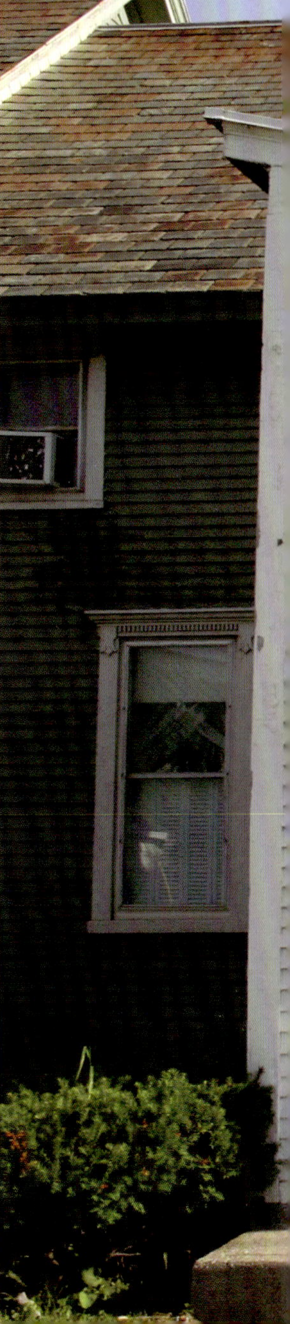

THELMA & LOUISE, Rutland, Vermont, 6/13/09

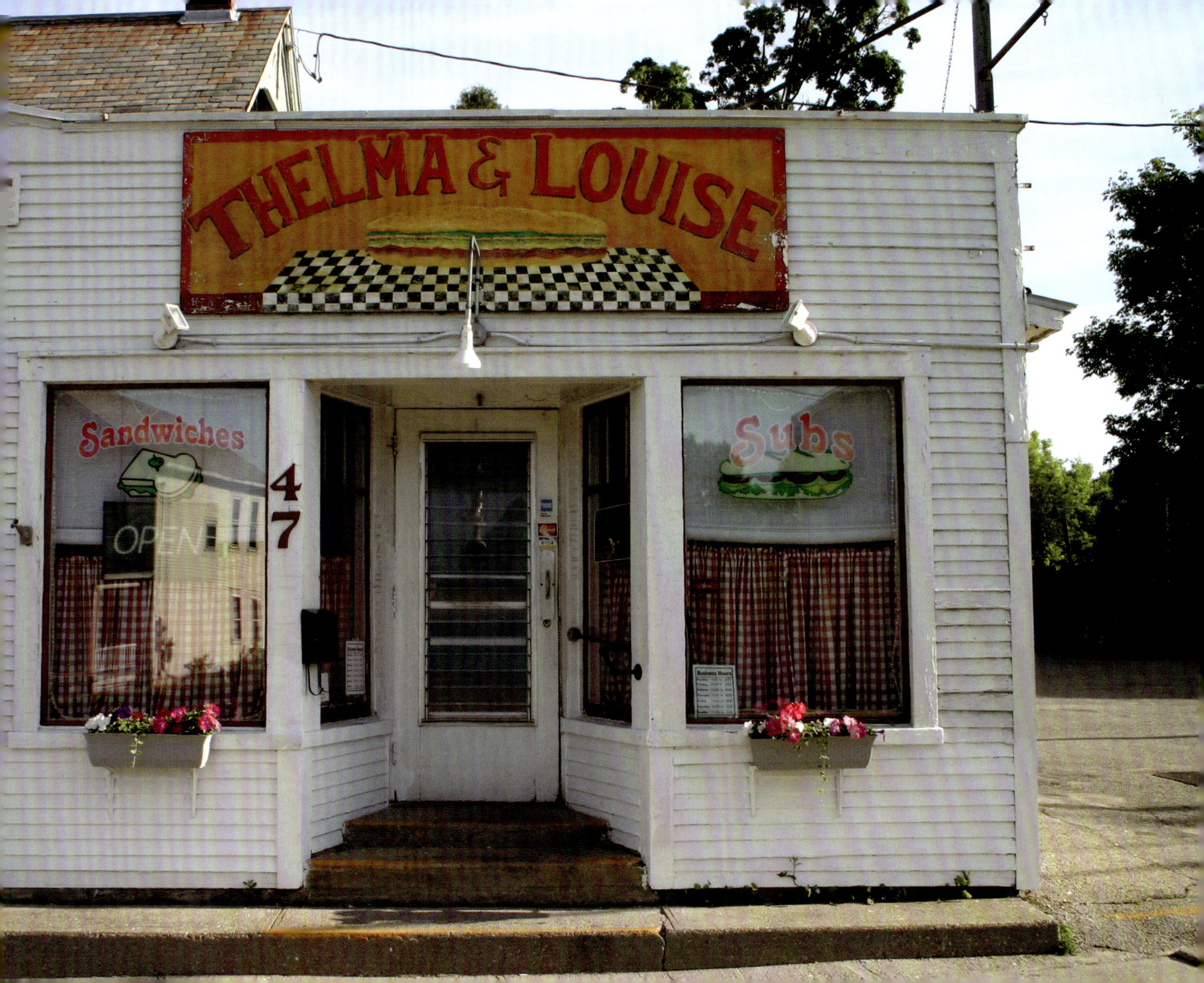
THELMA & LOUISE
Sandwiches
Subs
47
OPEN

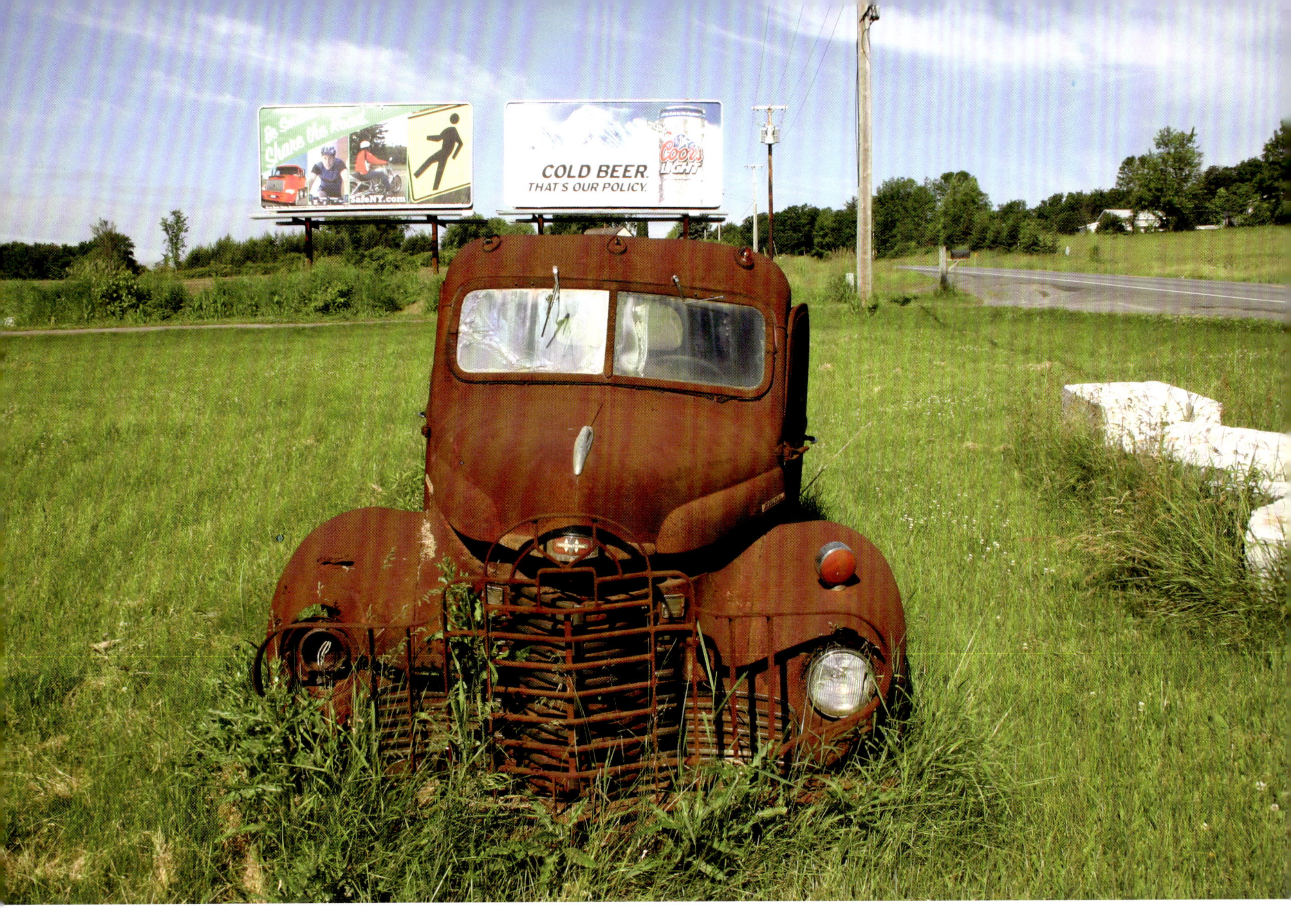

INTERNATIONAL HARVESTER TRUCK, Fort Ann, New York, 6/13/09

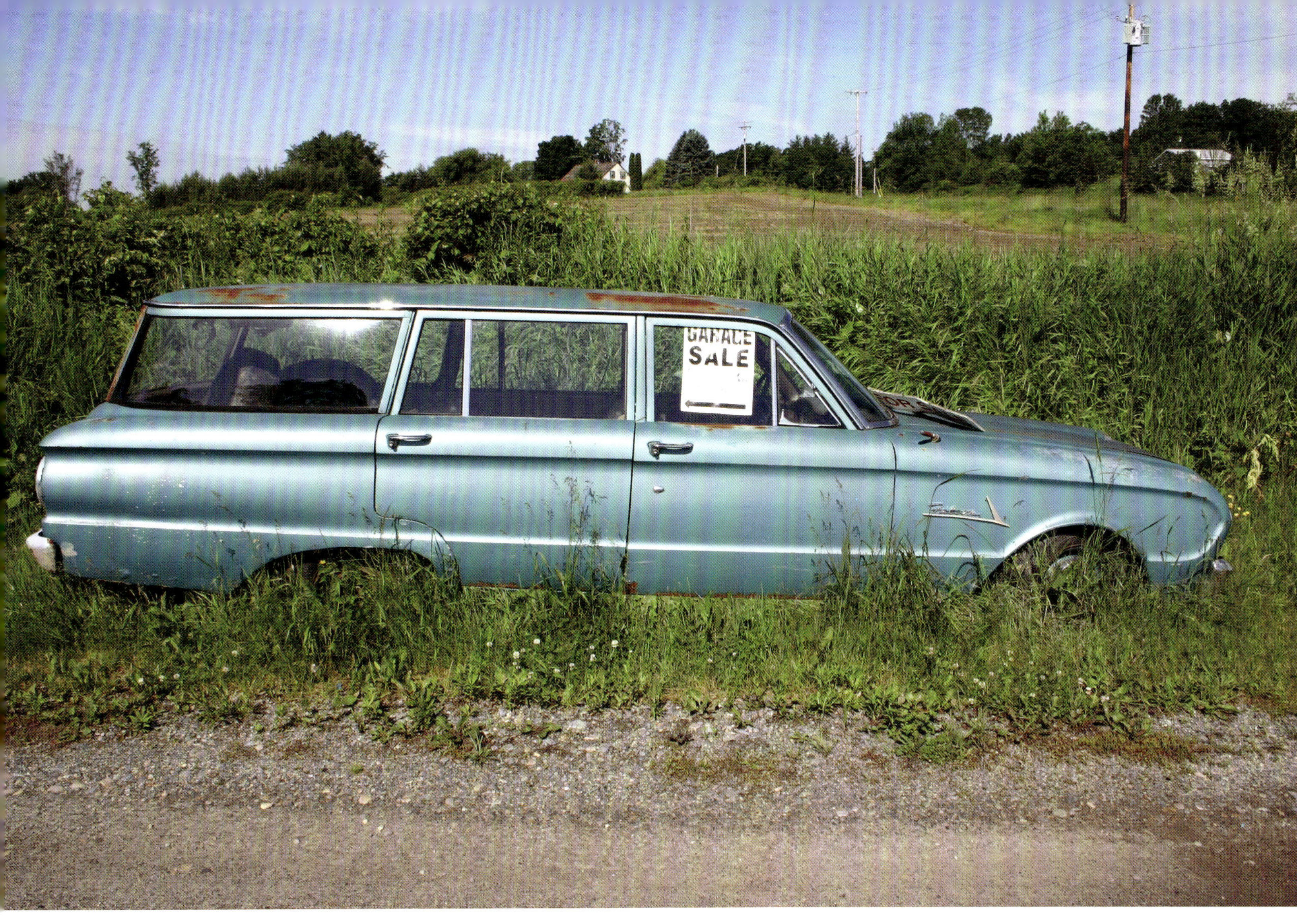

FORD FALCON, Fort Ann, New York, 6/13/09

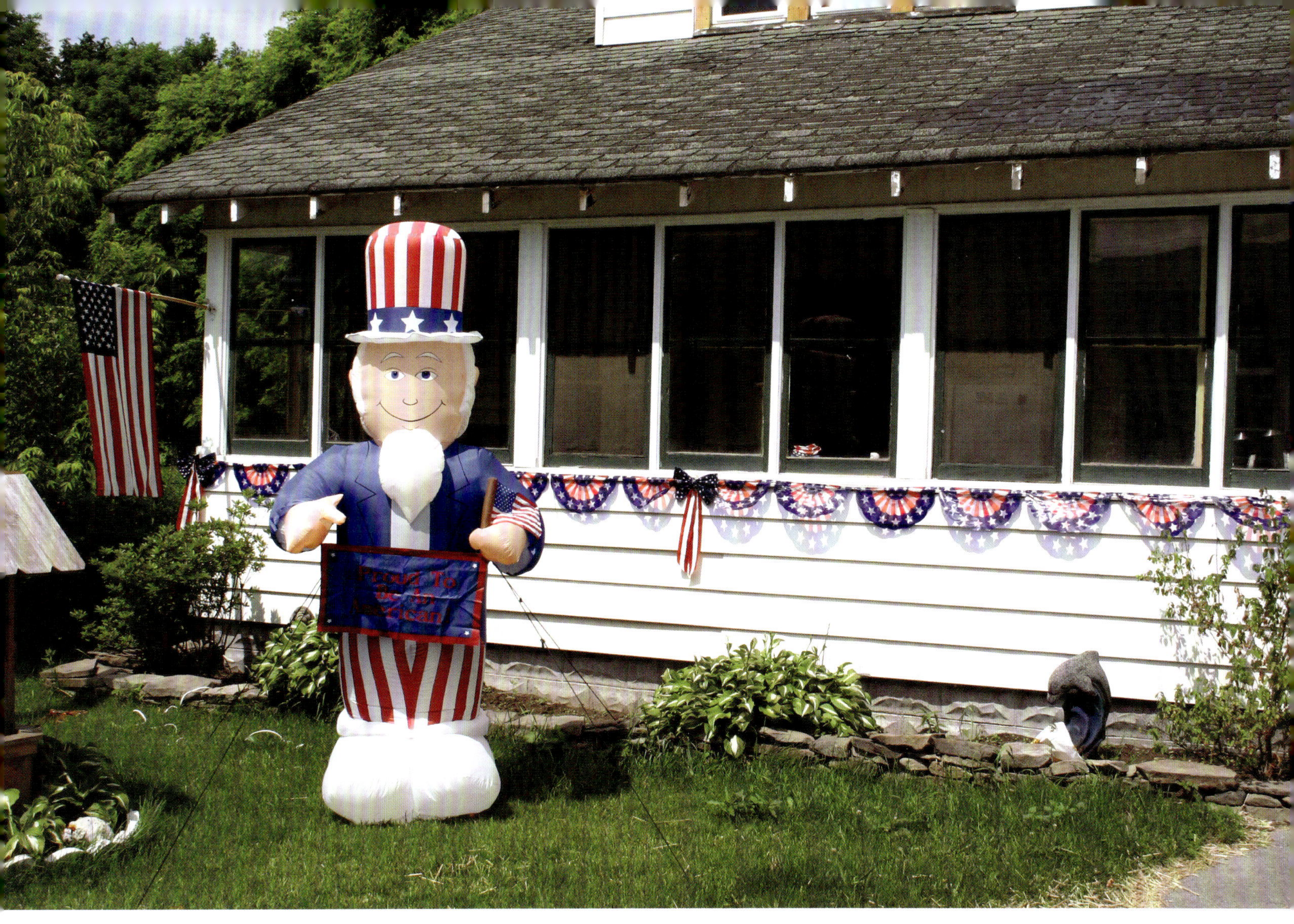

PROUD TO BE AN AMERICAN, Fultonham, New York, 6/13/09

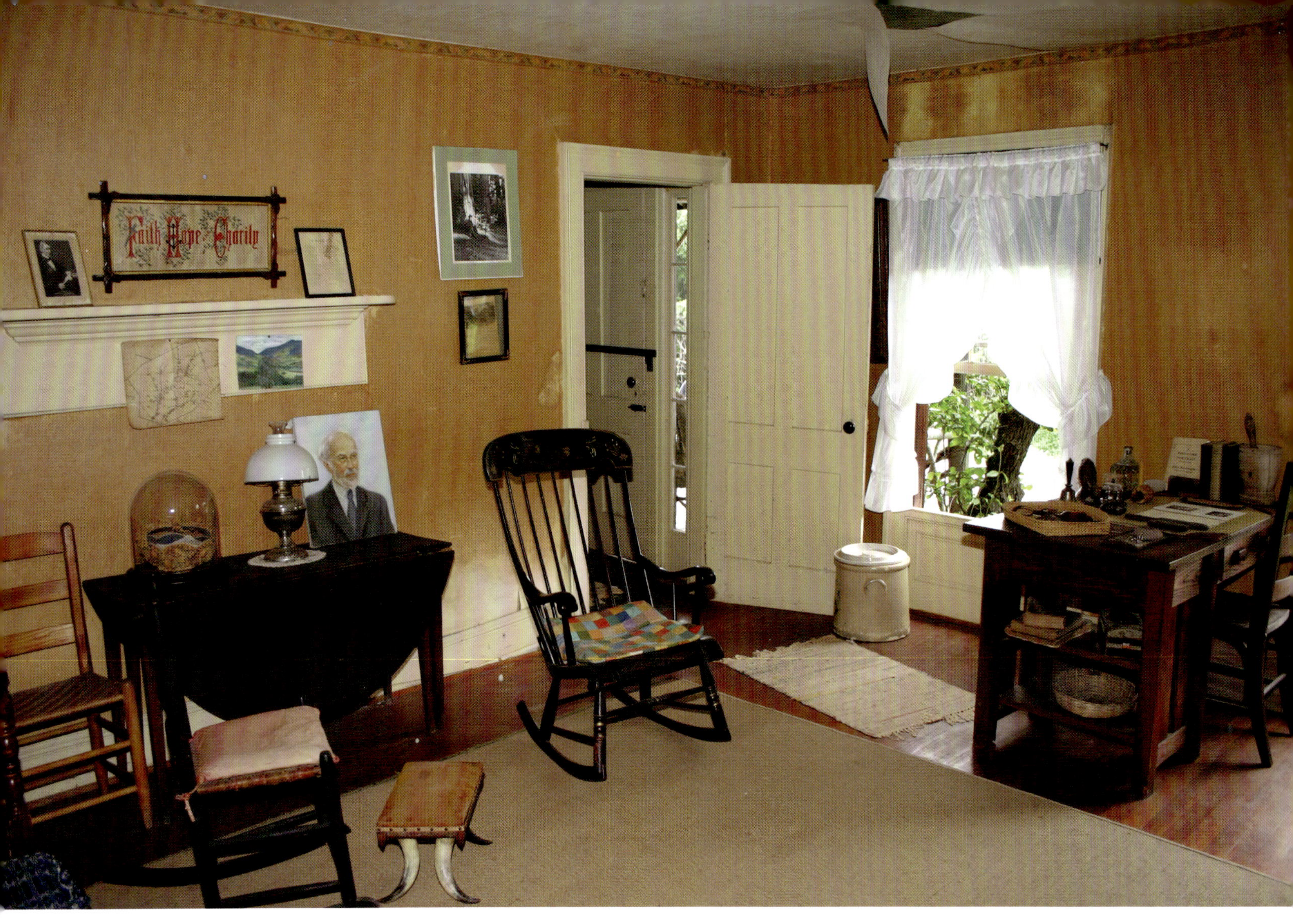

WOODCHUCK LODGE, Roxbury, New York, 6/13/09

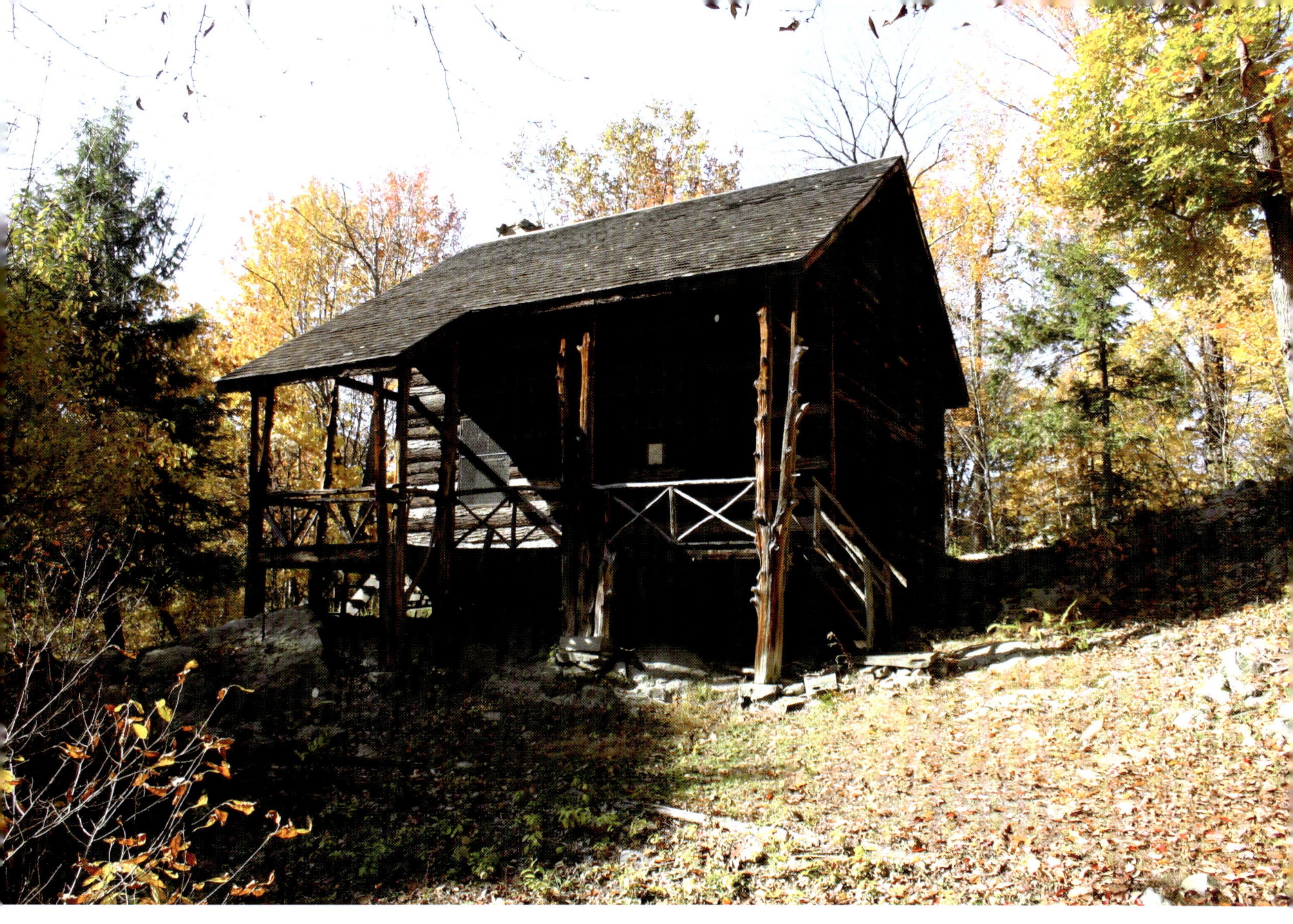

SLABSIDES, West Park, New York, 10/26/04

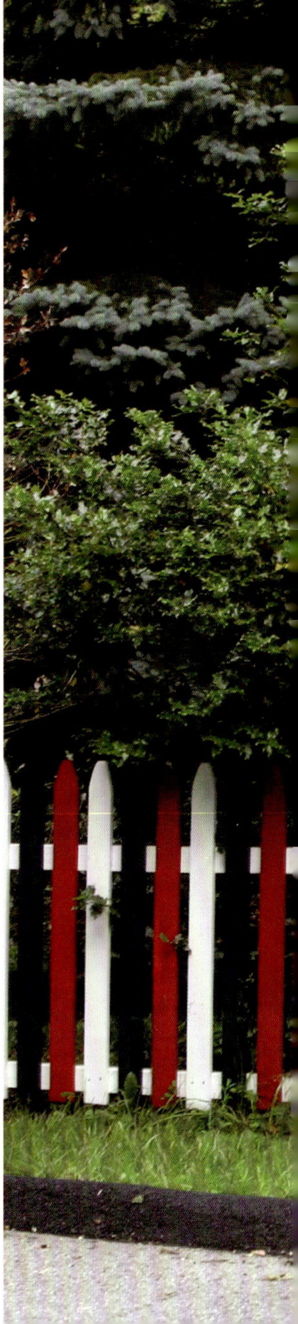

PATRIOTIC FENCE, Pleasantville, New York, 6/19/09

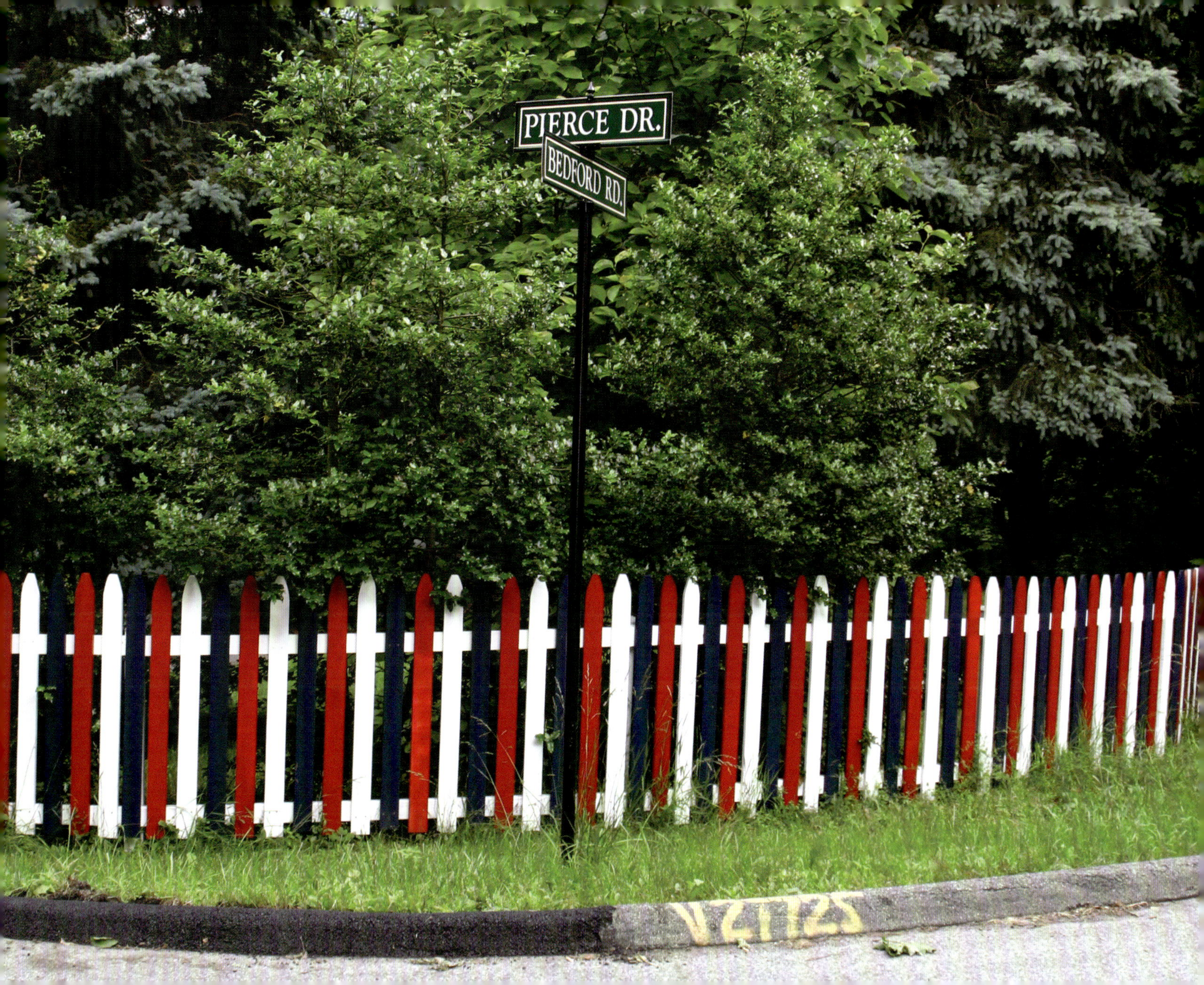
PIERCE DR.
BEDFORD RD.

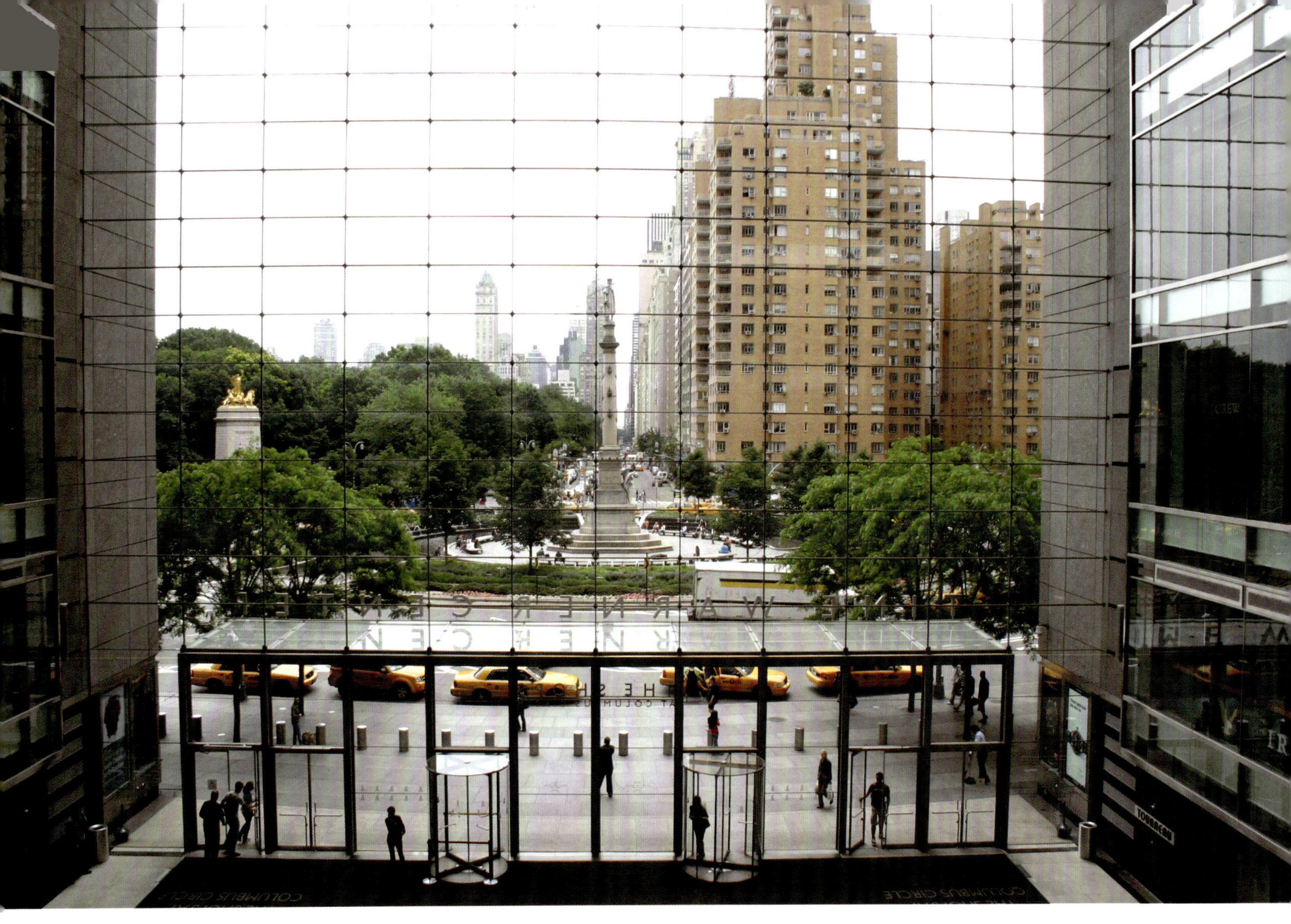

TIME WARNER CENTER, Columbus Circle, New York City, 6/16/09

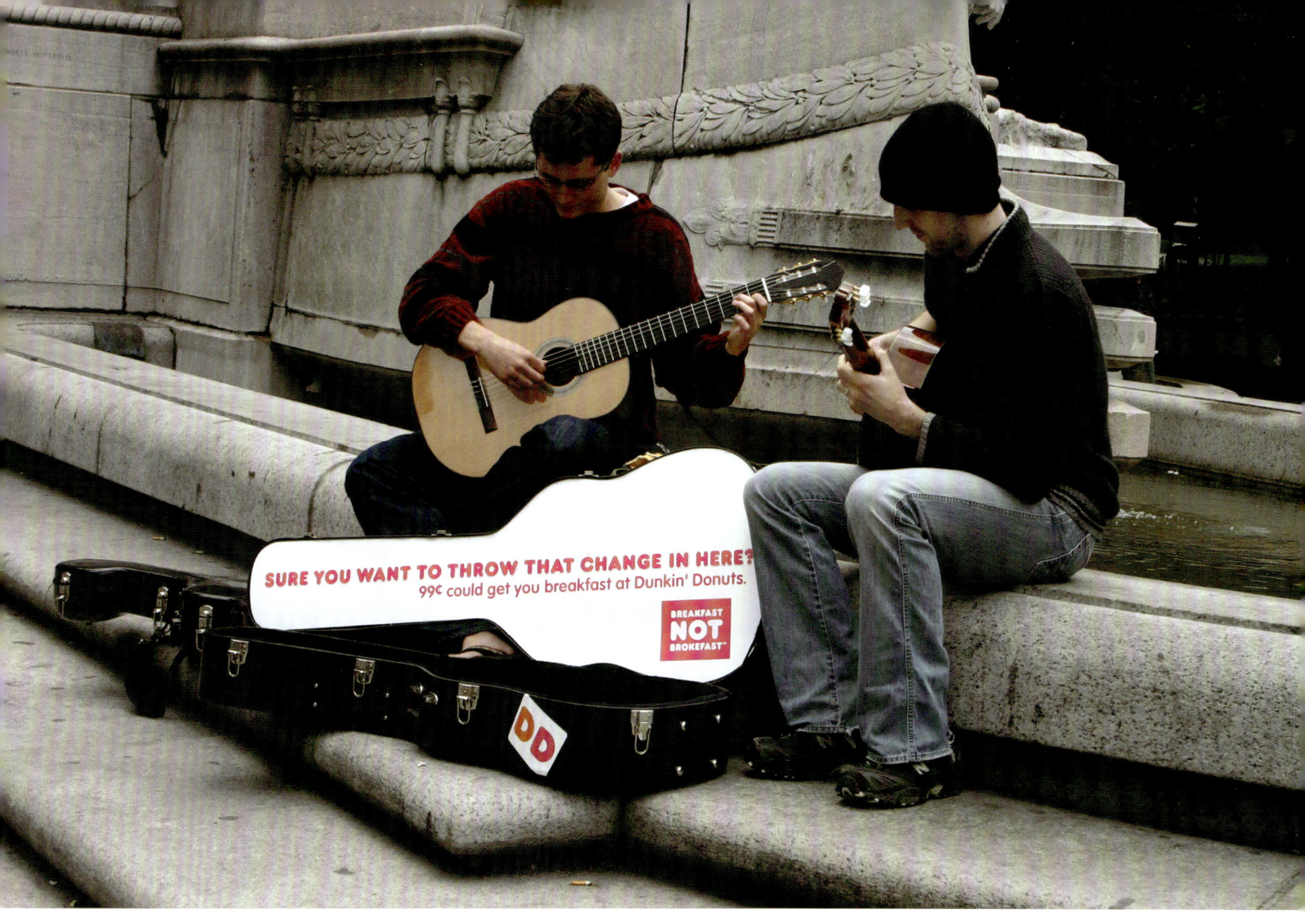

BUSKERS, Columbus Circle, New York City, 6/16/09

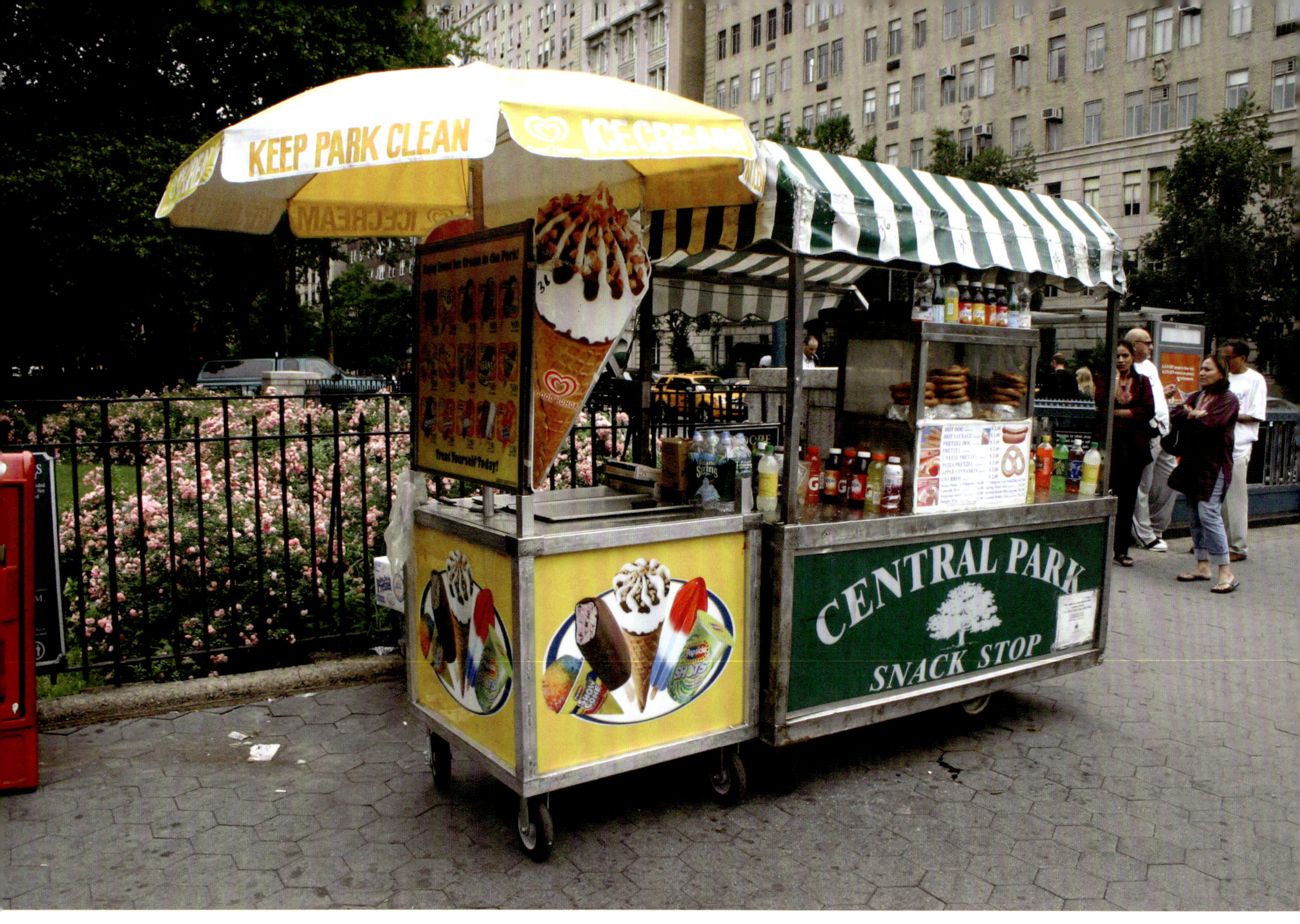

CENTRAL PARK SNACK STOP, Central Park West and 81st Street, New York City, 6/17/09

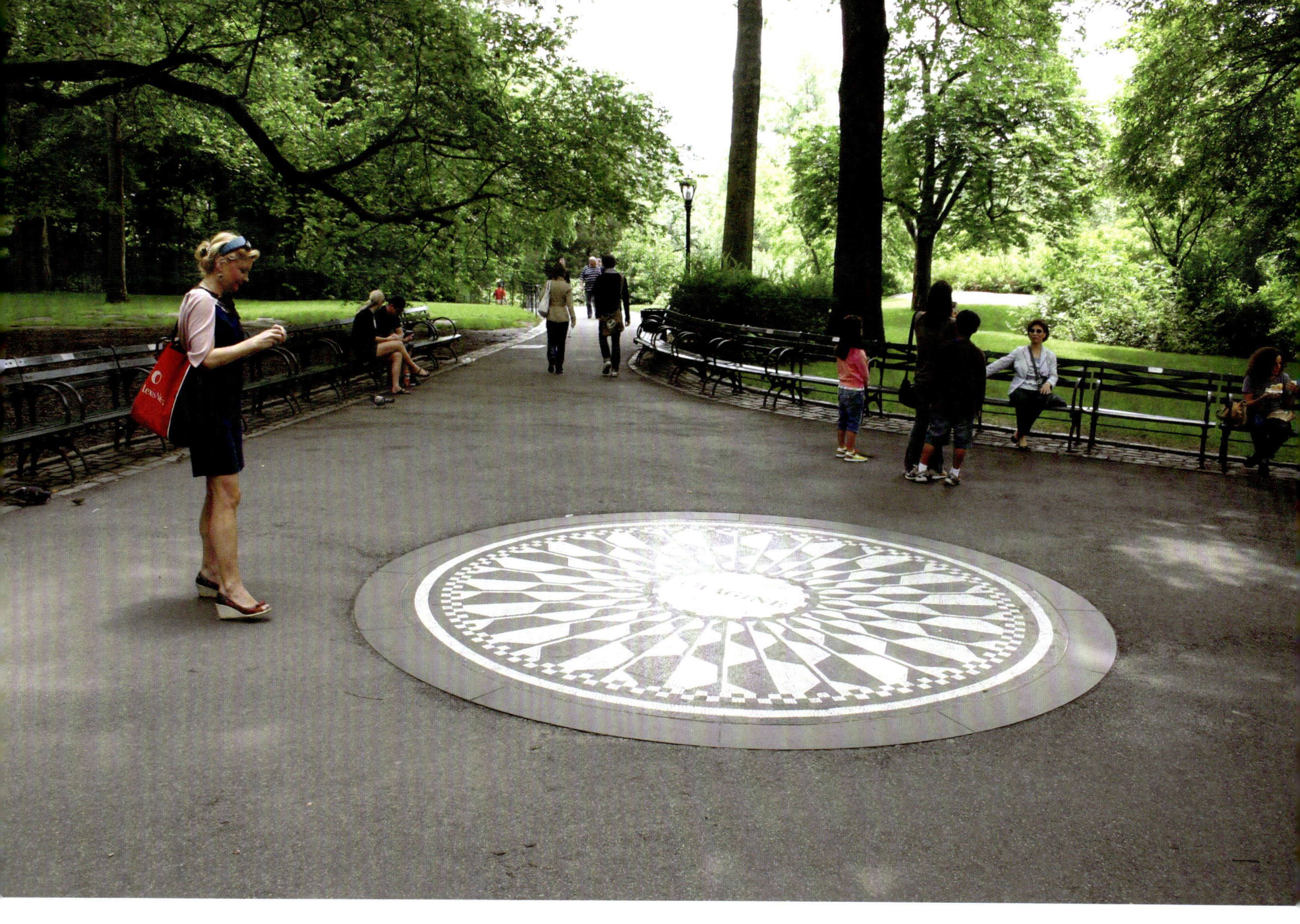

IMAGINE MOSAIC, Strawberry Fields, Central Park, New York City, 6/16/09

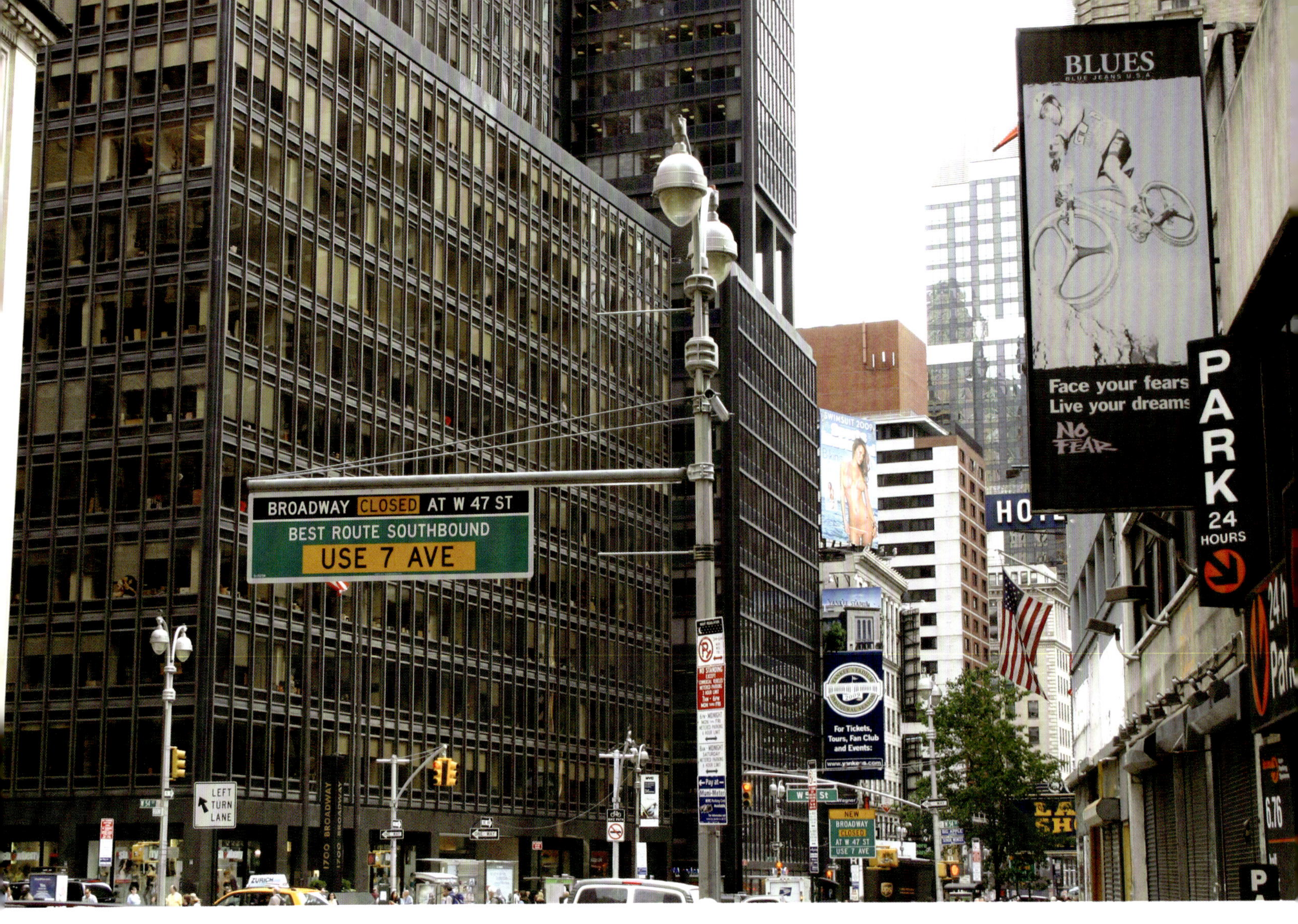

BROADWAY AND 54TH STREET, New York City, 6/17/09

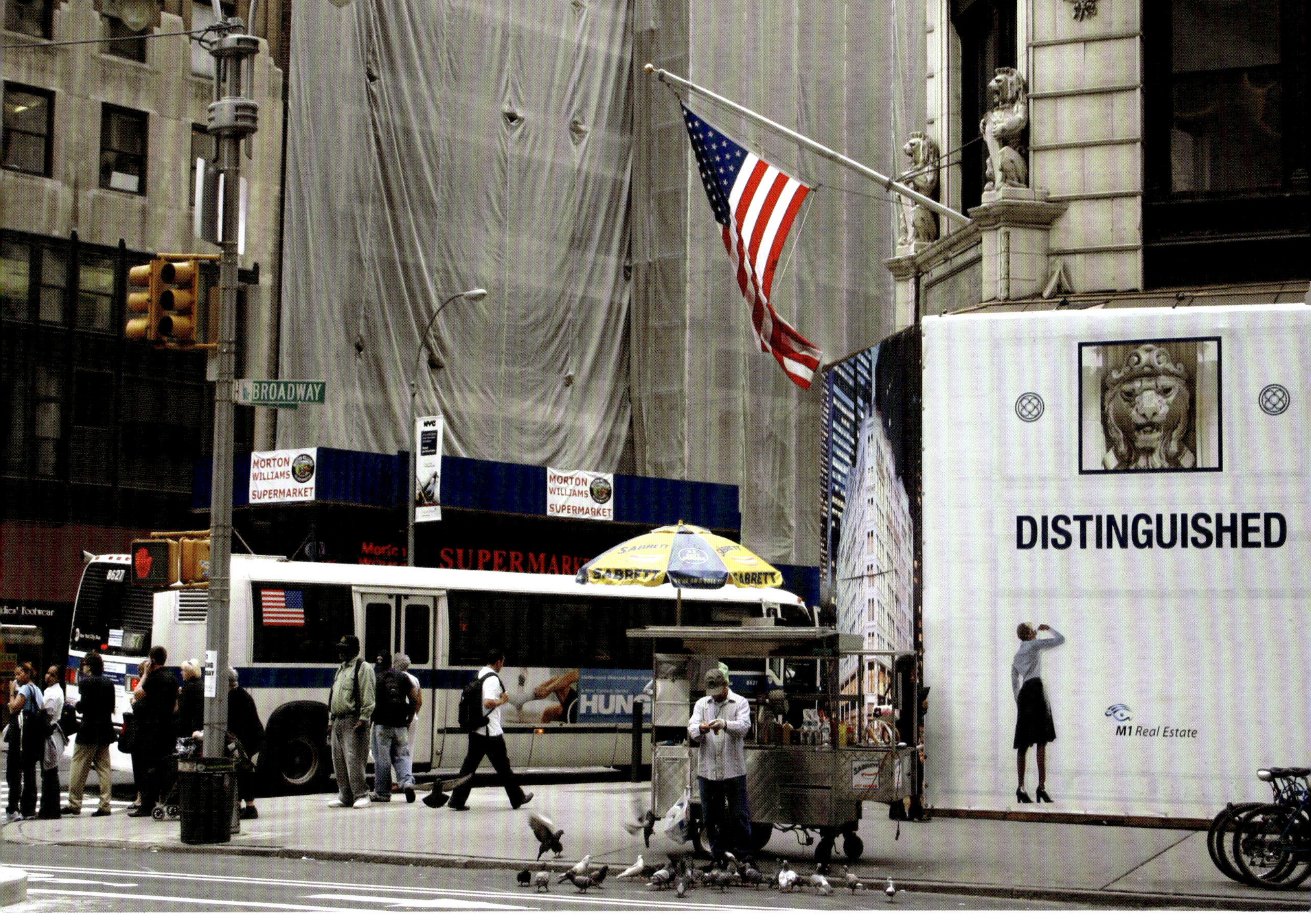

FOOD VENDOR WITH PIGEONS, Broadway and 57th Street, New York City, 6/17/09

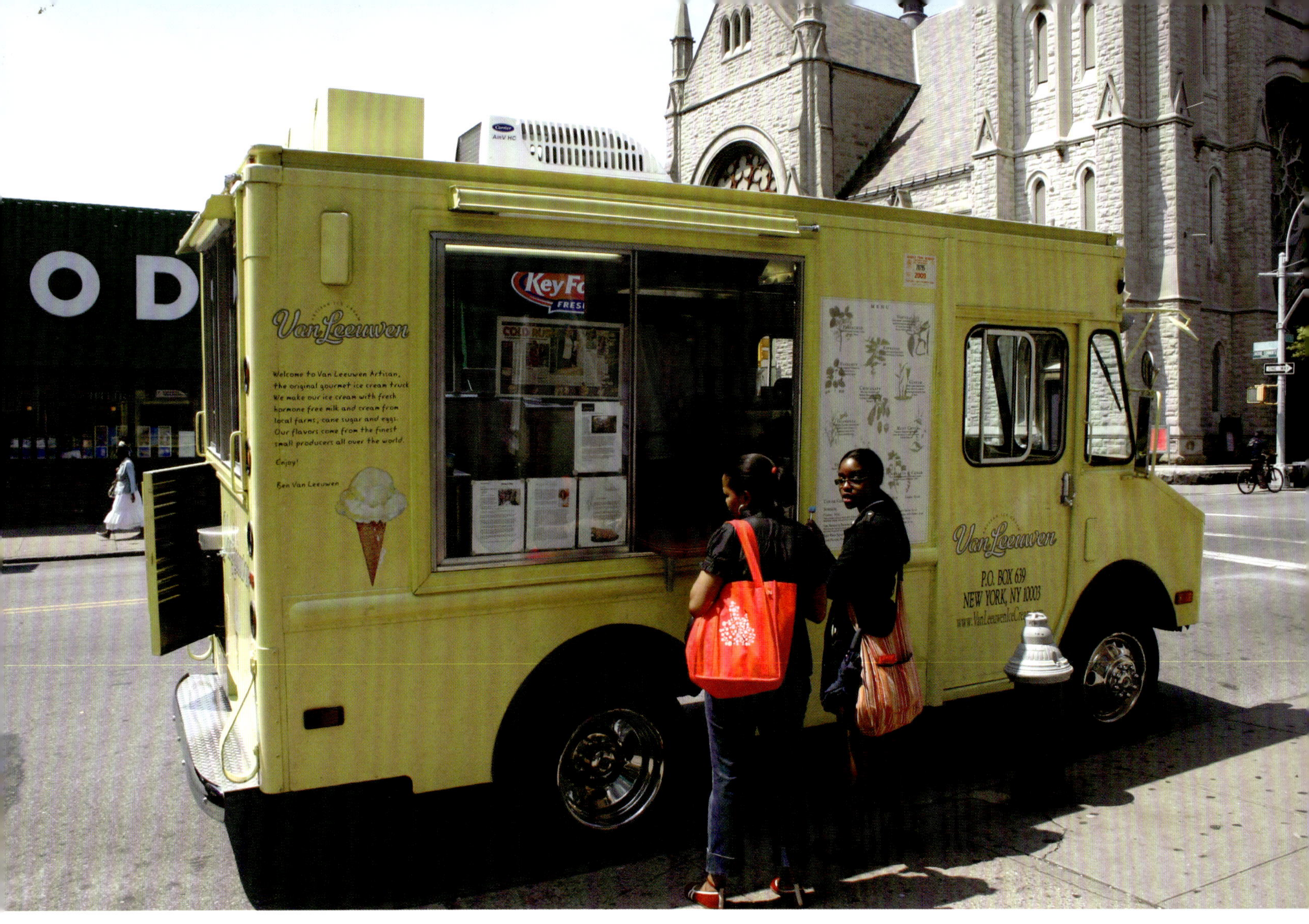

ICE CREAM TRUCK, Brooklyn, New York City, 6/15/09

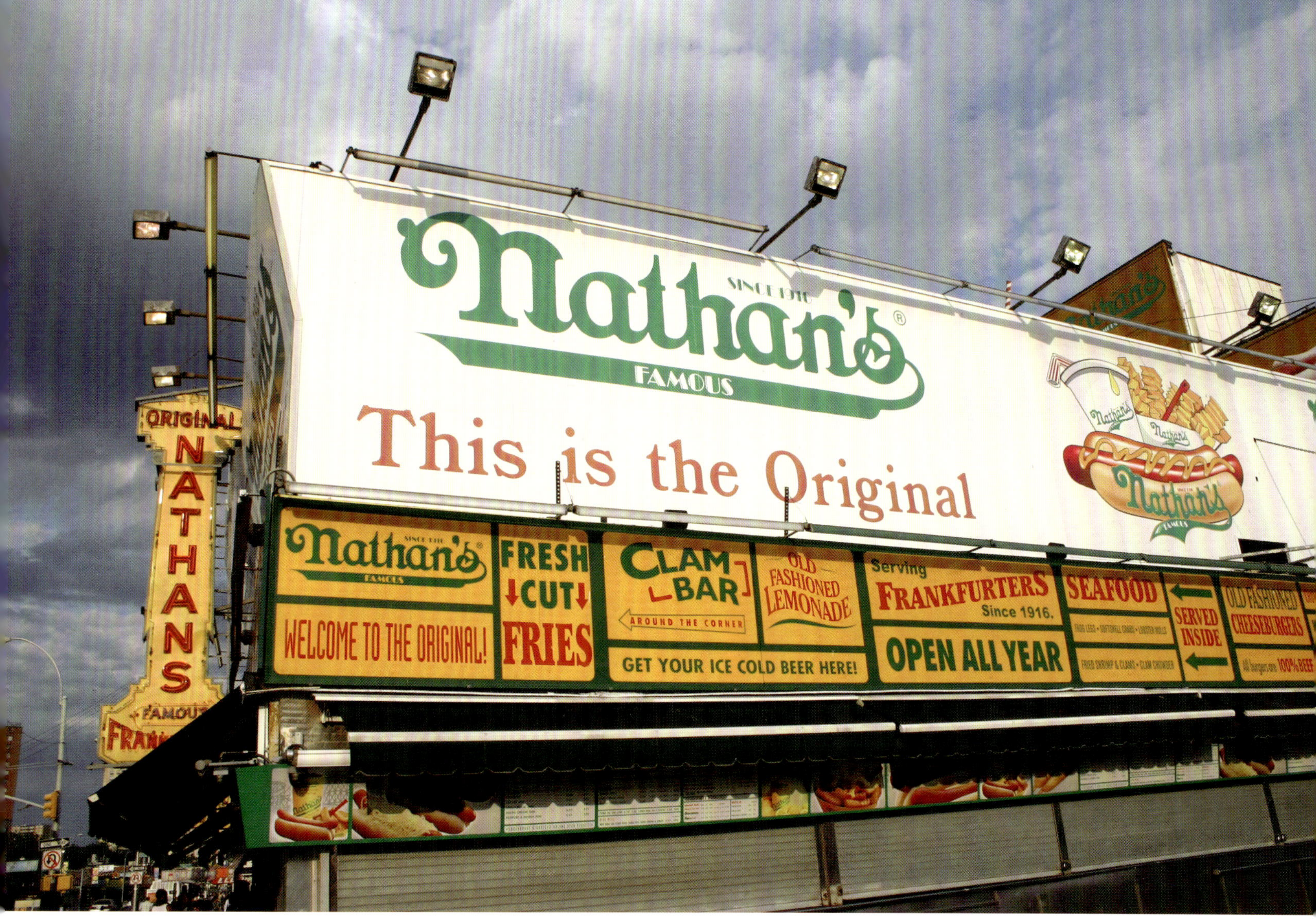

NATHAN'S, Coney Island, New York City, 6/15/09

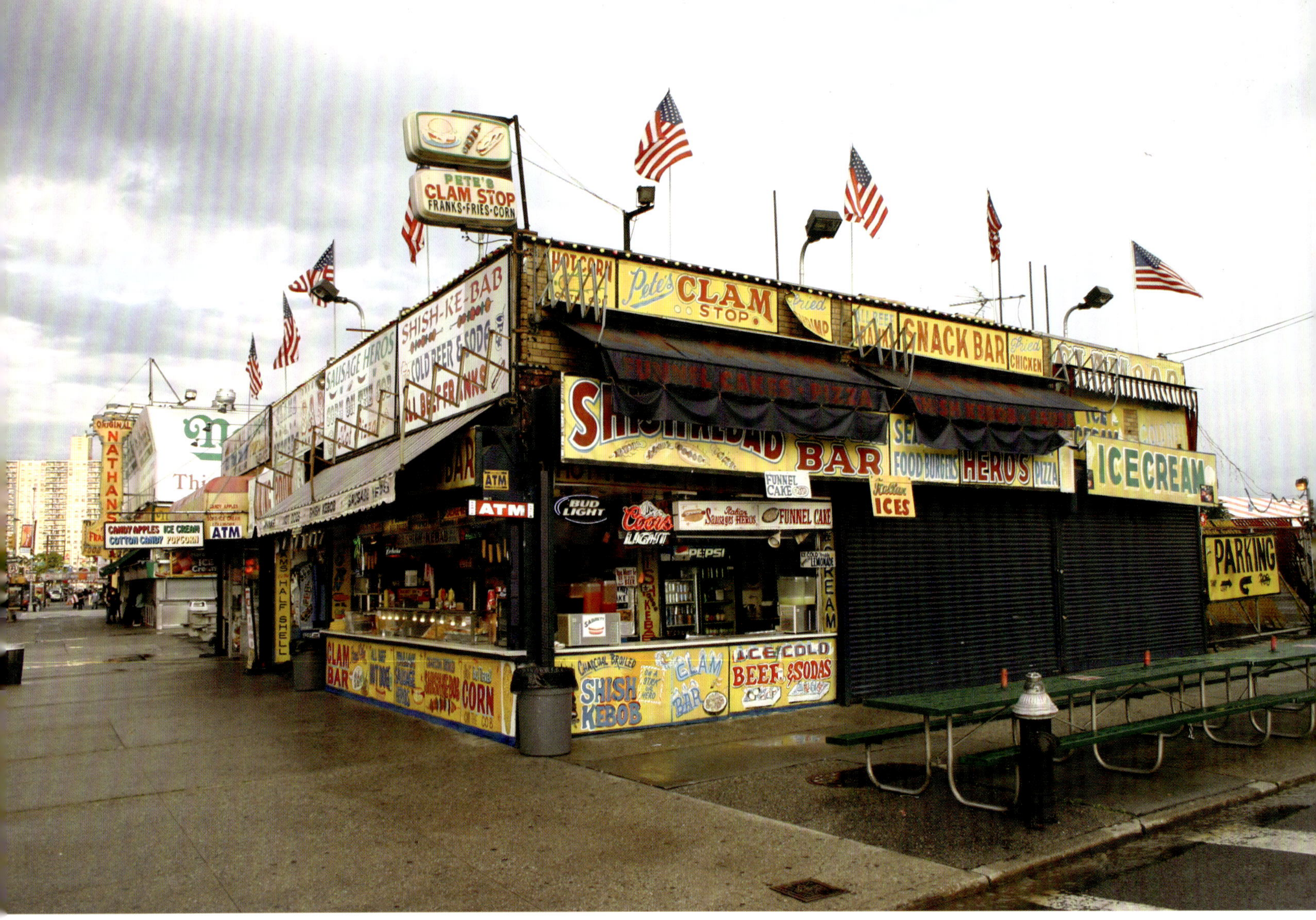

PETE'S CLAM STOP, Coney Island, New York City, 6/15/09

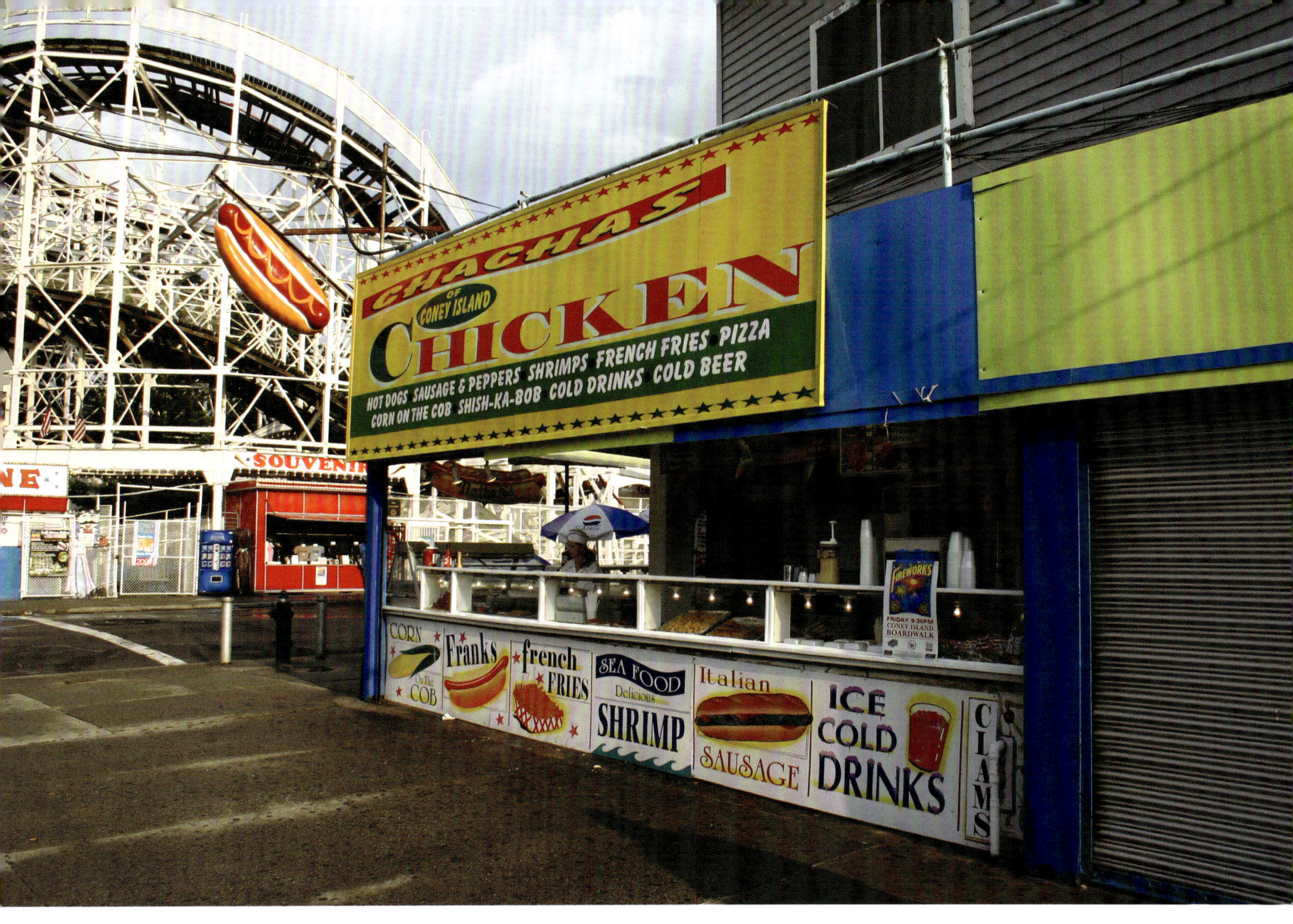

CHACHAS CHICKEN, Coney Island, New York City, 6/15/19

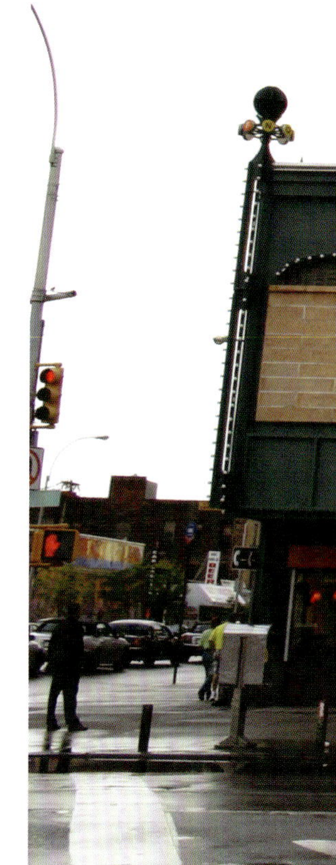

CONEY ISLAND TERMINAL, Coney Island, New York City, 6/15/09

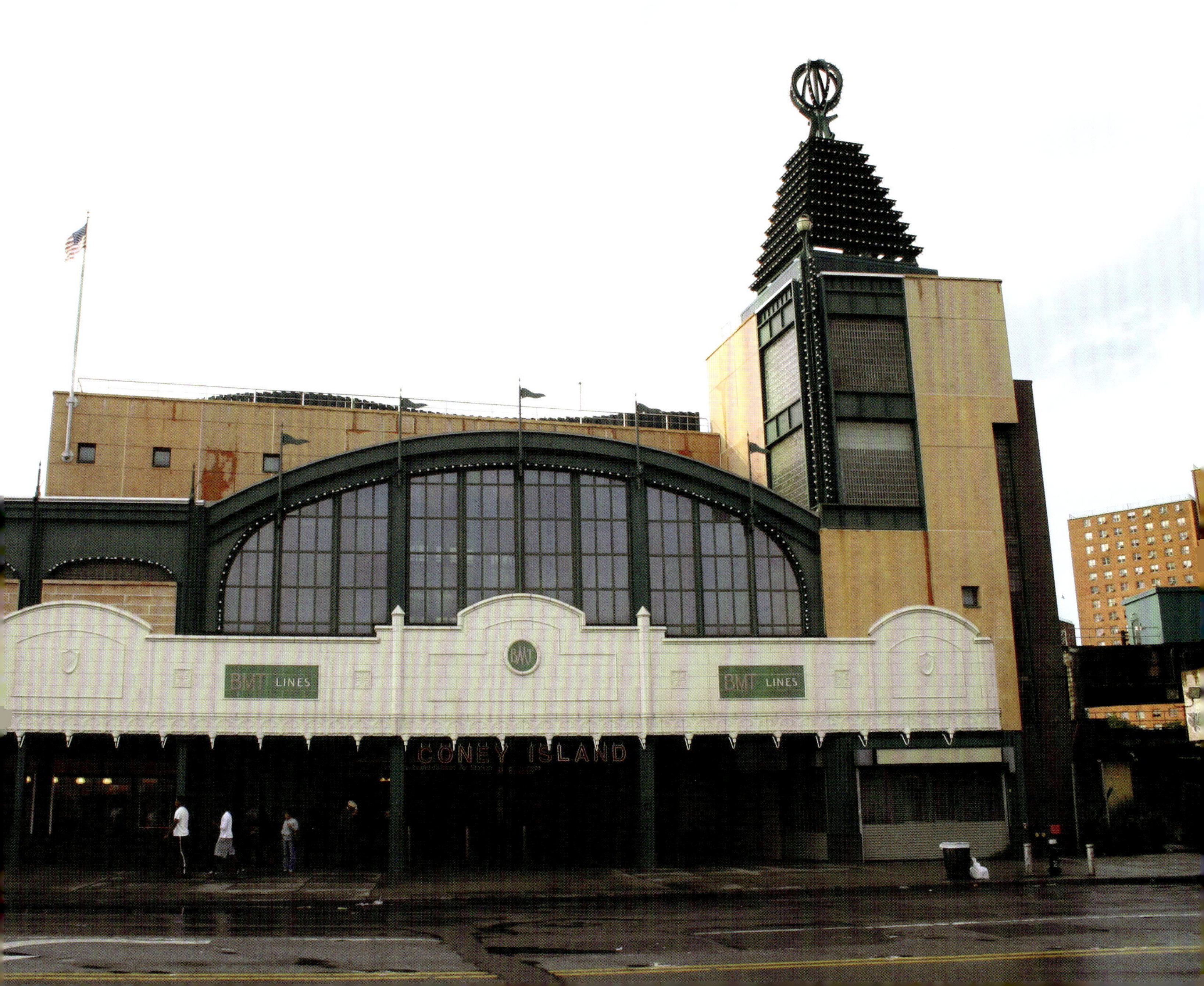
BMT
BMT LINES
BMT LINES
CONEY ISLAND

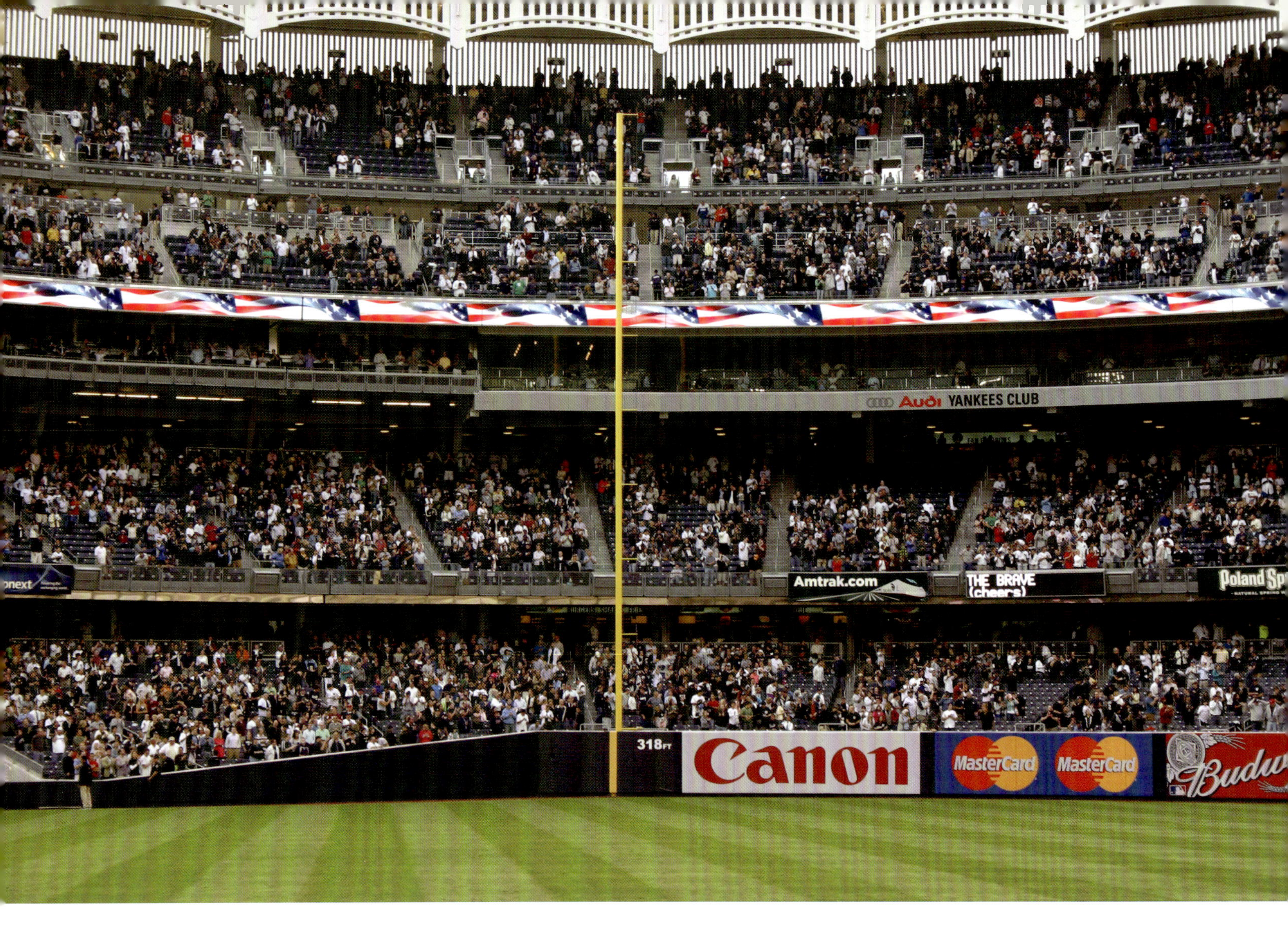

NATIONAL ANTHEM, Yankee Stadium, New York City, 6/16/09

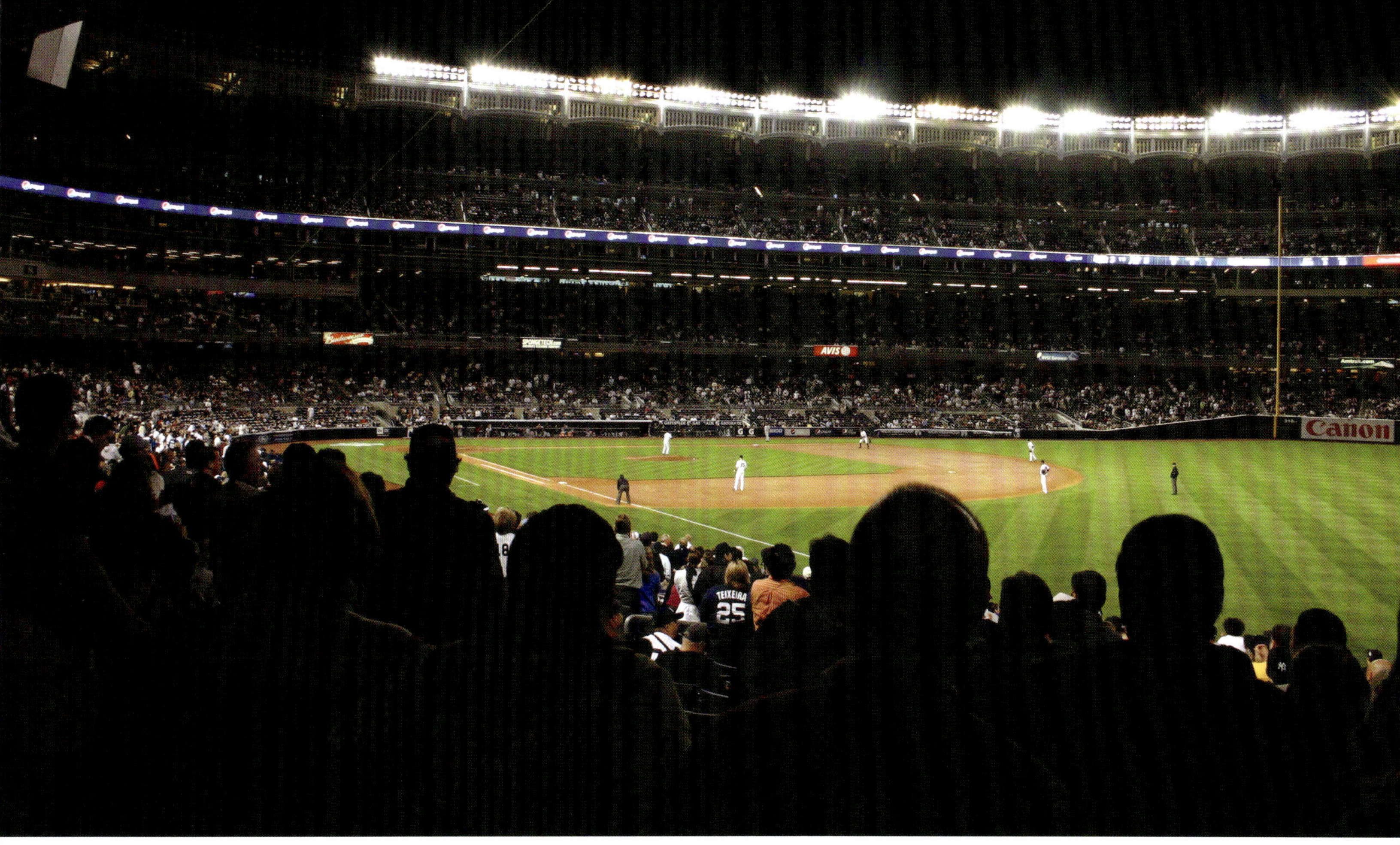

MARIANO RIVERA, Yankee Stadium, New York City, 6/16/09

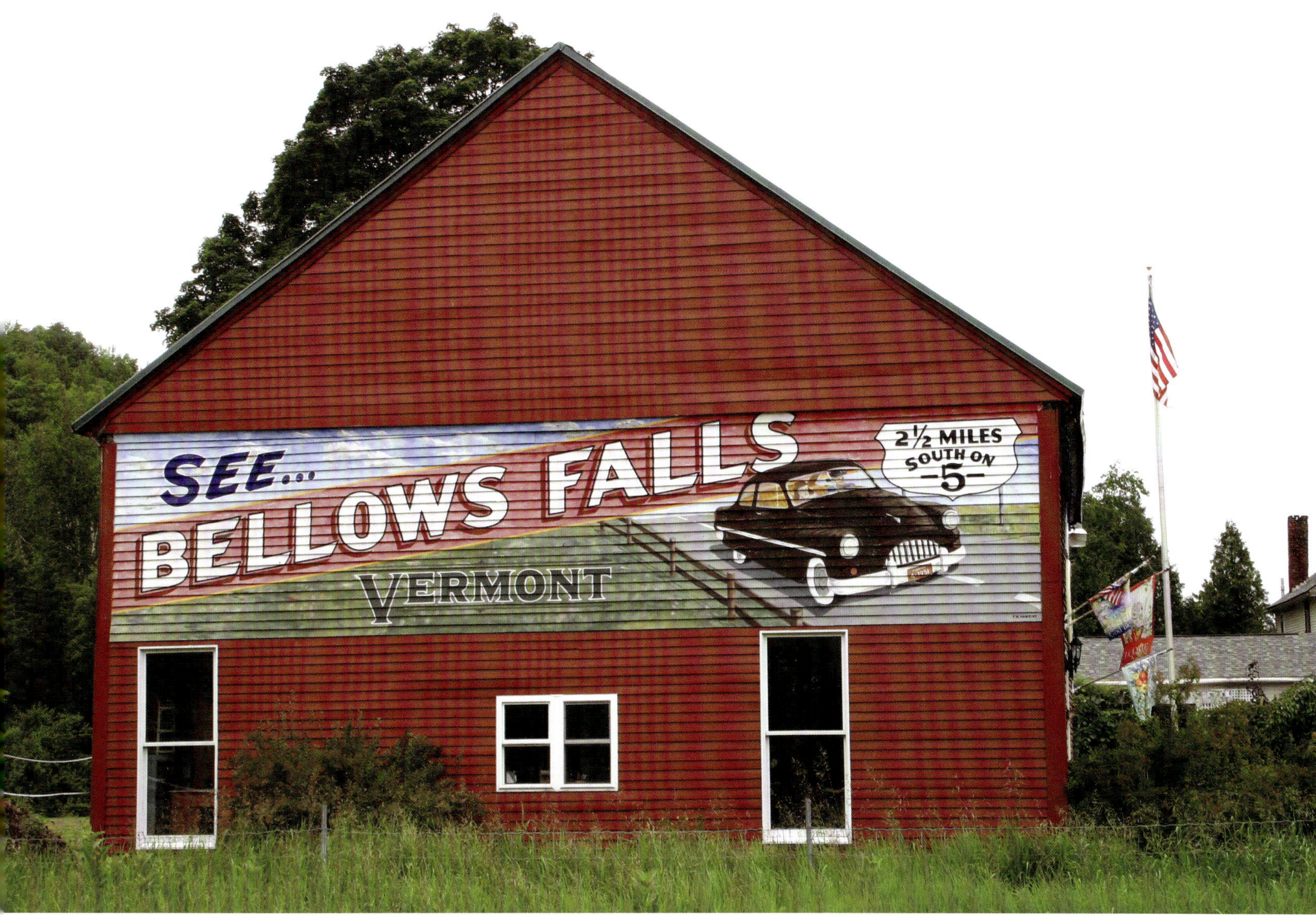

BARN, Bellows Falls, Vermont, 6/21/09

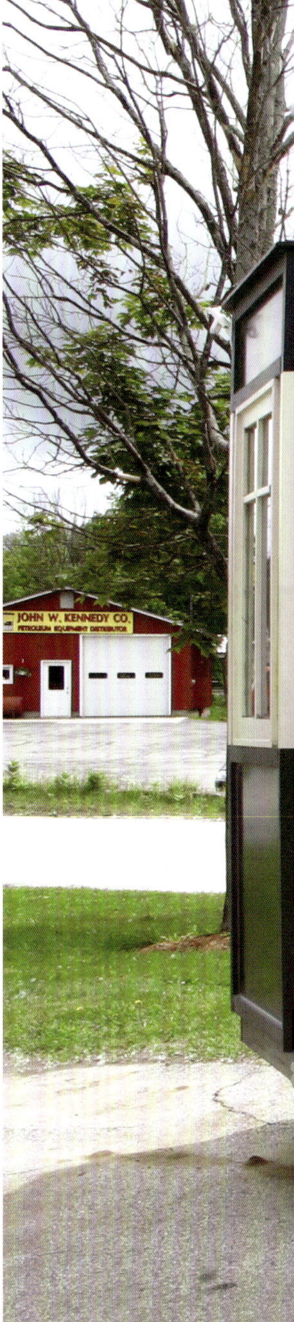

FOOD TRAILER, Montpelier, Vermont, 6/21/09

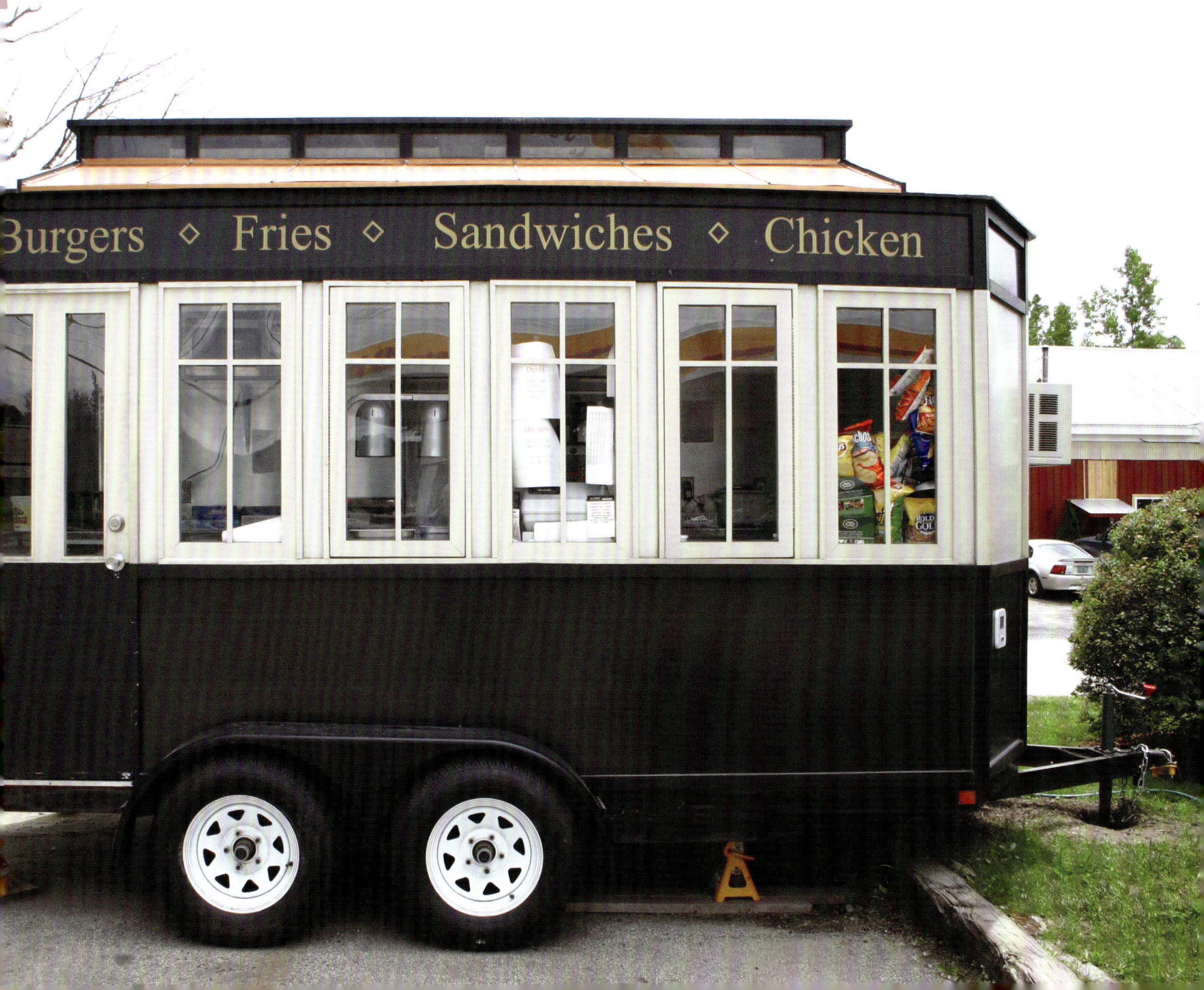
Burgers ◇ Fries ◇ Sandwiches ◇ Chicken

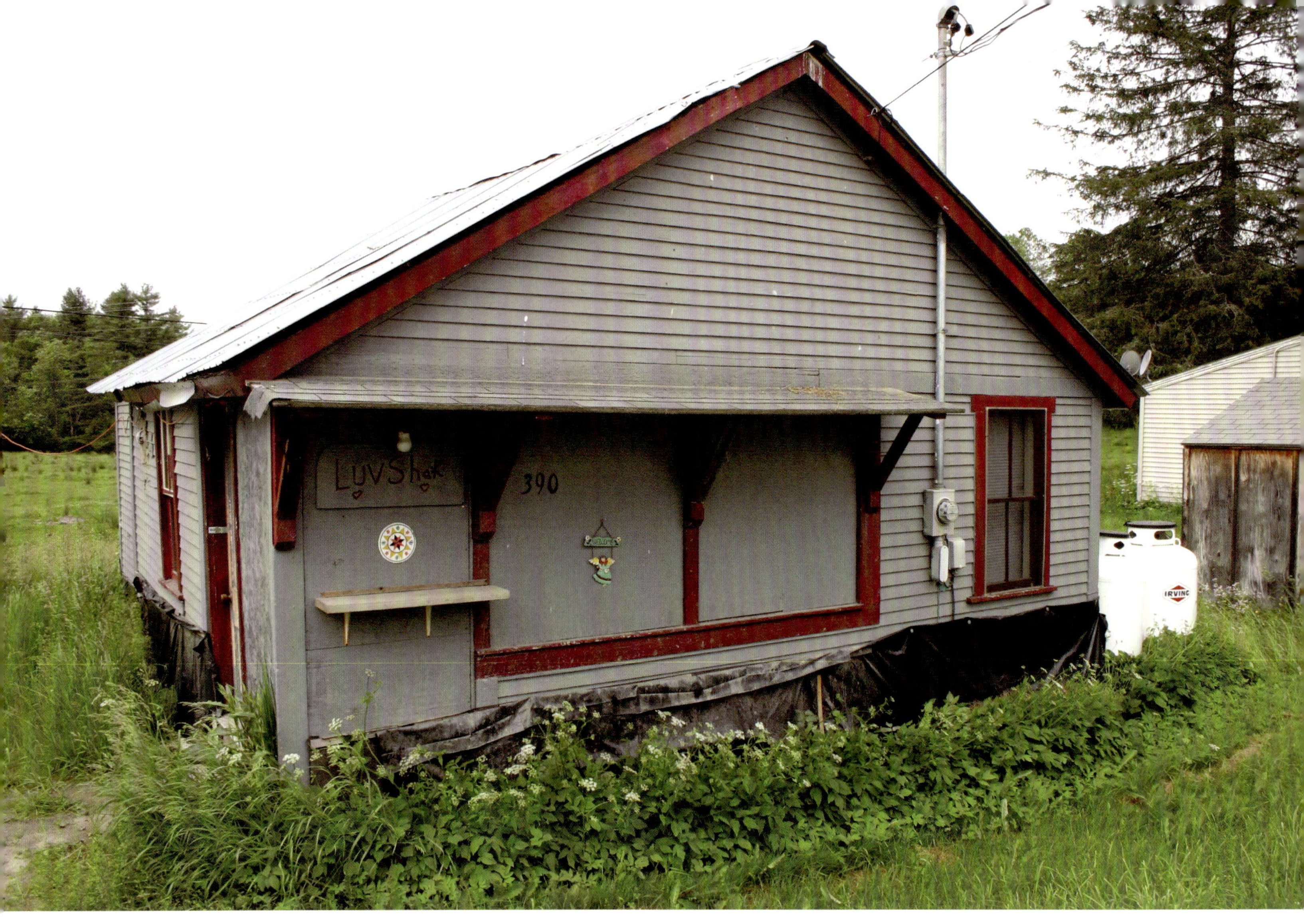

LUV SHAK, Calais, Vermont, 6/22/09

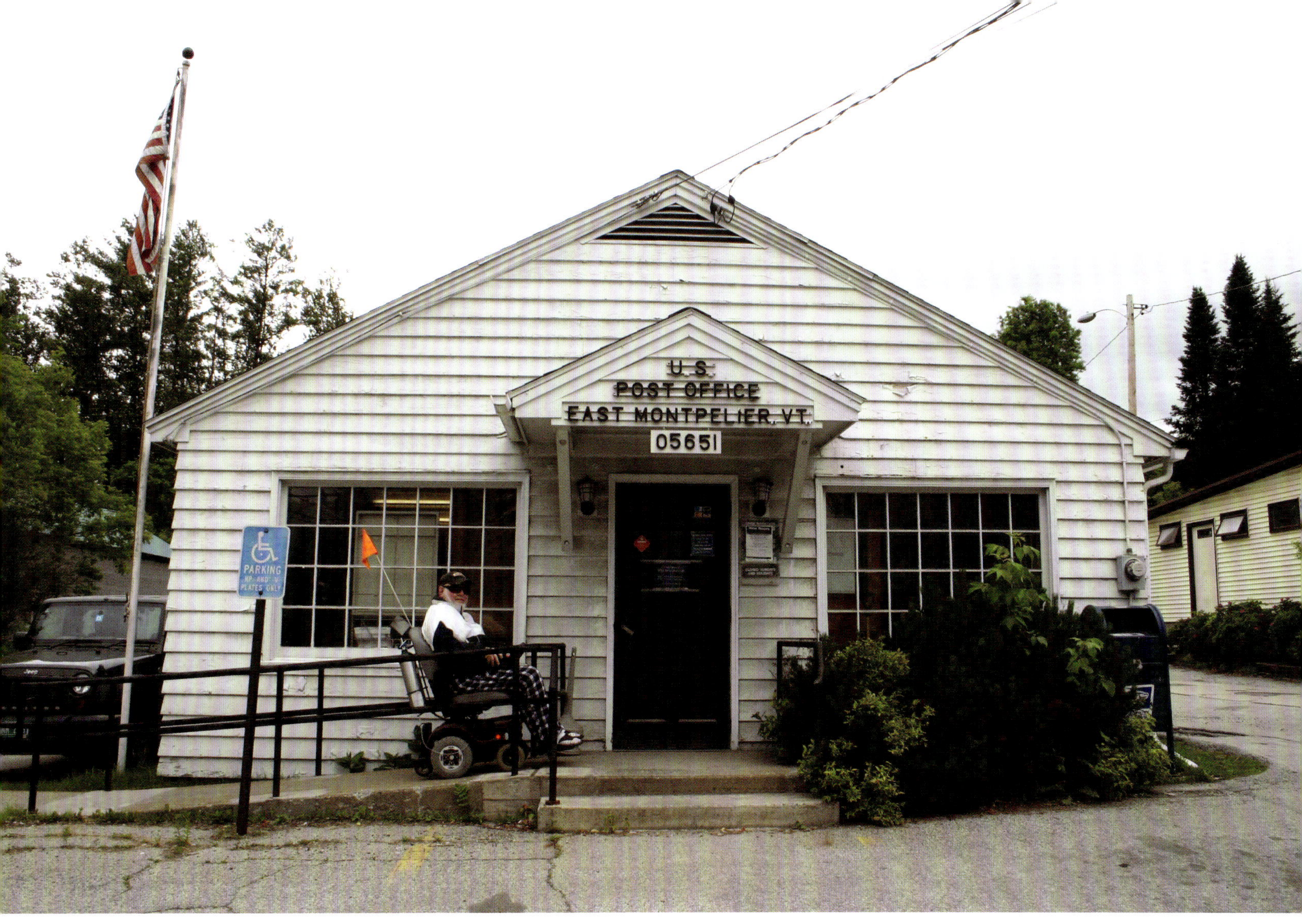

EAST MONTPELIER POST OFFICE, East Montpelier, Vermont, 6/22/09

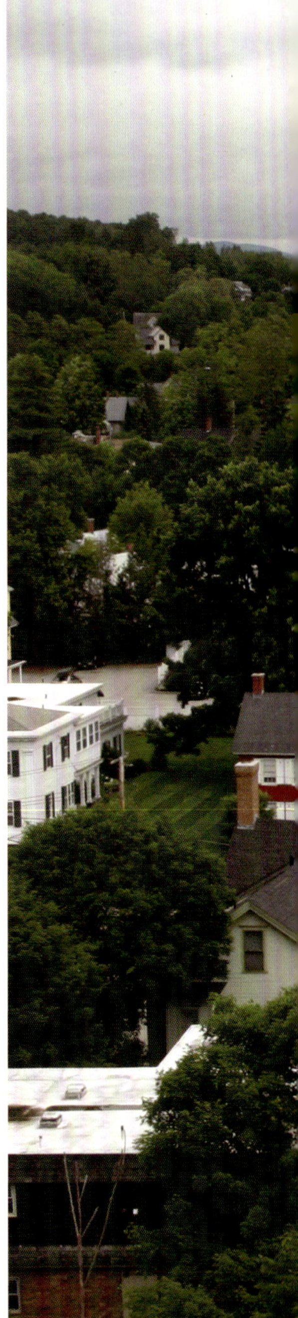

MONTPELIER FROM CORSE STREET, Montpelier, Vermont 6/22/09

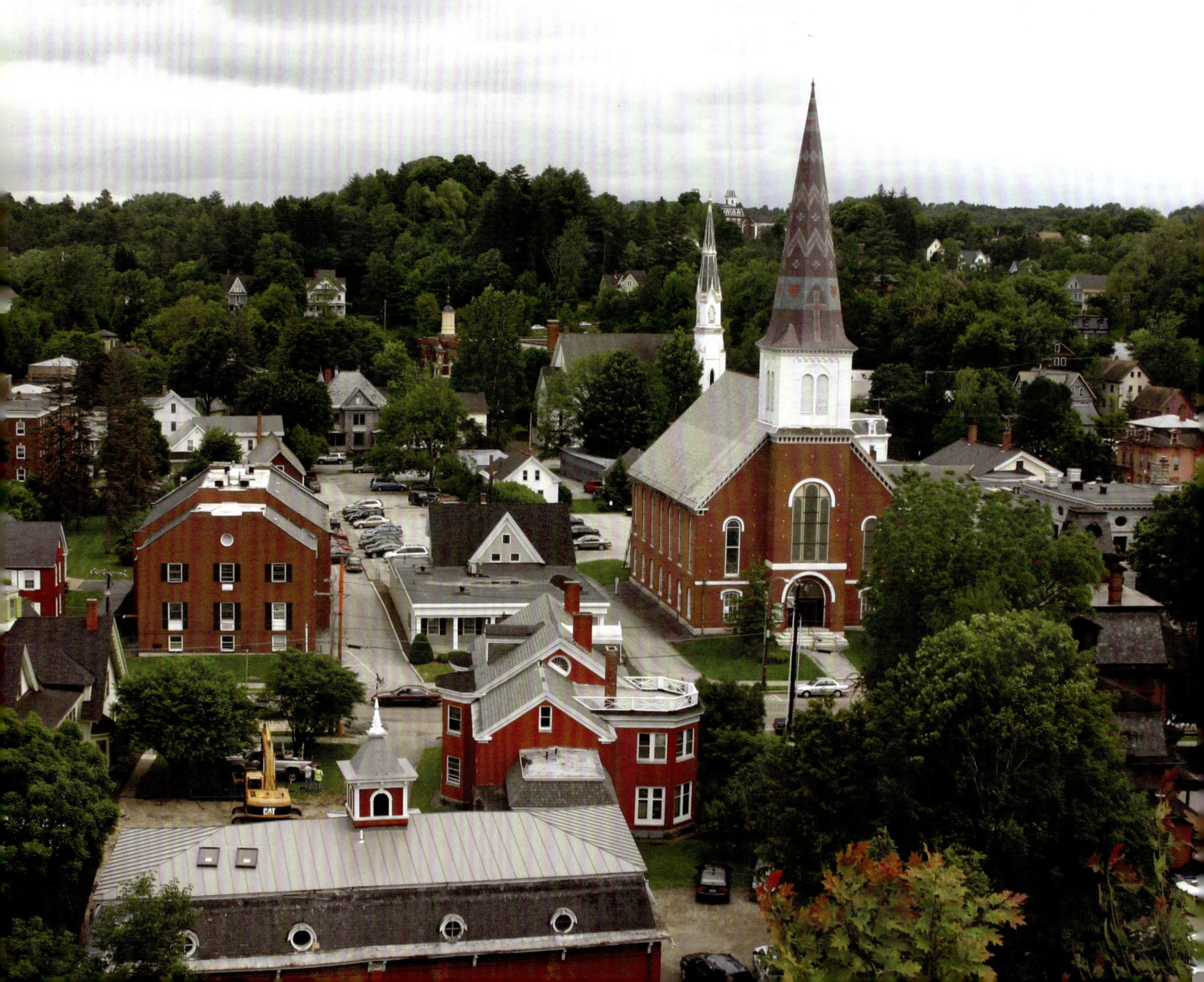
CAT

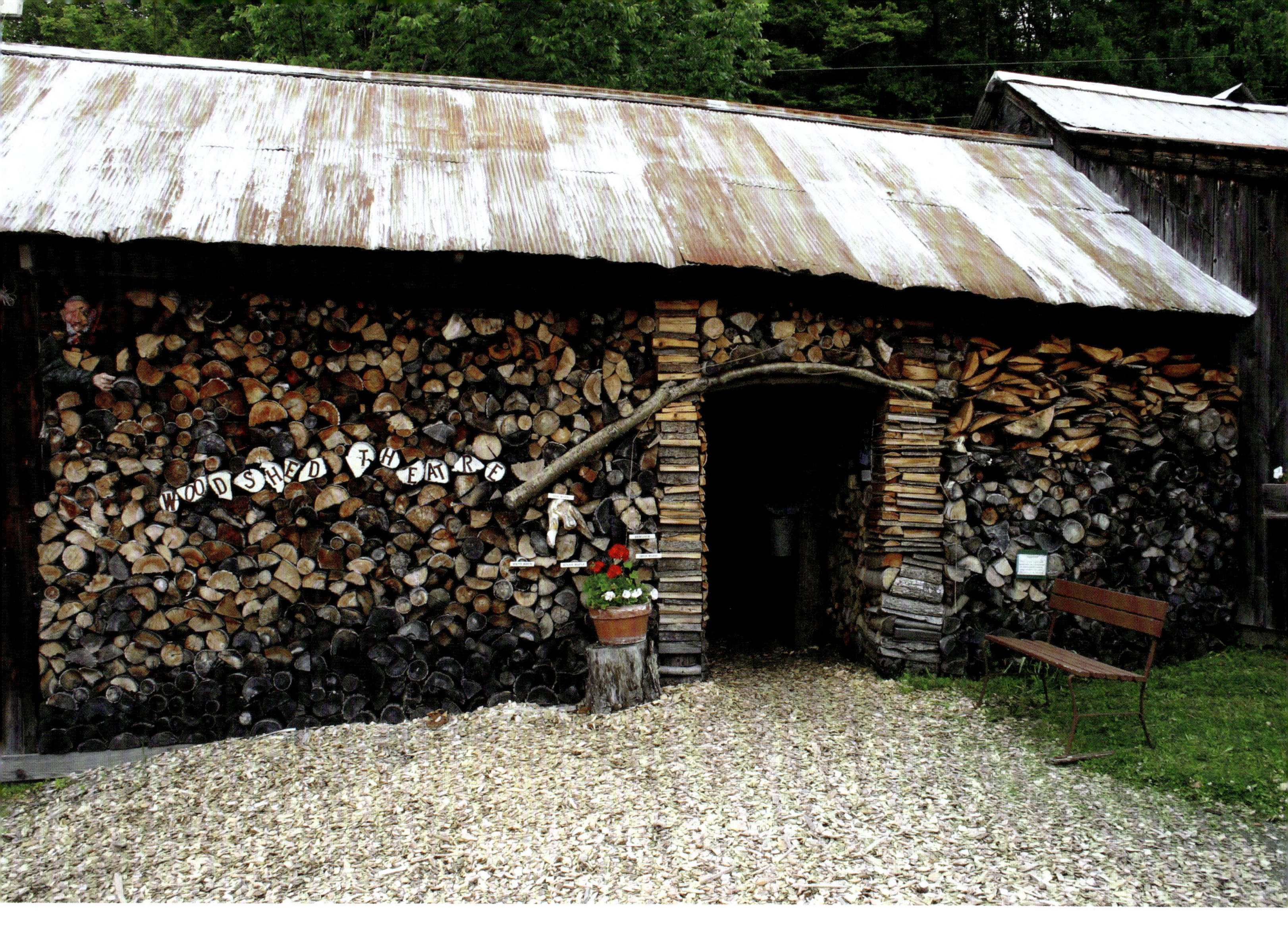

WOODSHED THEATRE, East Montpelier, Vermont, 6/22/09

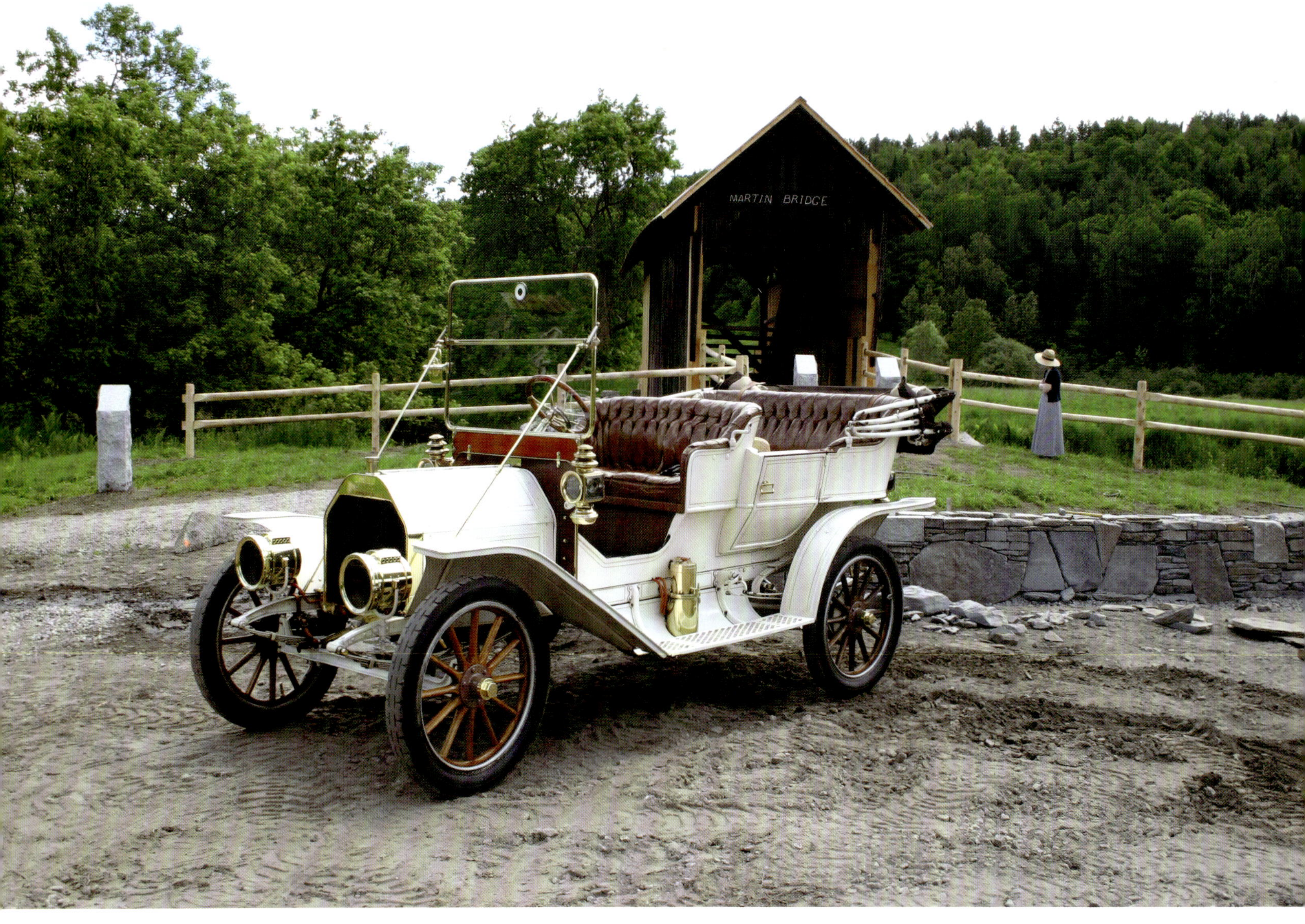

MARTIN COVERED BRIDGE WITH 1909 EMF MODEL 30, Marshfield, Vermont, 6/24/09

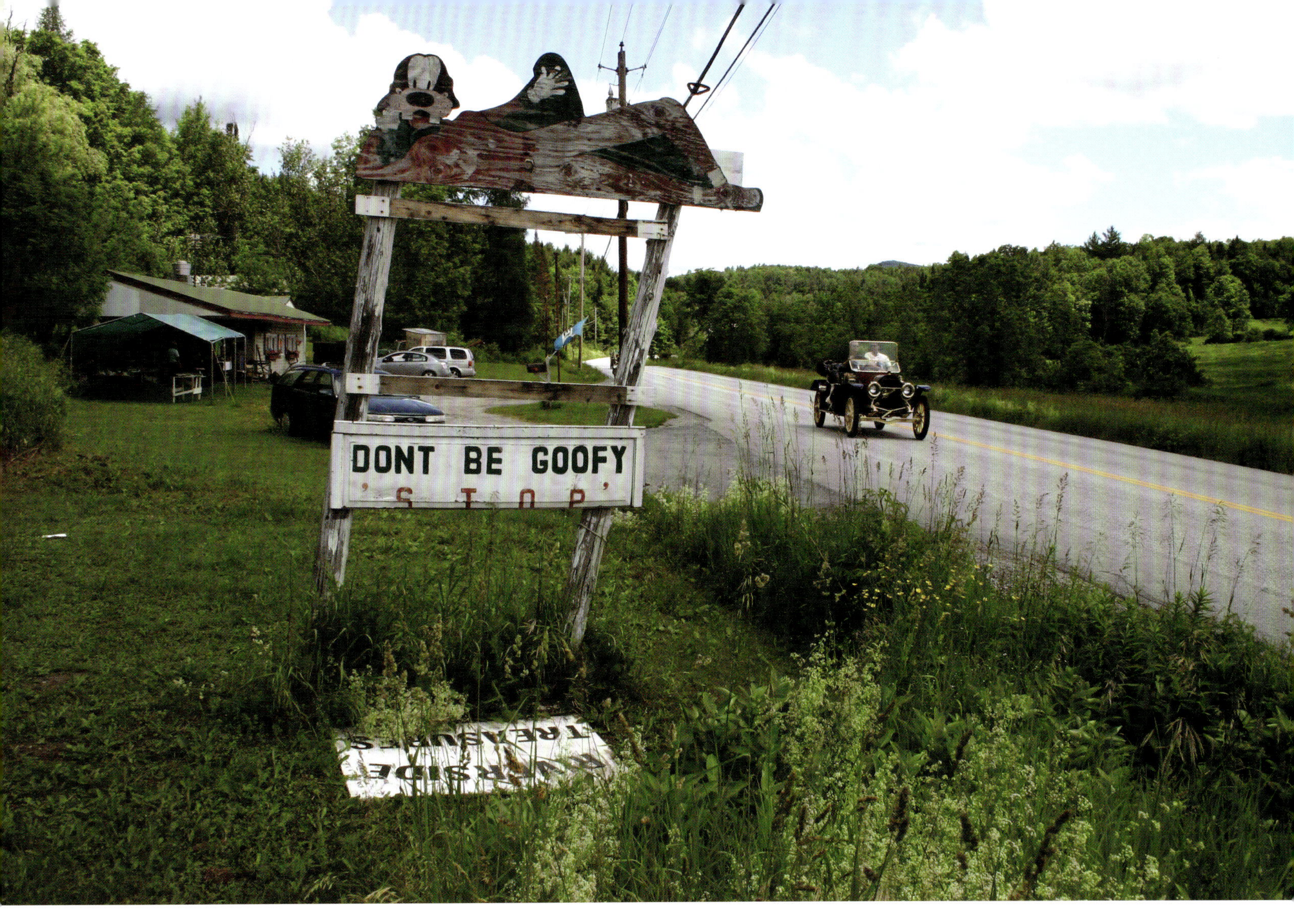

DON'T BE GOOFY, Marshfield, Vermont, 6/24/09

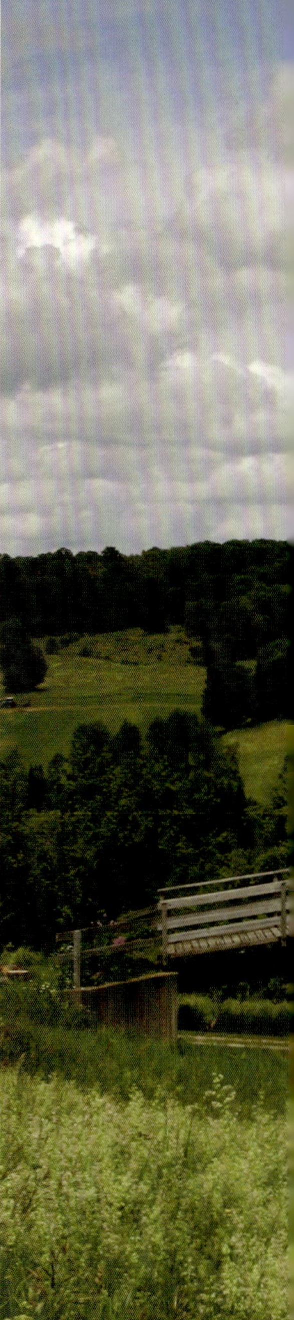

BARN, Center Road, East Montpelier, Vermont, 6/25/09

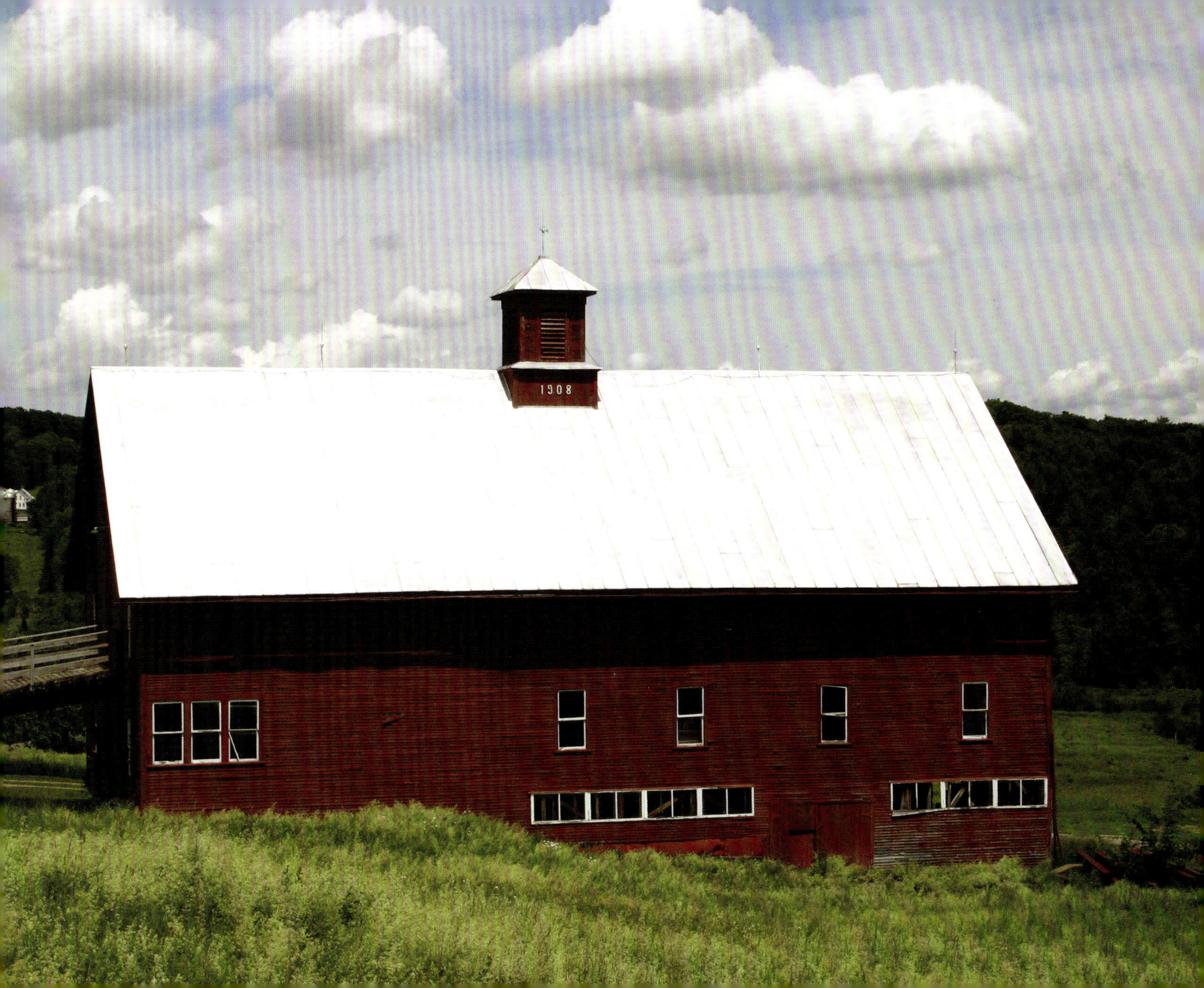
1908

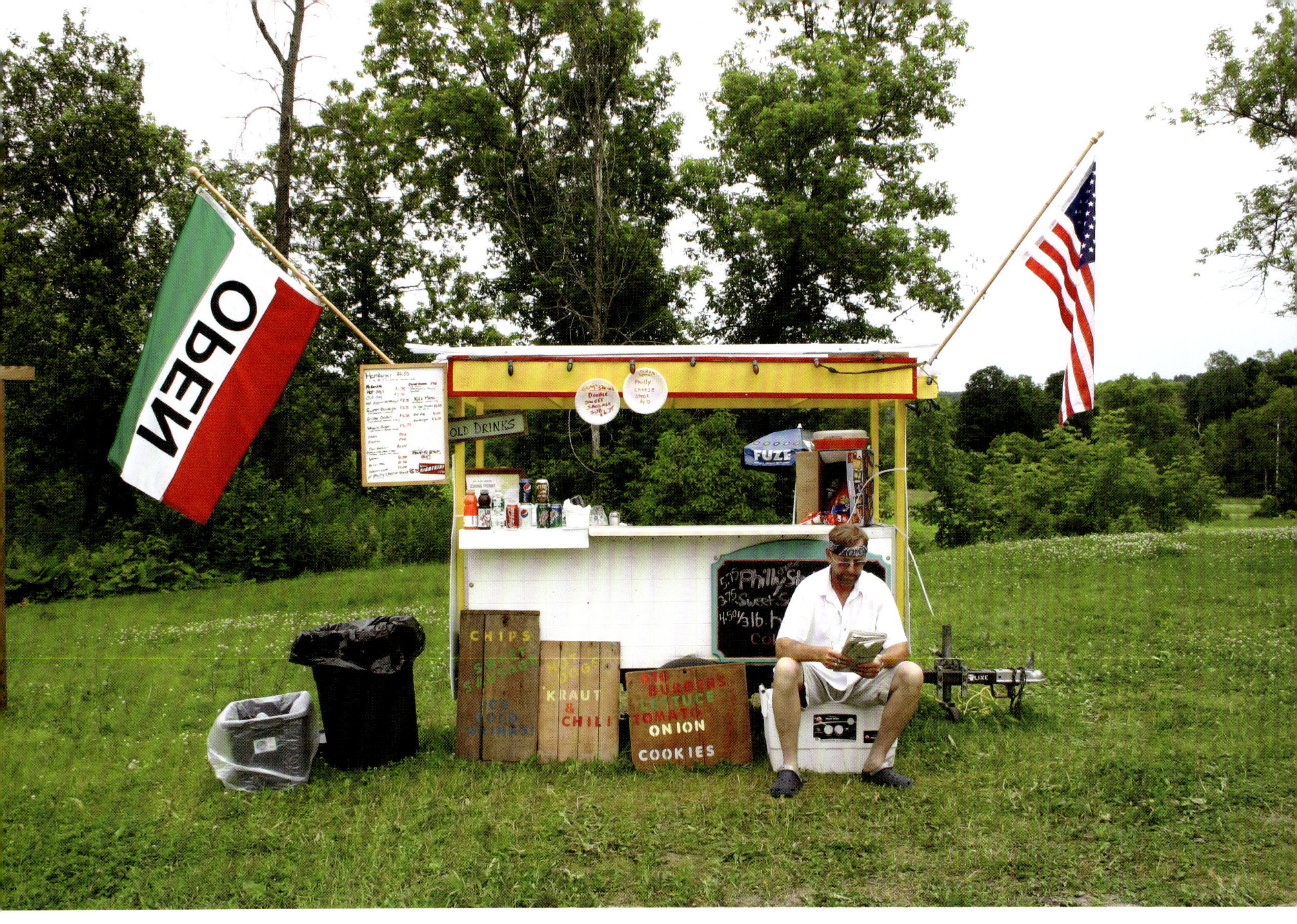

FOOD VENDOR, East Montpelier, Vermont, 6/26/09

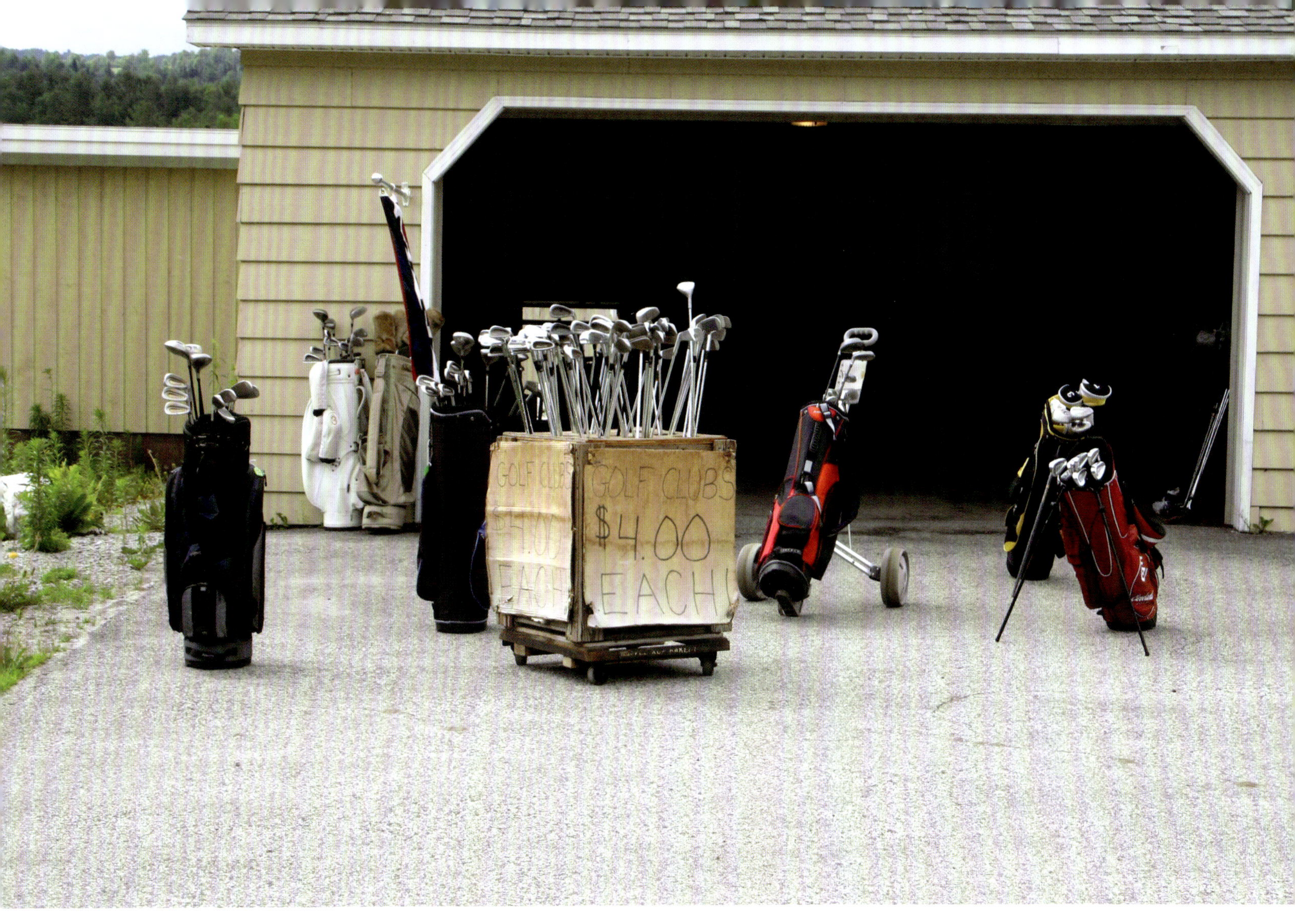

GOLF CLUBS, East Montpelier, Vermont, 6/27/09

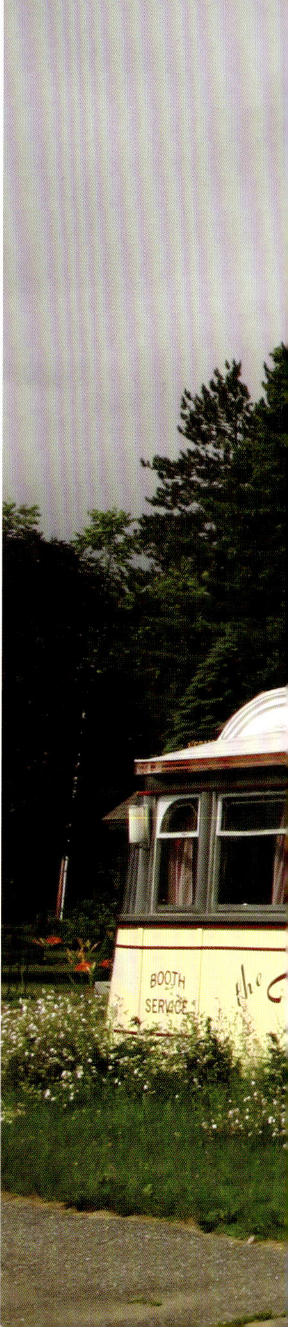

FARMERS DINER, Quechee, Vermont, 6/28/09

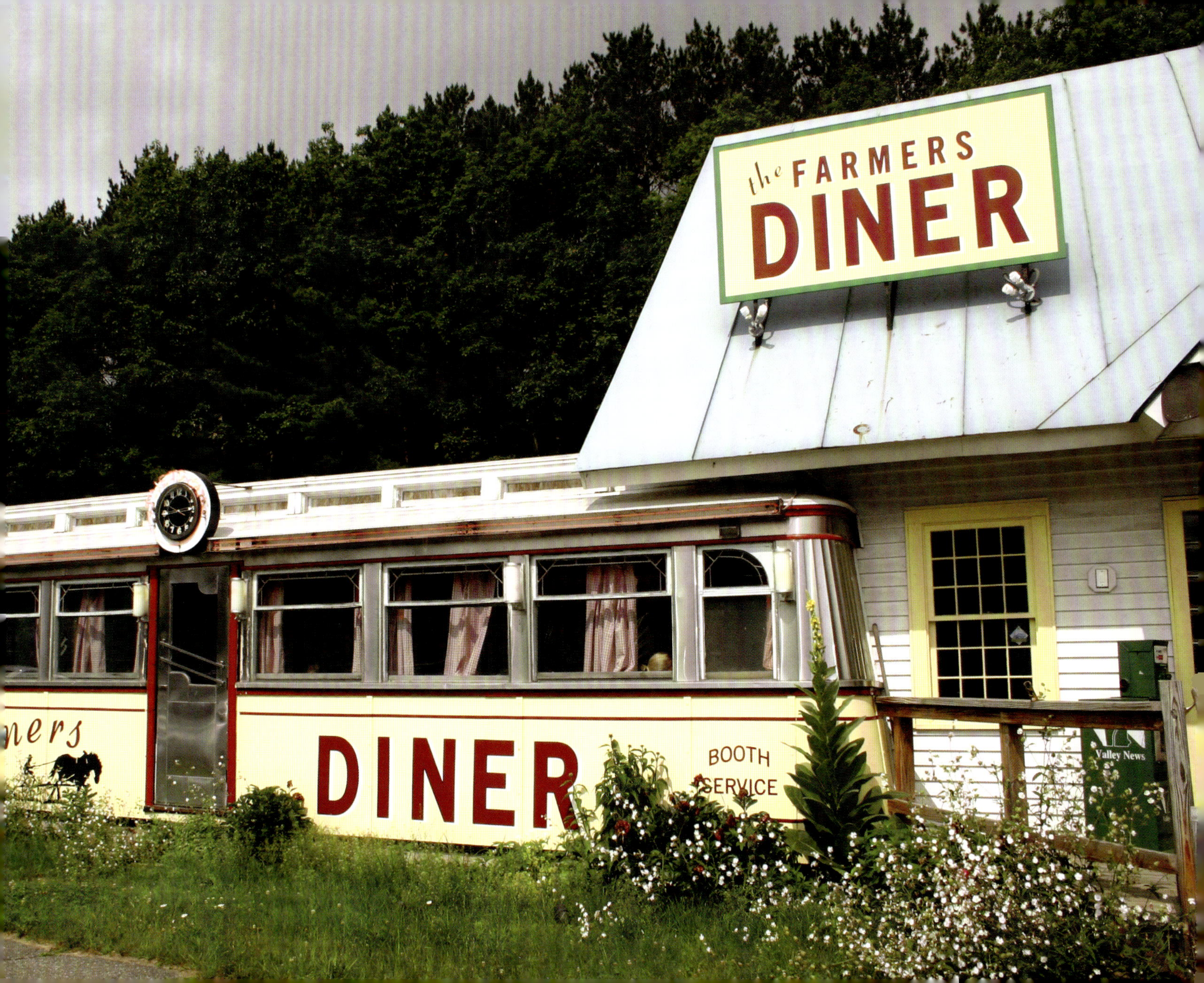

the FARMERS
DINER
DINER
BOOTH
SERVICE
Valley News

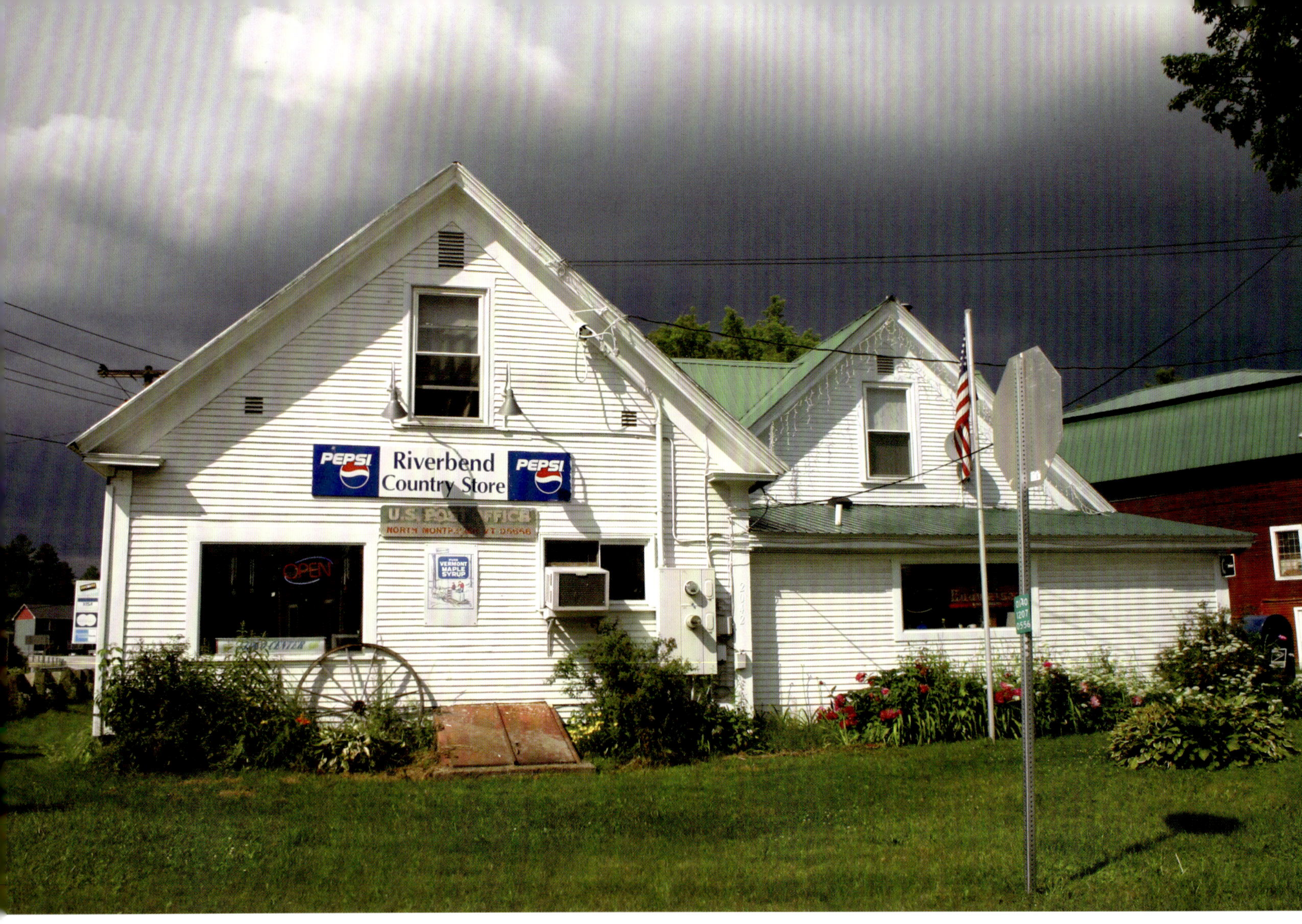

RIVERBEND COUNTRY STORE, East Montpelier, Vermont, 6/28/09

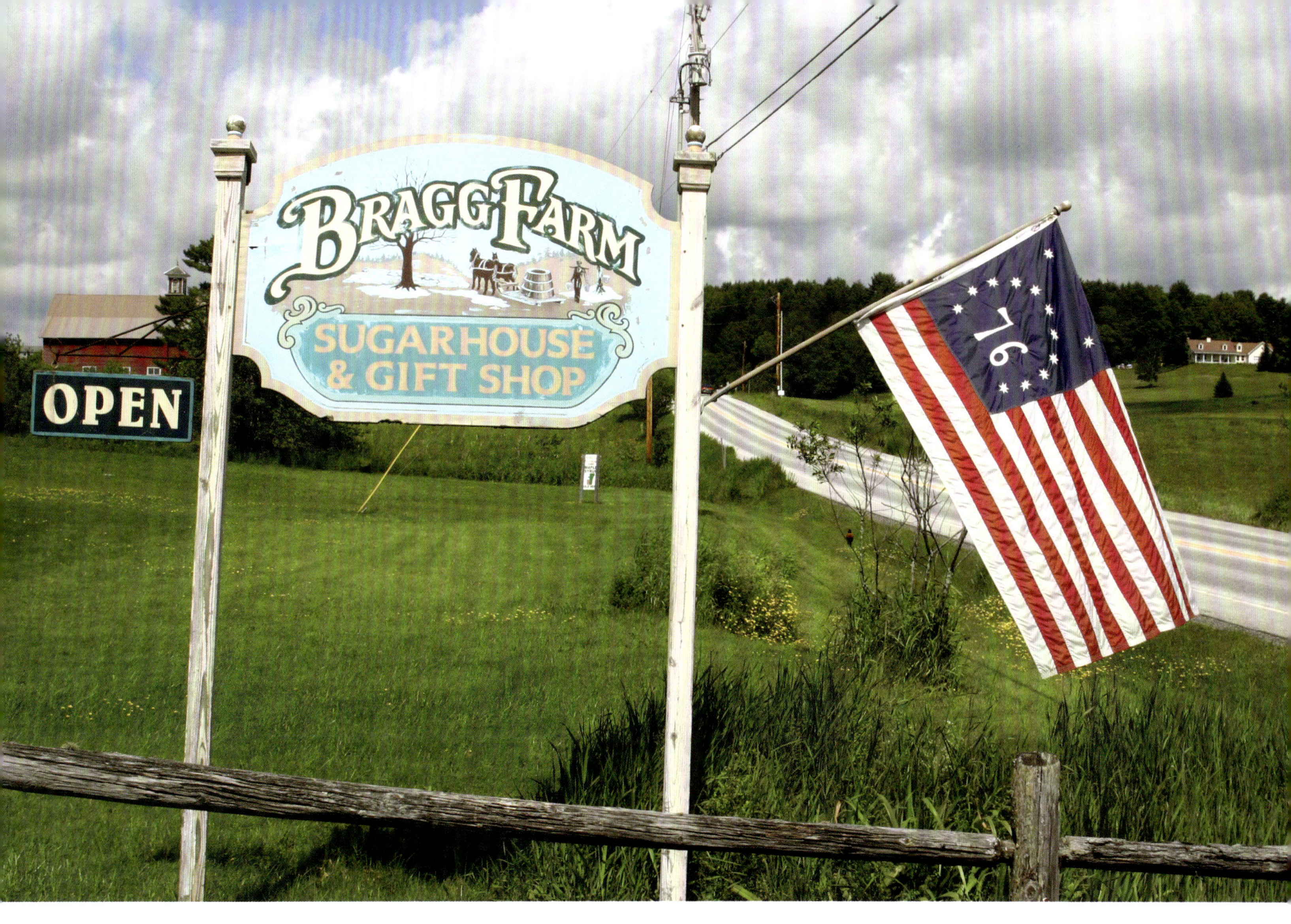

BRAGG FARM AND AMERICAN FLAG 76, East Montpelier, Vermont, 6/12/09

COCA-COLA TRUCK AND CITY HALL, Montpelier, Vermont, 6/28/12

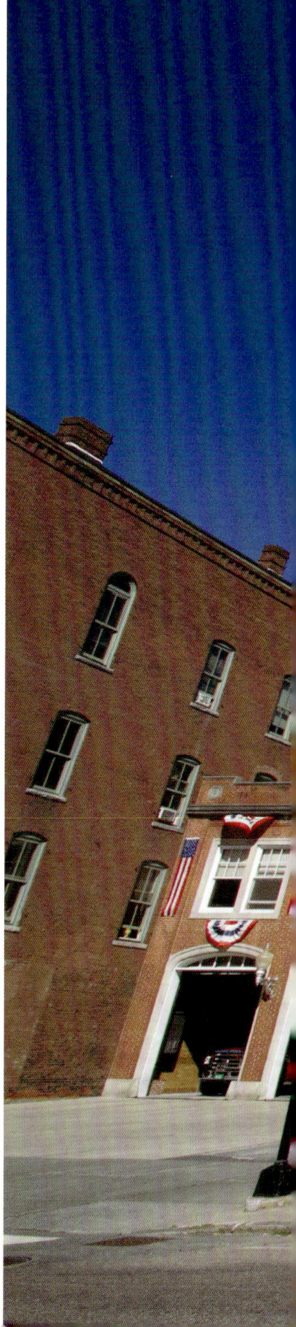

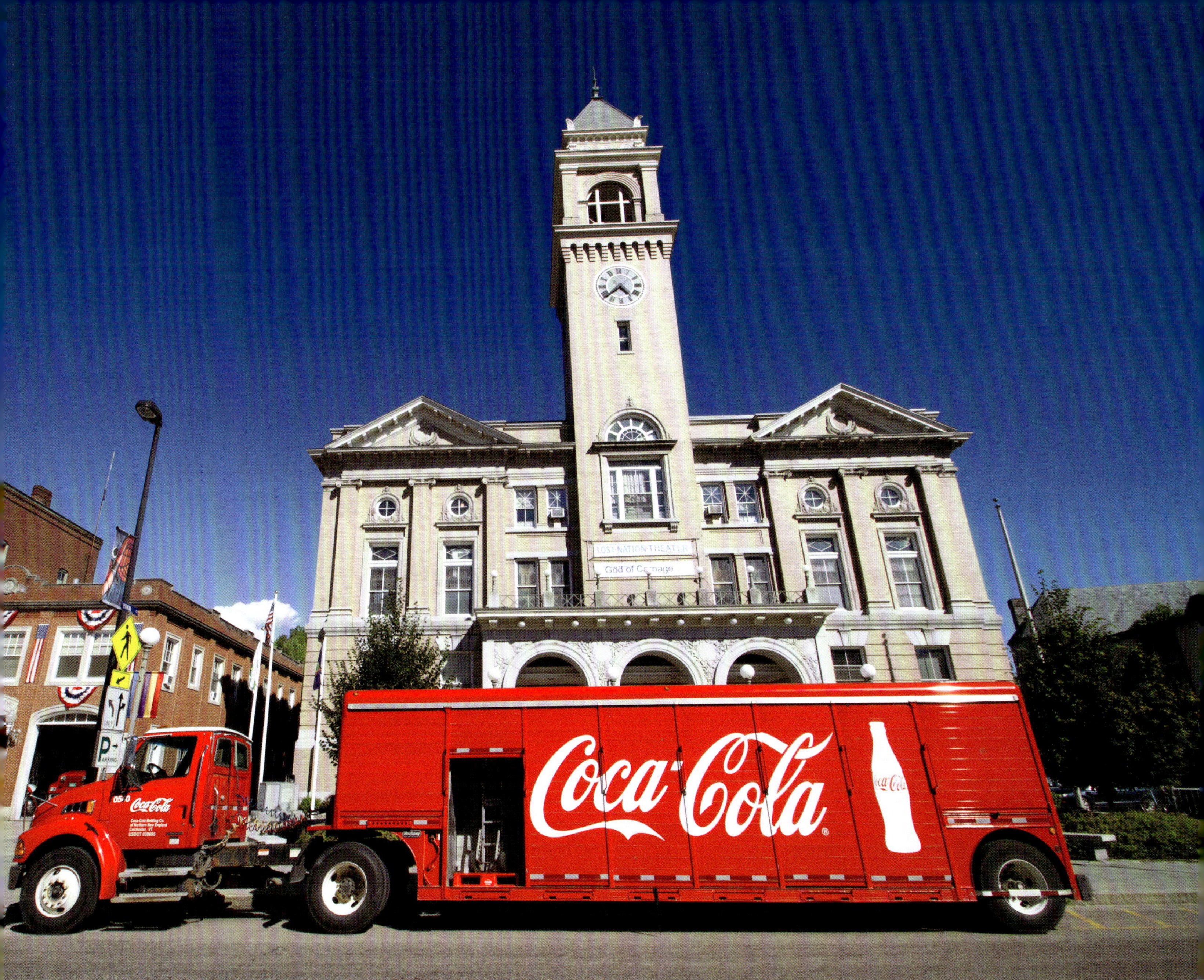
LOST NATION THEATER
Coca-Cola
Coca-Cola

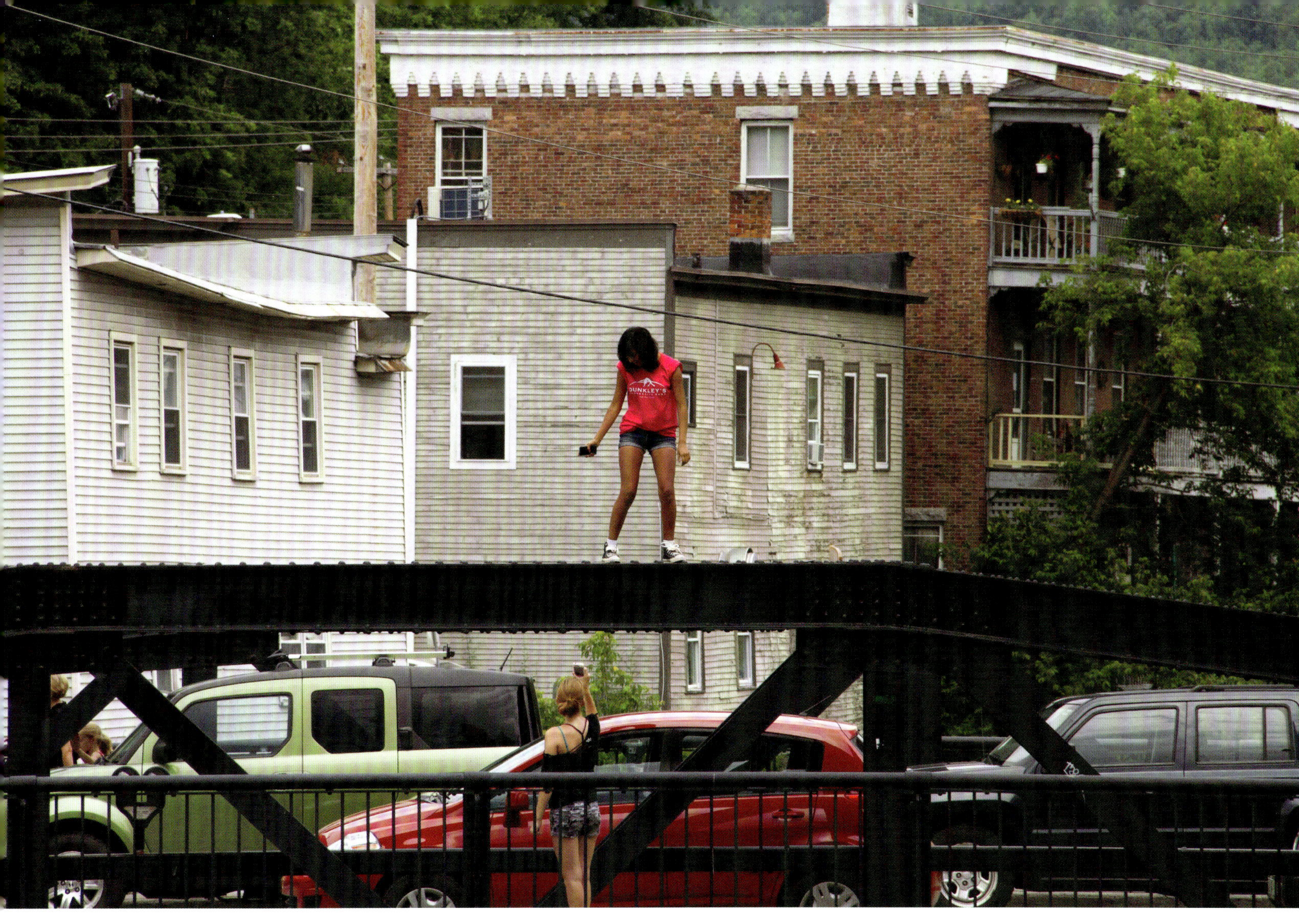

GIRLS ON BRIDGE, Montpelier, Vermont, 7/7/12

WOODPILE AND AMERICAN FLAG, Calais, Vermont, 7/8/12

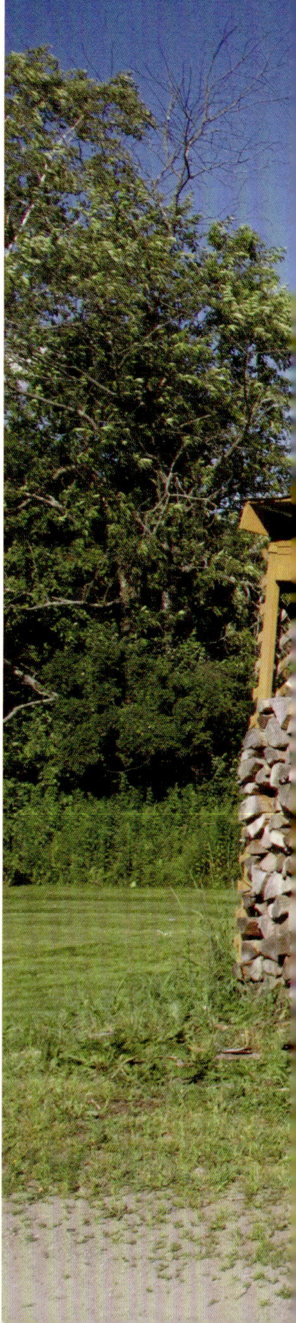

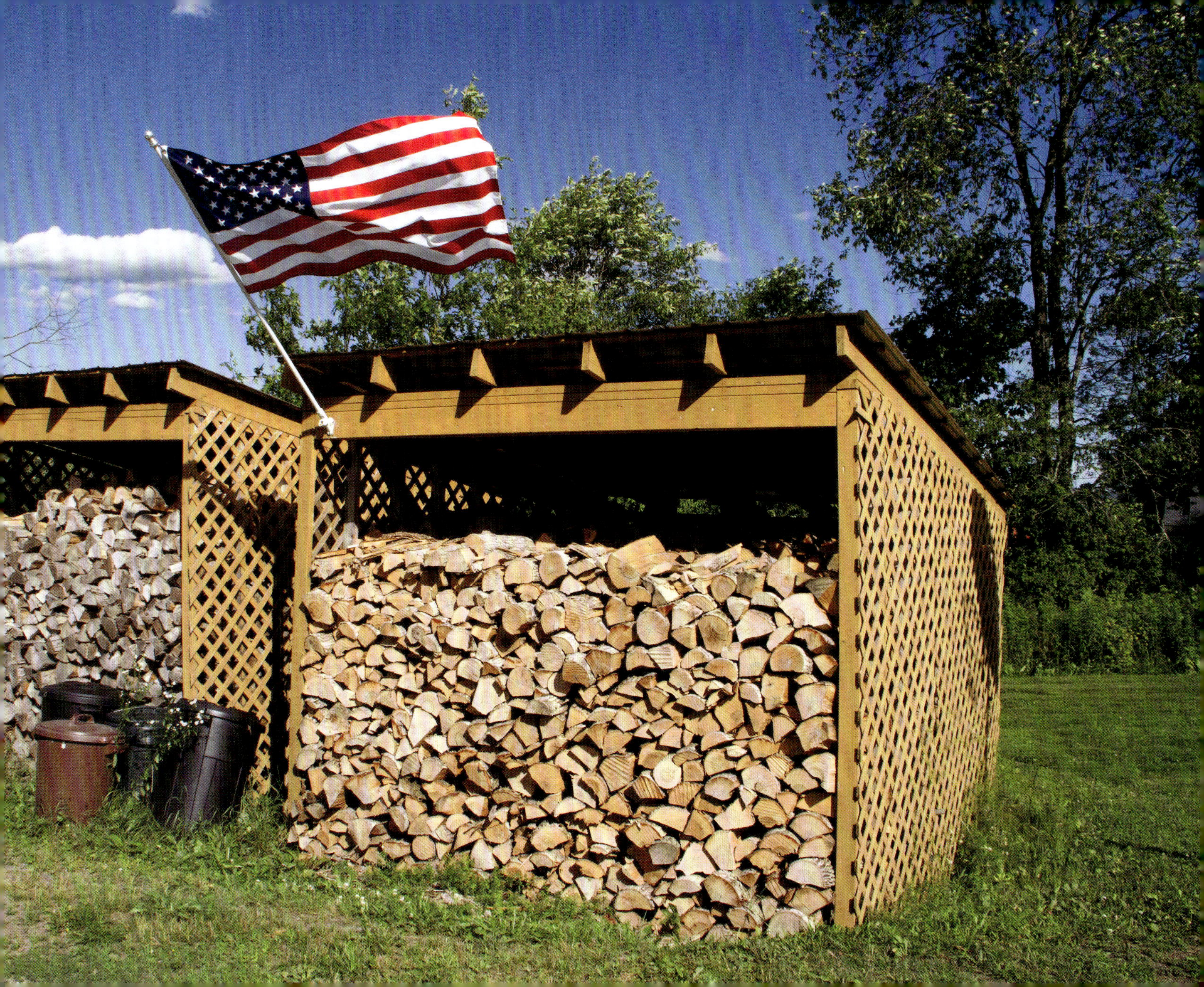

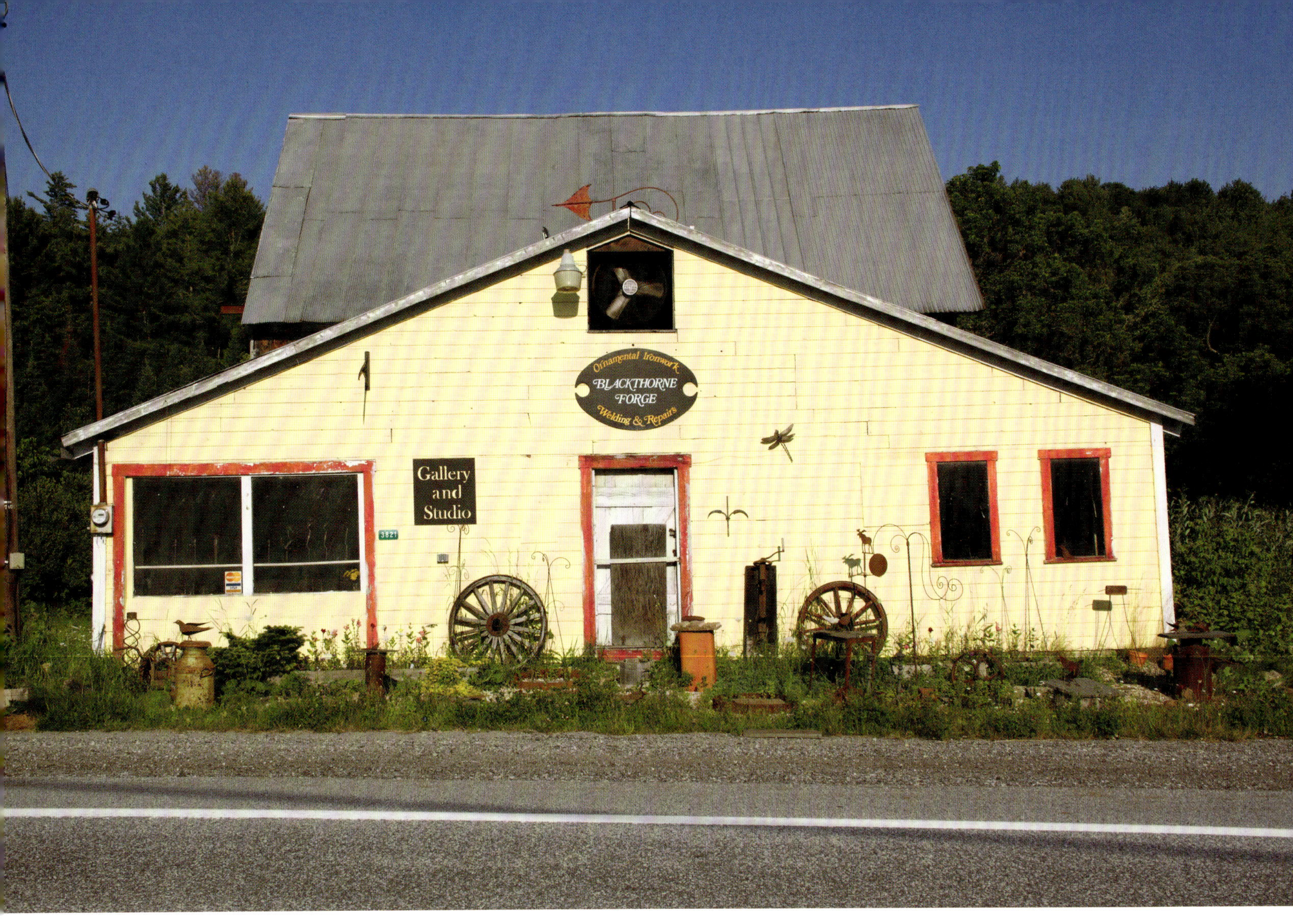

BLACKTHORNE FORGE, Marshfield, Vermont, 7/12/12

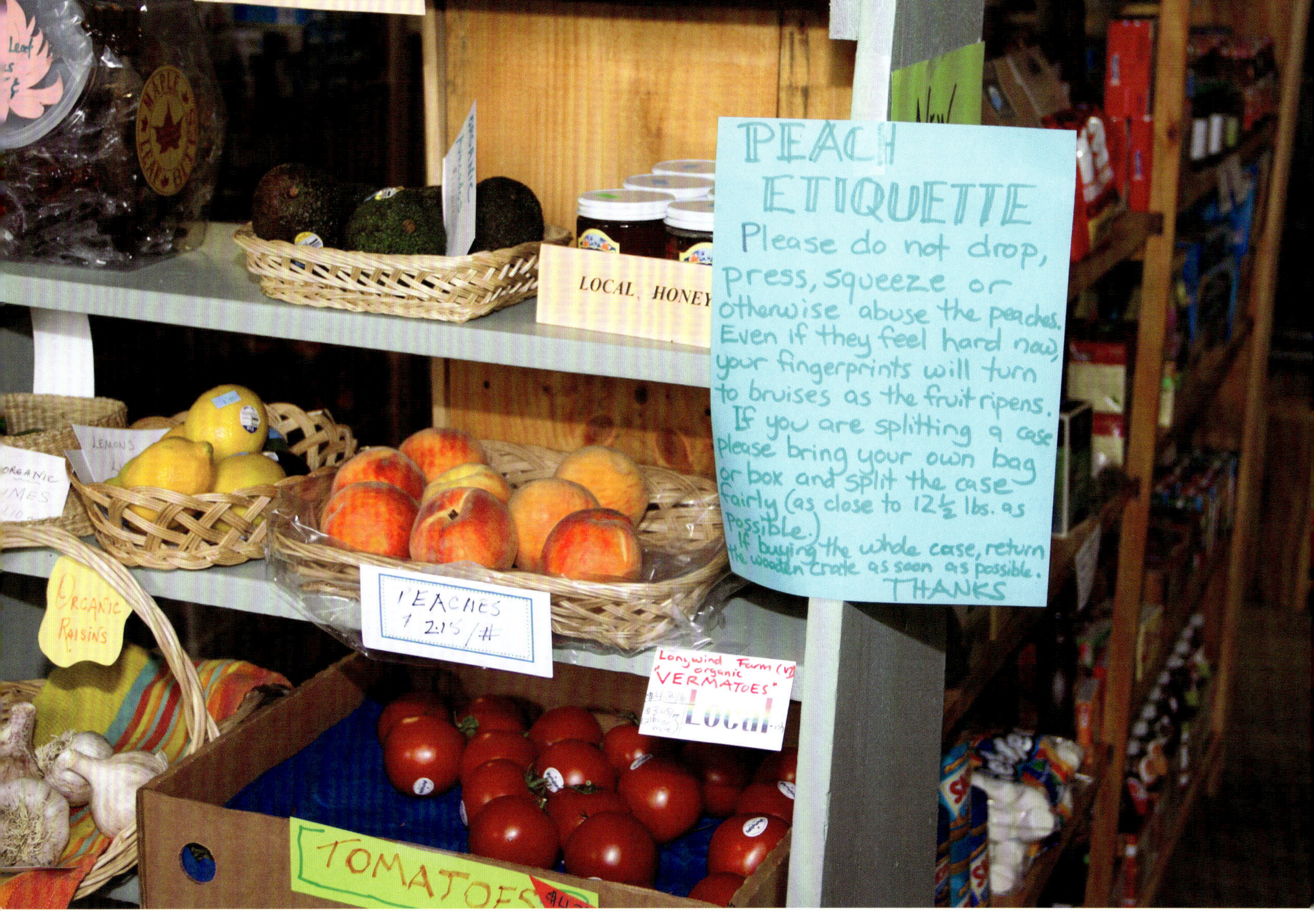

PEACH ETIQUETTE, Adamant, Vermont, 7/28/12

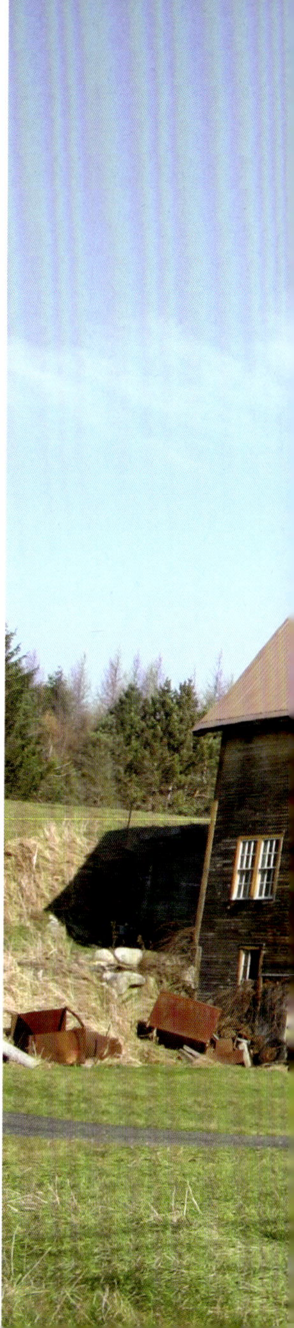

BARN AND WILLYS JEEP STATION WAGON, Marshfield, Vermont, 11/20/05

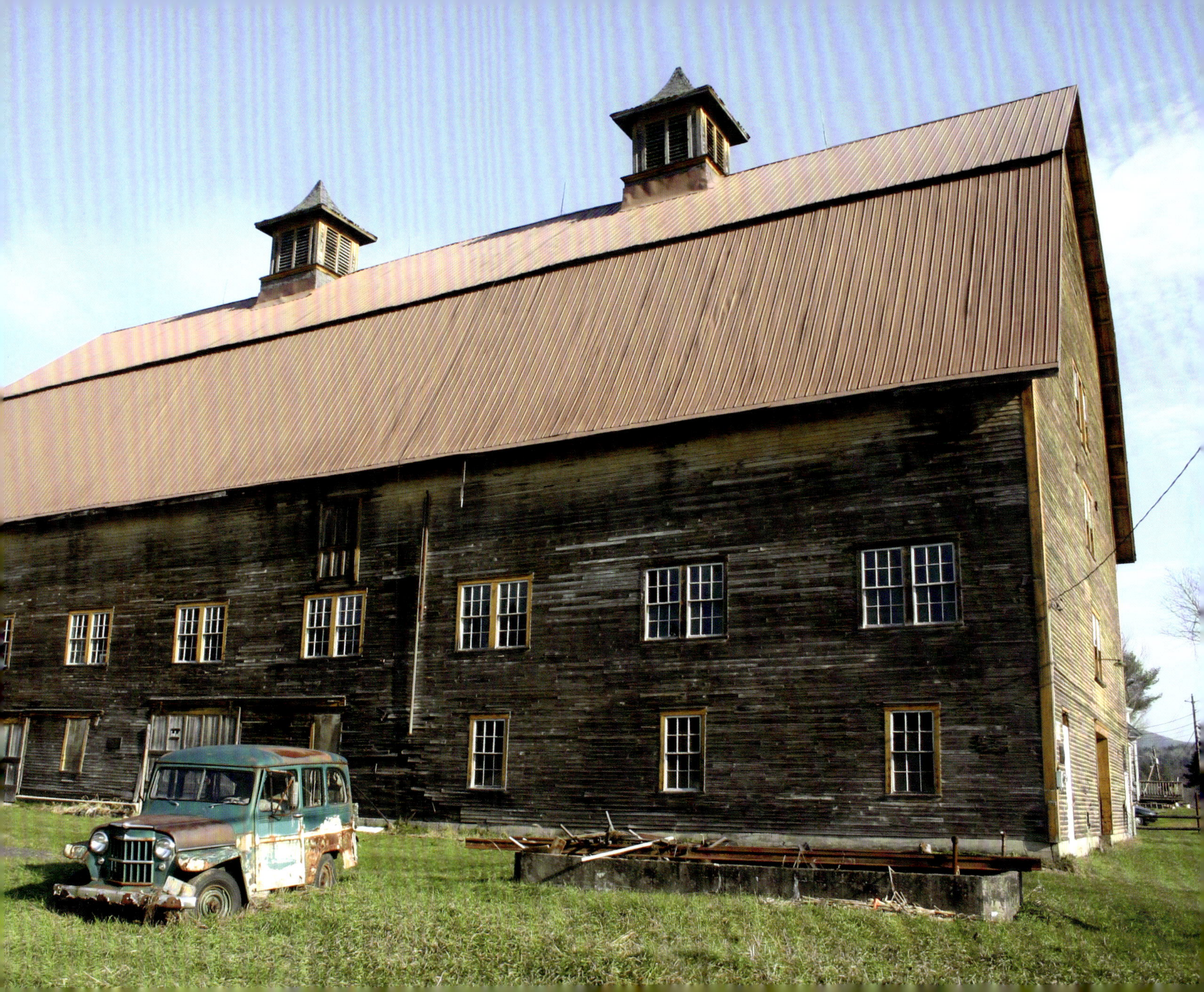

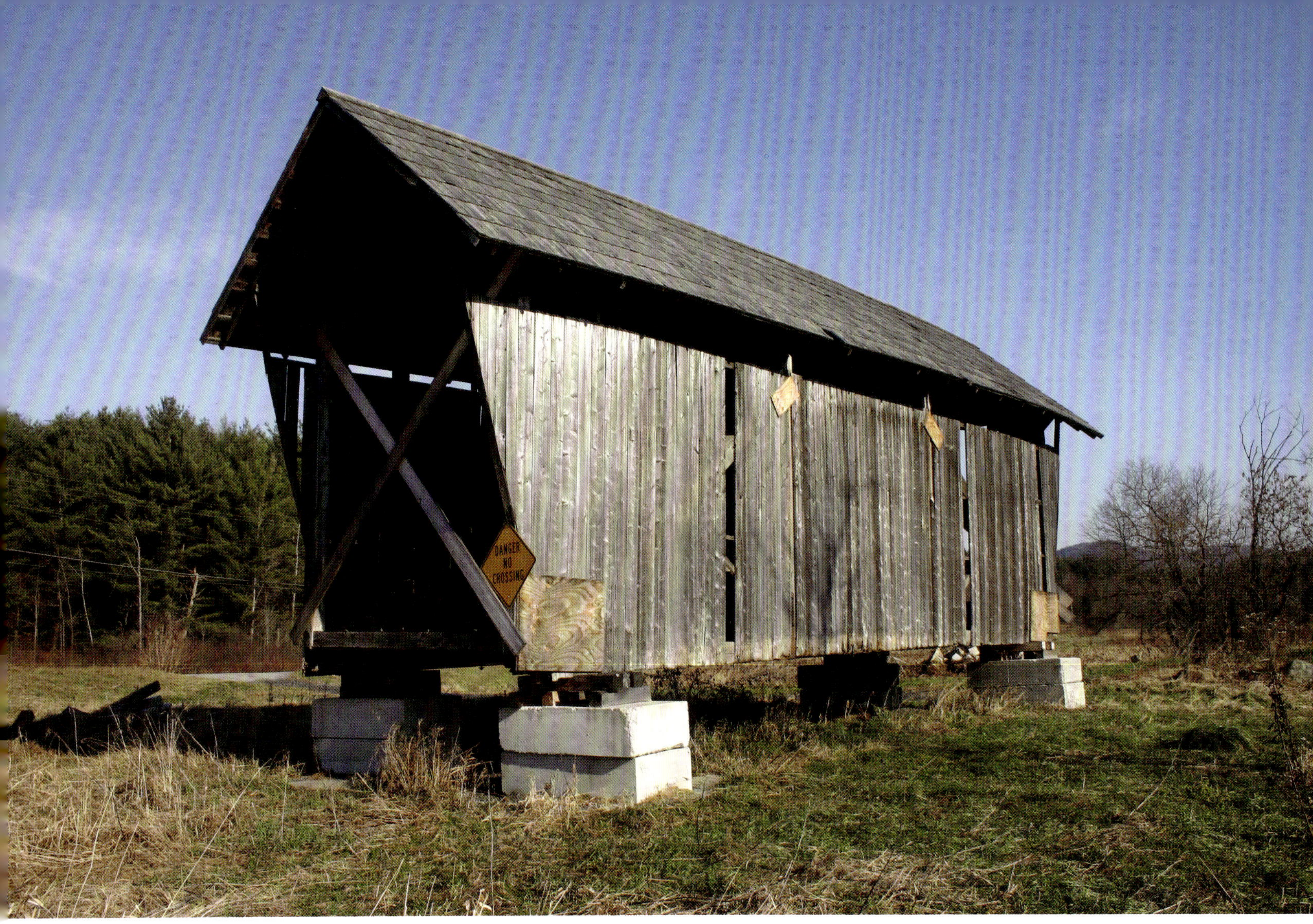

MARTIN COVERED BRIDGE, Marshfield, Vermont, 11/20/05

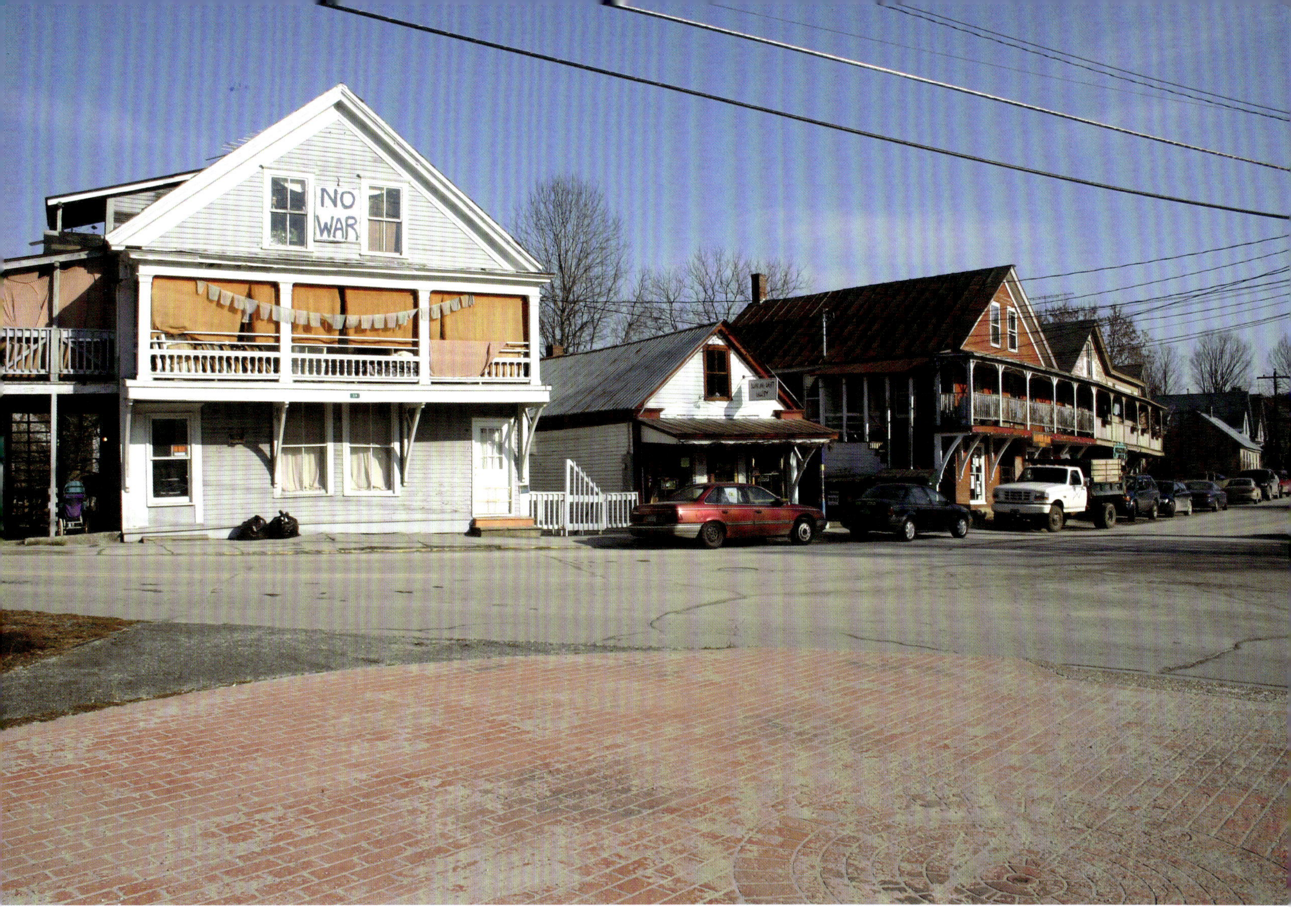

NO WAR, Plainfield, Vermont, 11/20/05

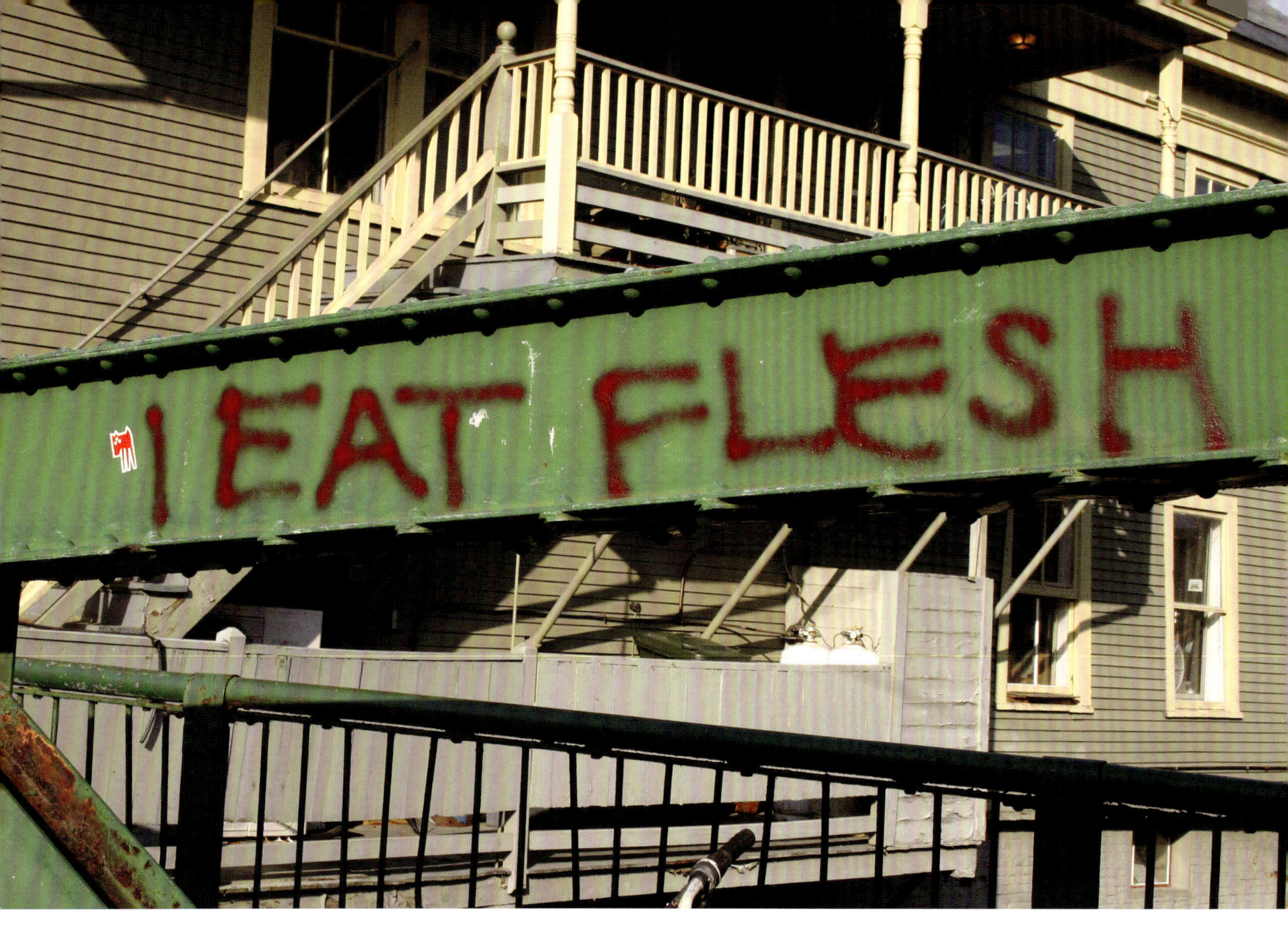

I EAT FLESH, Montpelier, Vermont, 11/20/05

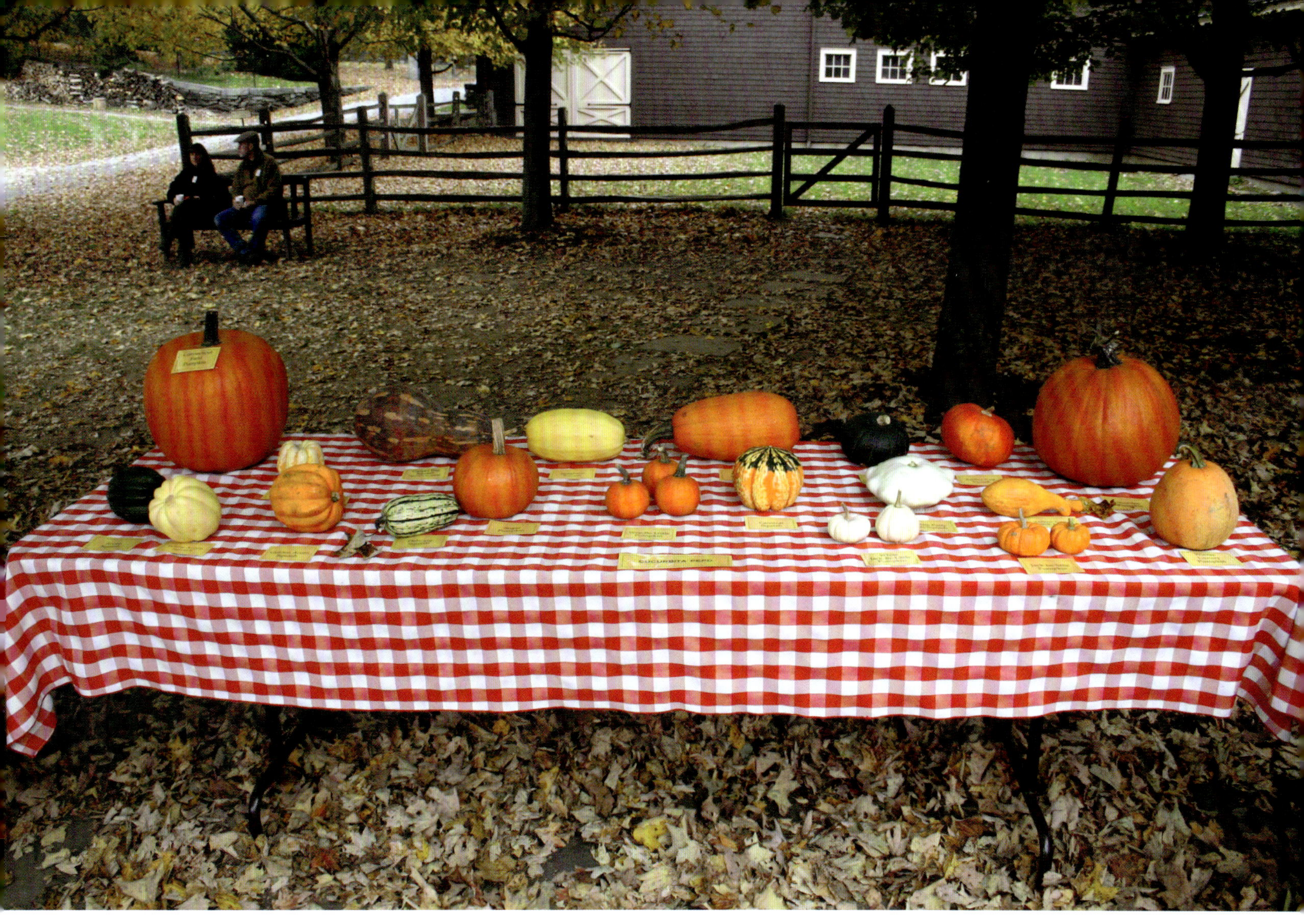

SQUASH AND PUMPKIN DISPLAY, Woodstock, Vermont, 10/10/04

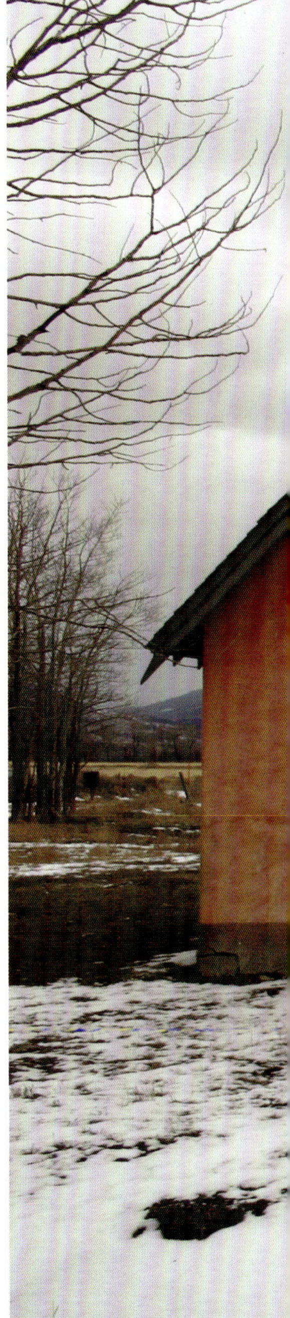

MOULTON PINK HOUSE, Mormon Row, Grand Teton National Park, Wyoming, 11/30/08

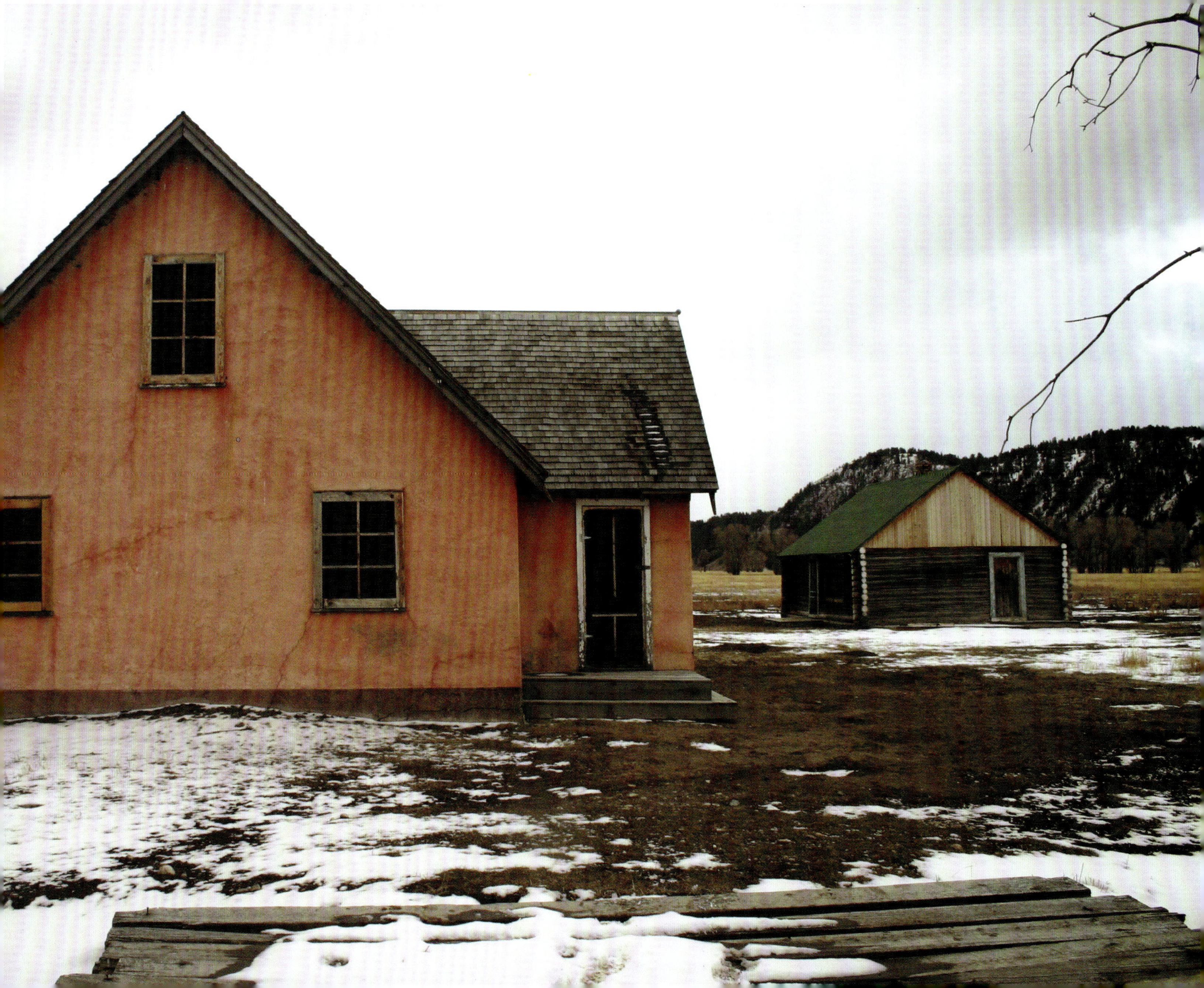

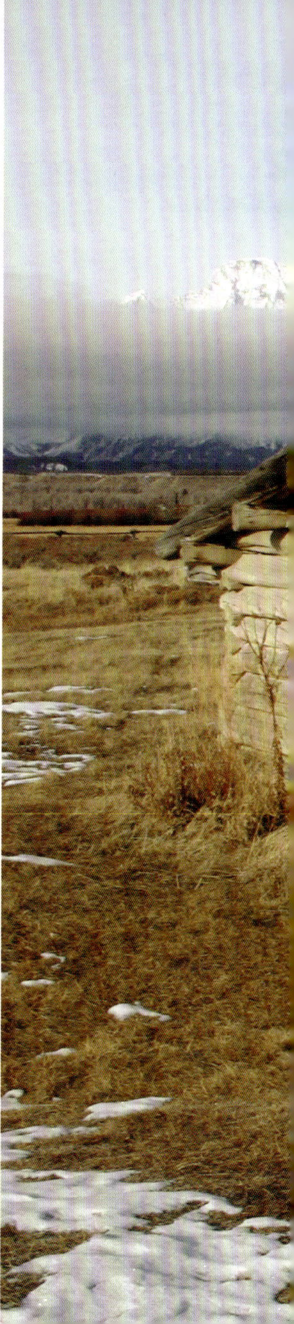

CUNNINGHAM CABIN, Grand Teton National Park, Wyoming, 12/1/08

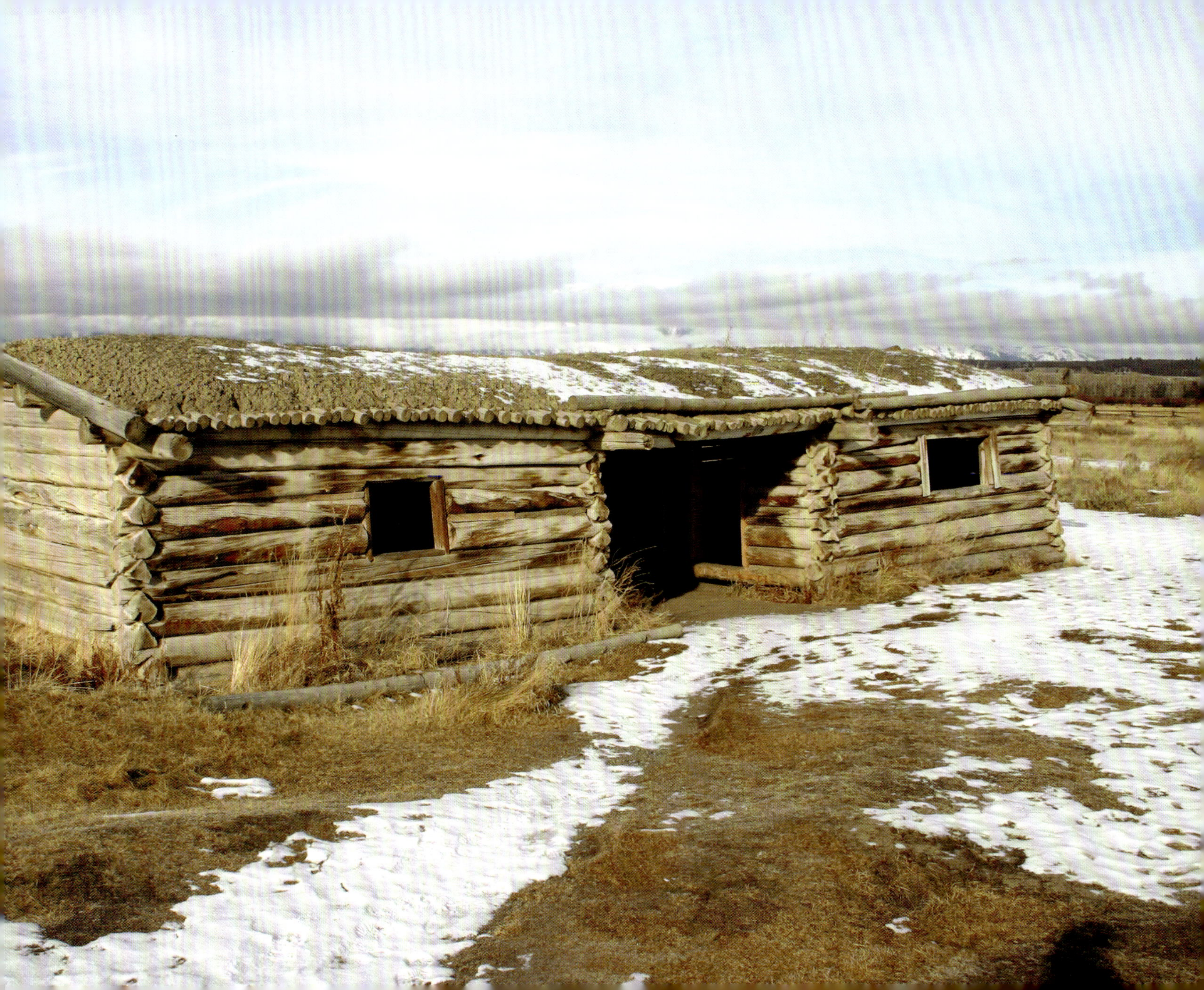

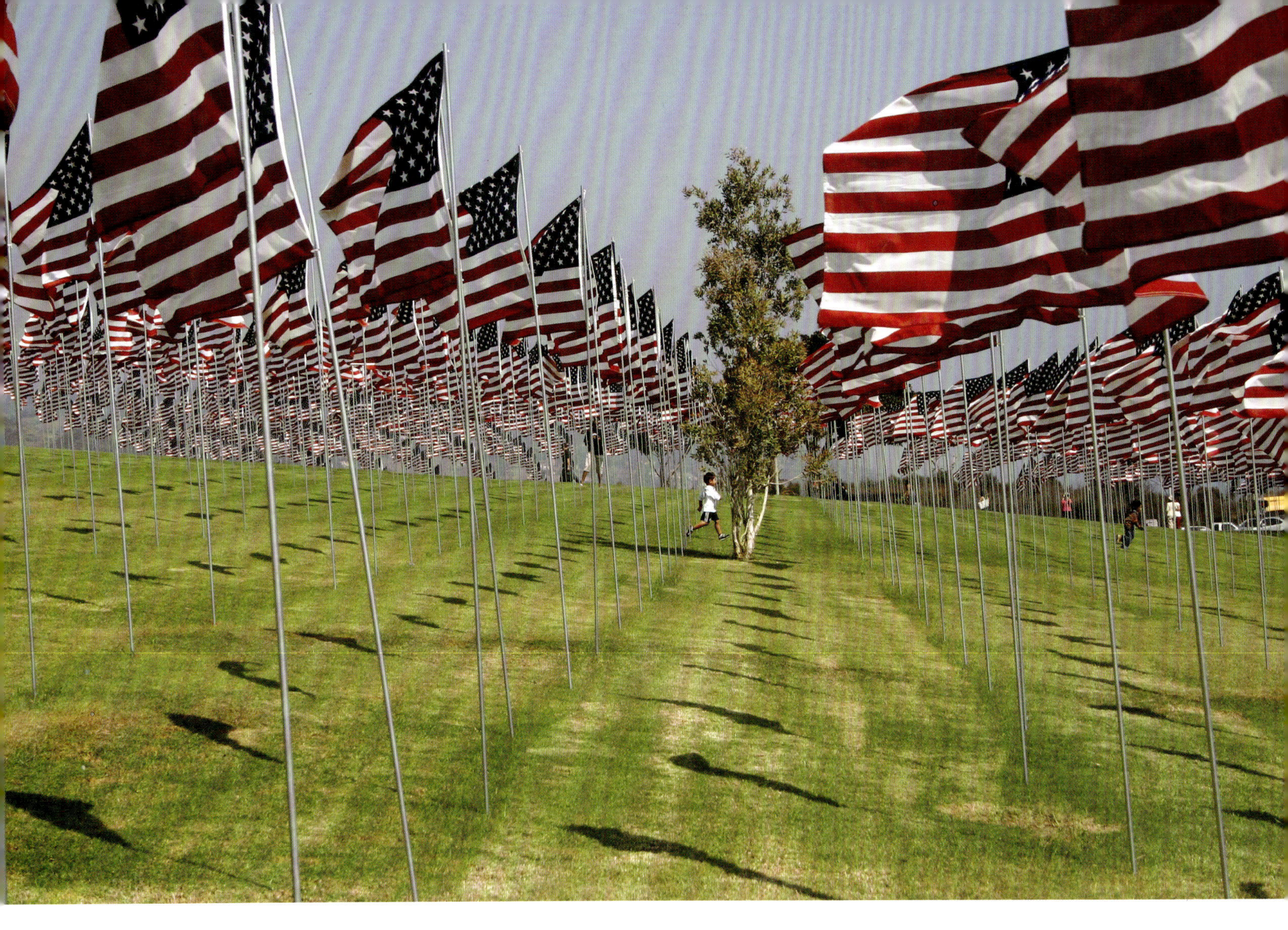

BOY AND AMERICAN FLAGS, Pepperdine University, Malibu, California, 9/11/08

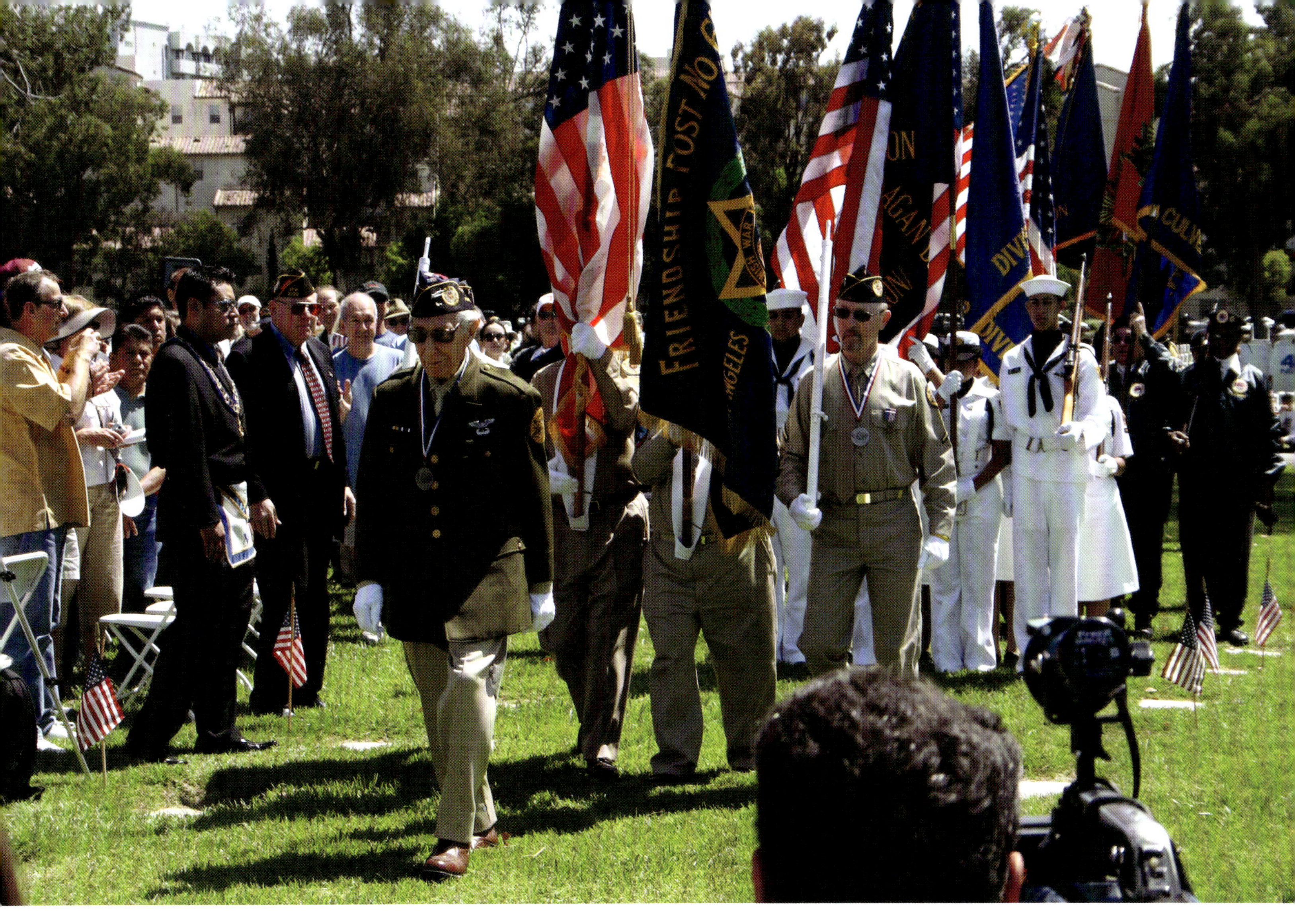

JEWISH WAR VETERANS, Los Angeles National Cemetery, Westwood, California, 5/26/08

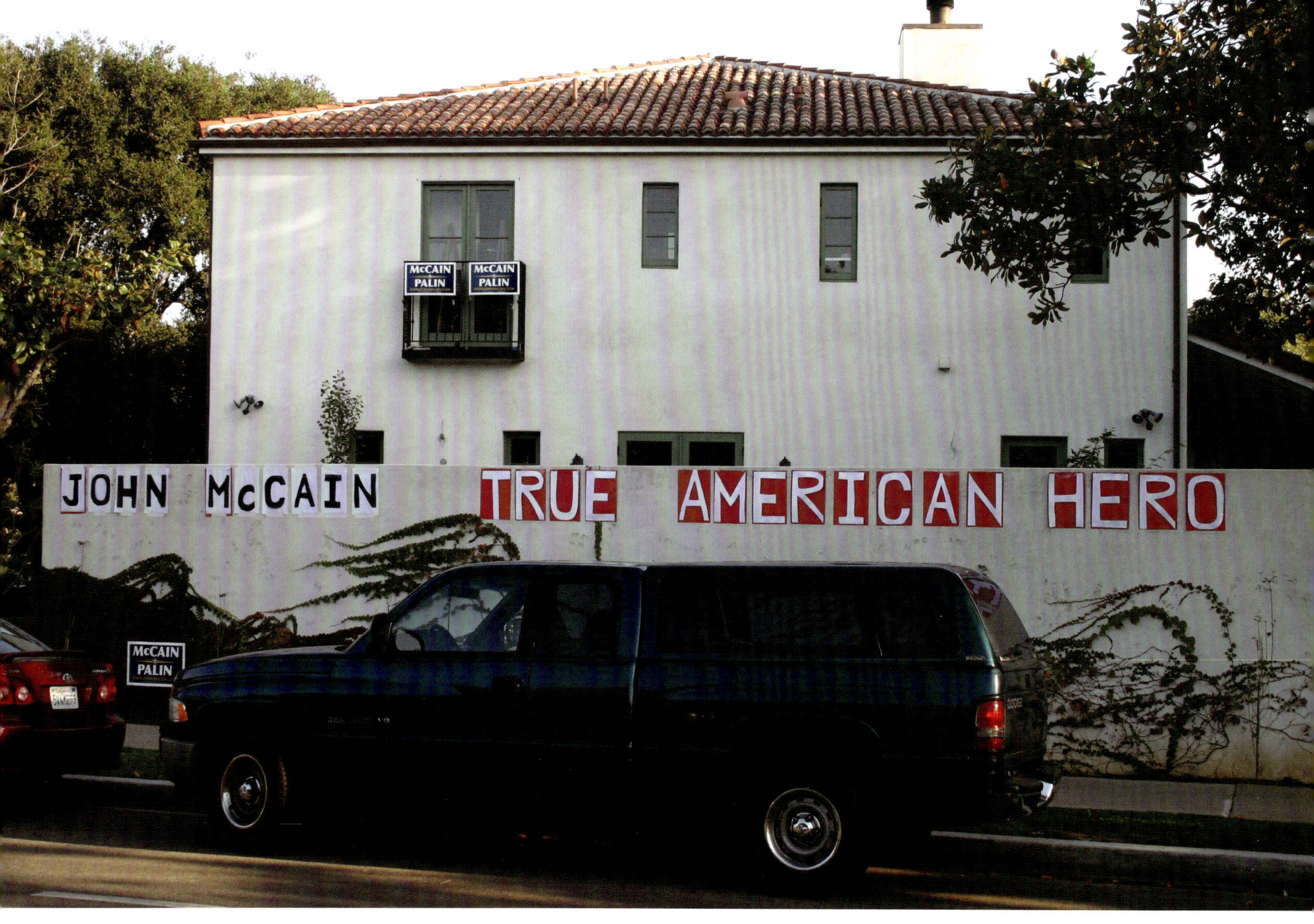

JOHN MCCAIN, TRUE AMERICAN HERO, Santa Monica, California, 11/3/08

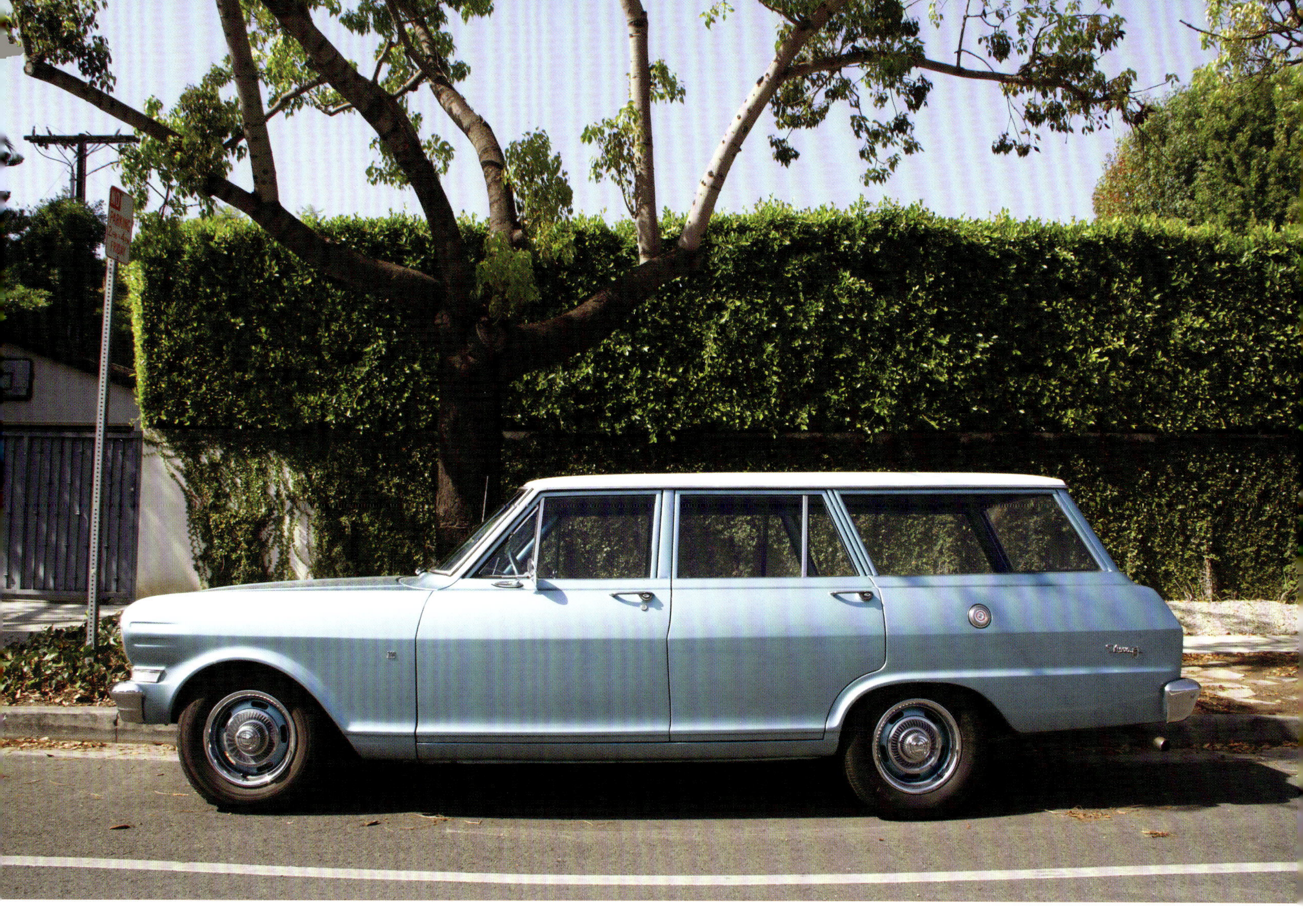

CHEVY NOVA, Santa Monica, California, 10/10/13

ROLLER COASTER AT TWILIGHT, Santa Monica, California, 8/30/07

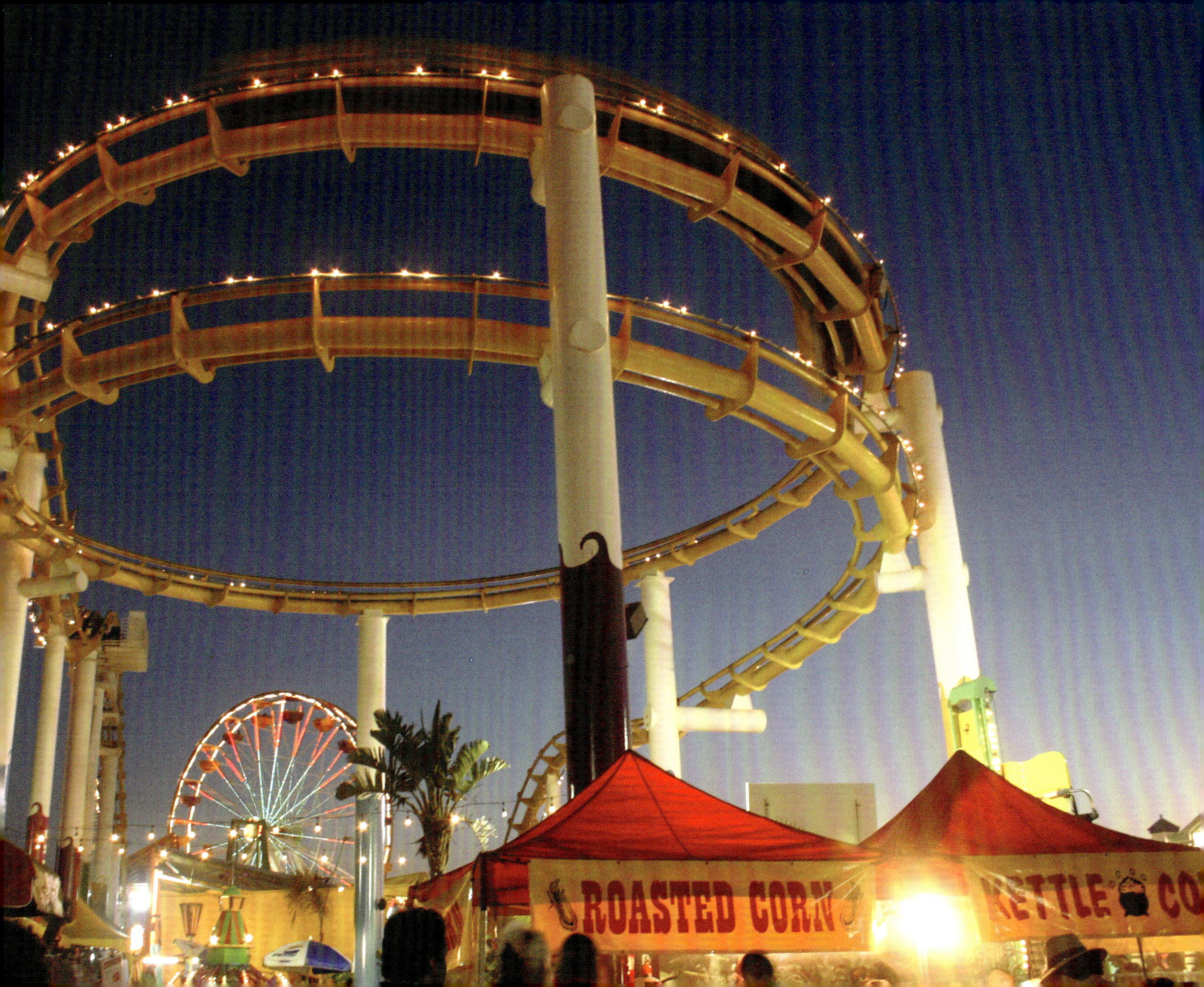
ROASTED CORN

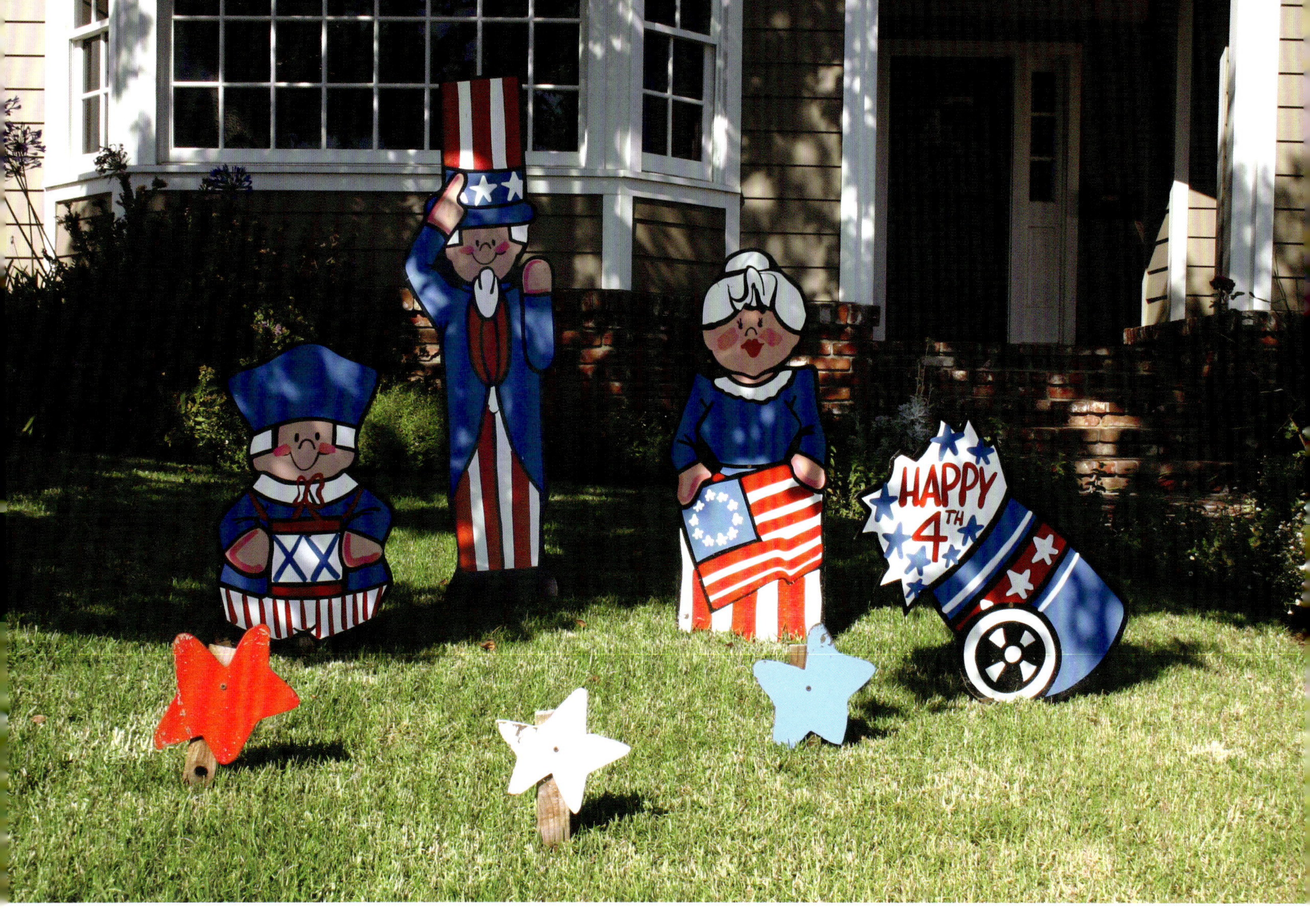

HAPPY 4TH, Pacific Palisades, California, 7/17/11

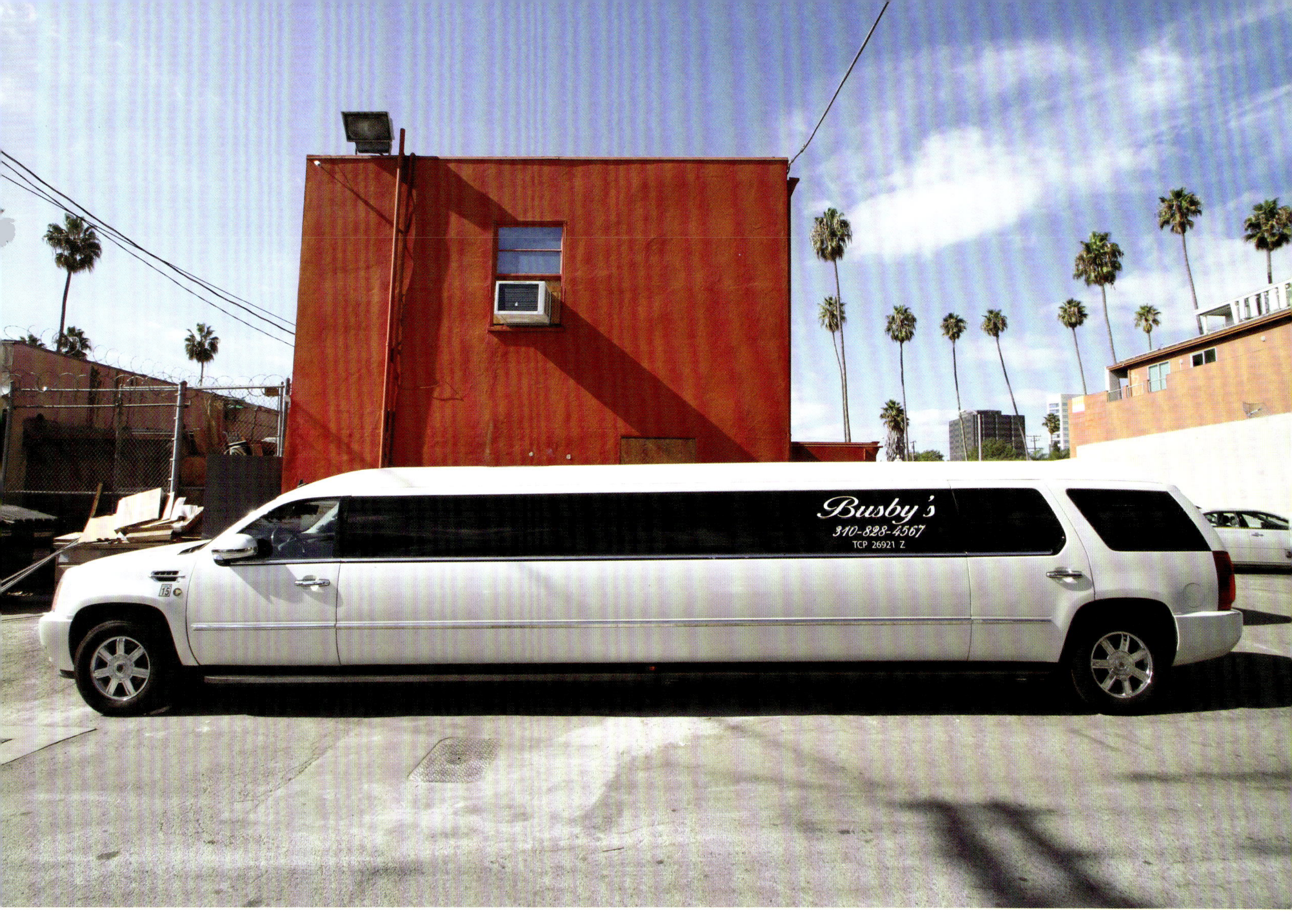

LIMOUSINE, Los Angeles, California, 10/18/12

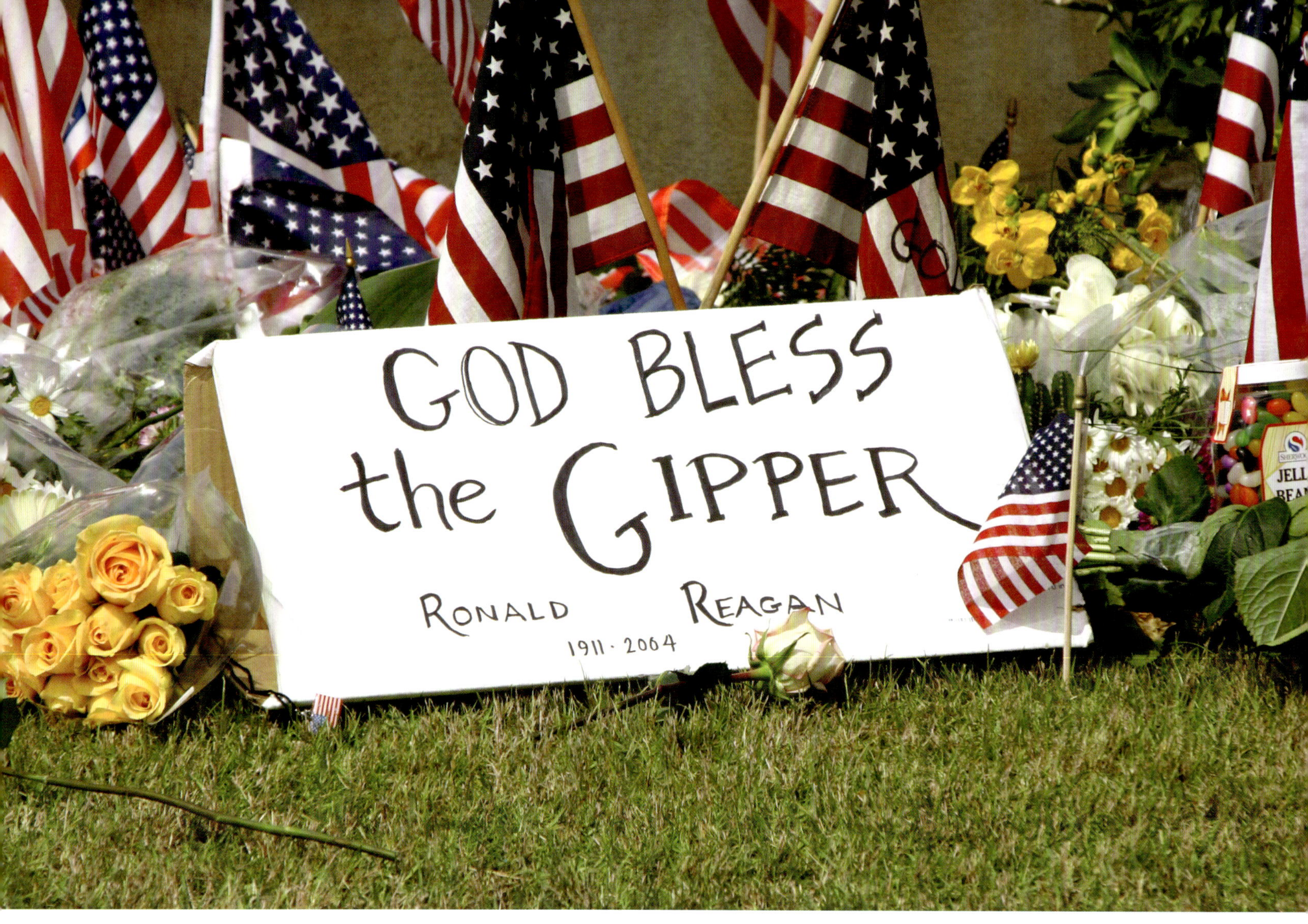

GOD BLESS THE GIPPER, Santa Monica, California, 6/6/04

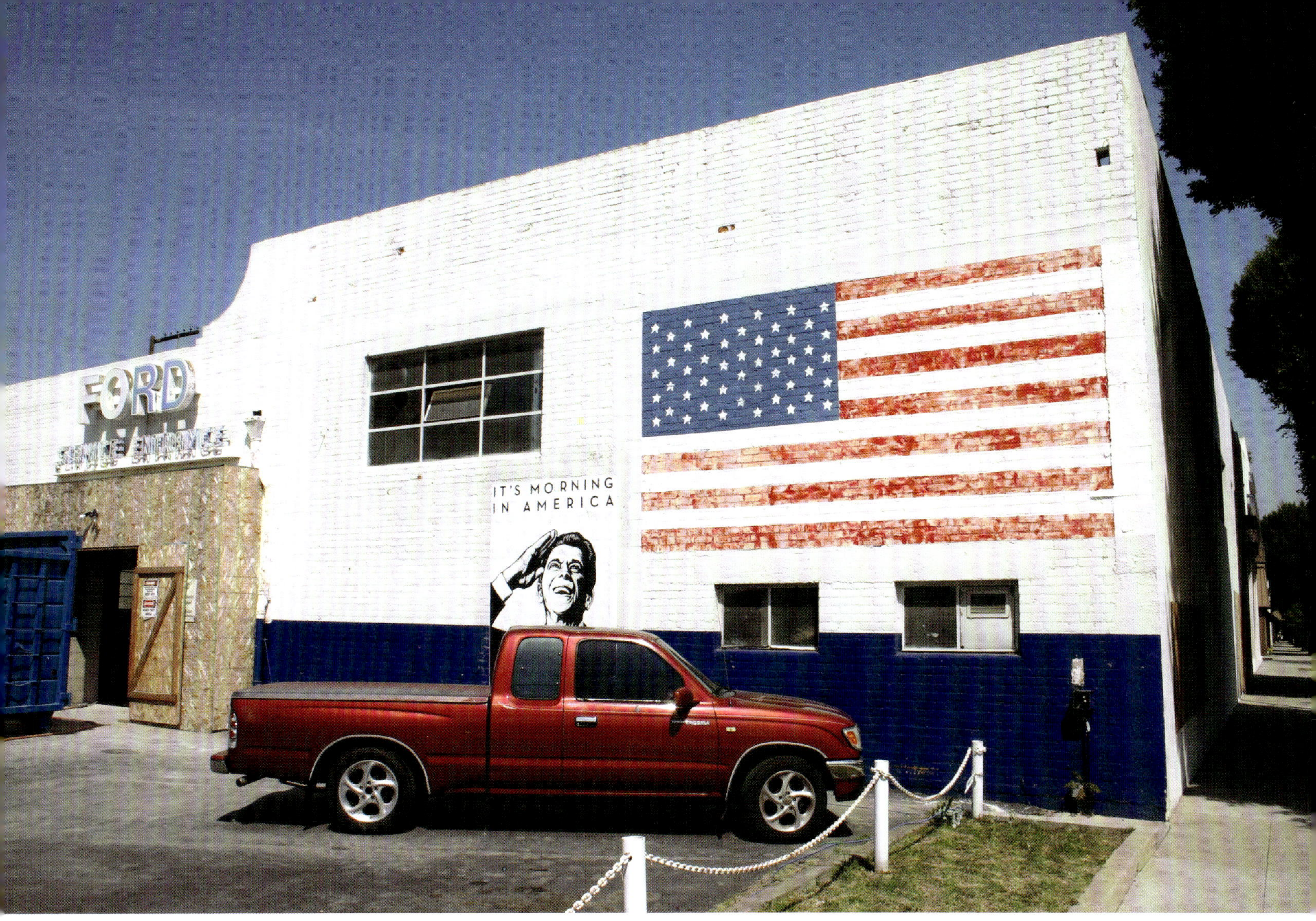

IT'S MORNING IN AMERICA, Beverly Hills, California, 4/9/12

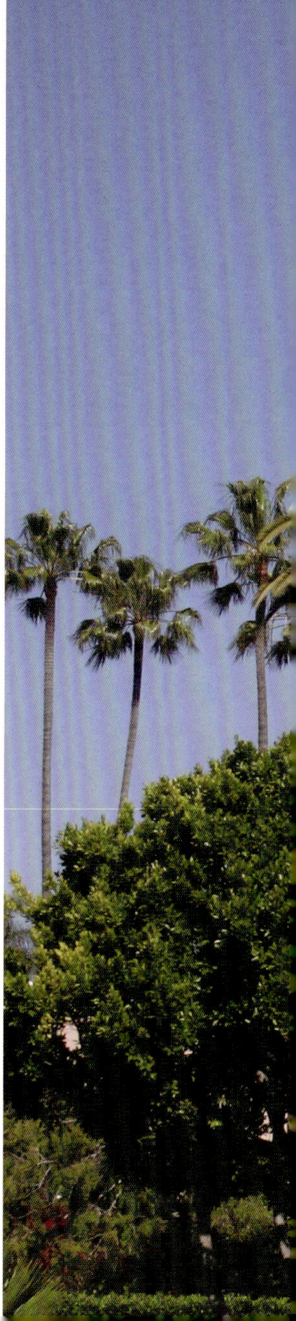

BEVERLY HILLS HOTEL, Beverly Hills, California, 4/27/07

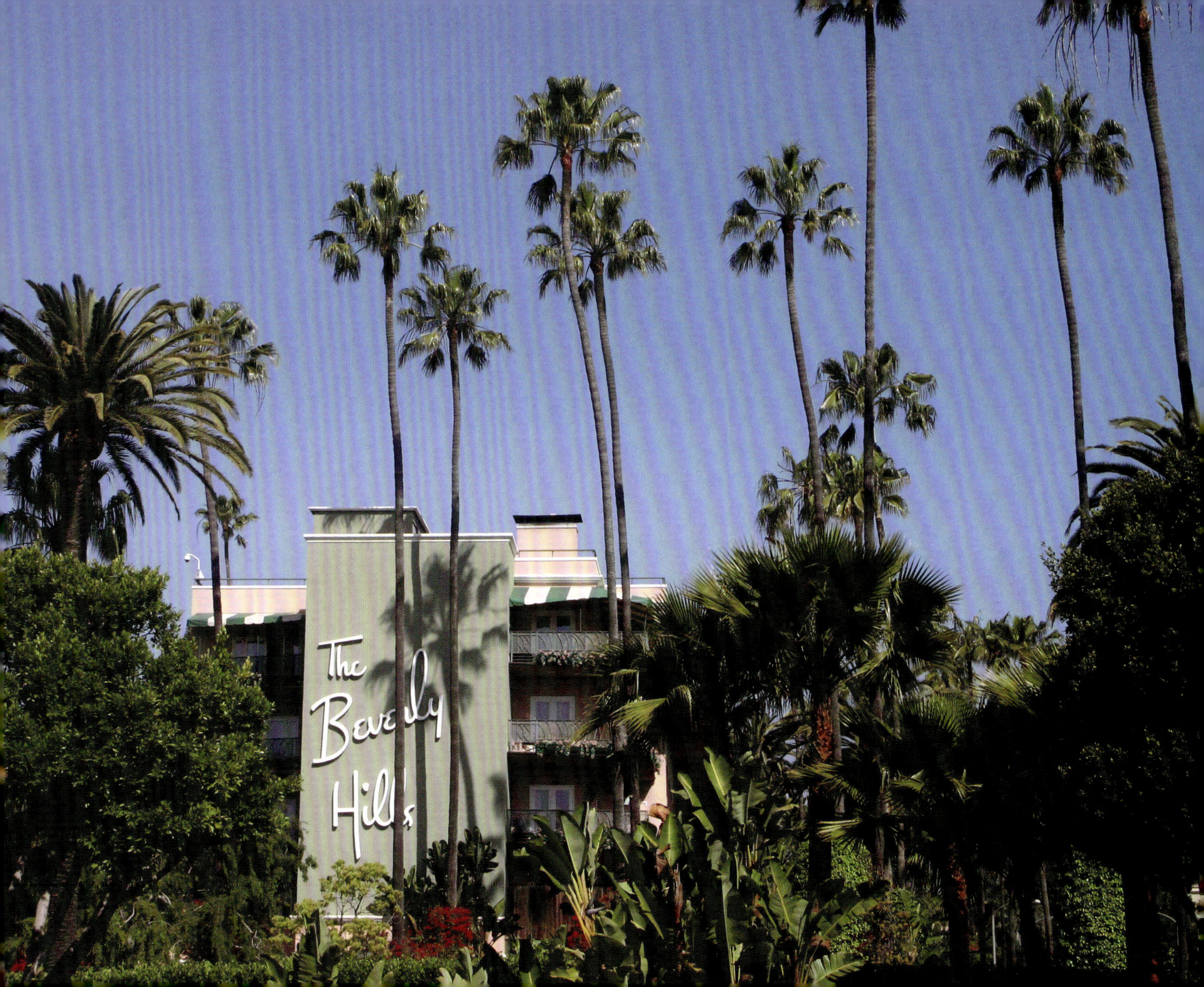
The Beverly Hills

GUITAR SCULPTURES, West Hollywood, California, 10/6/12

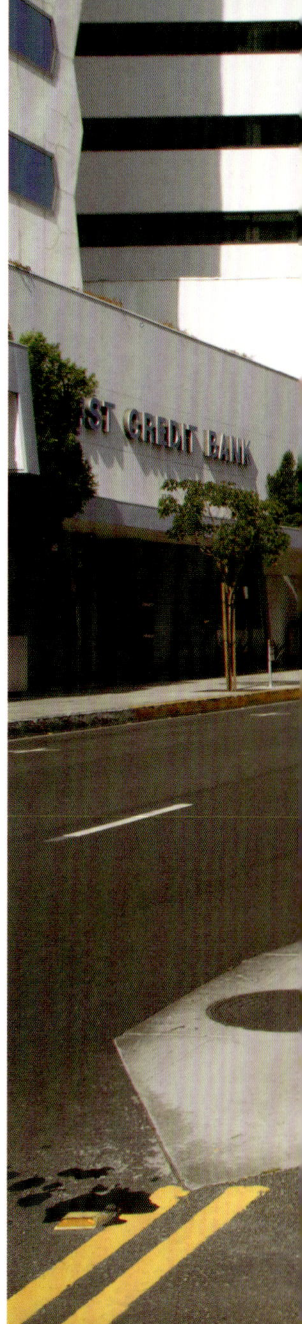

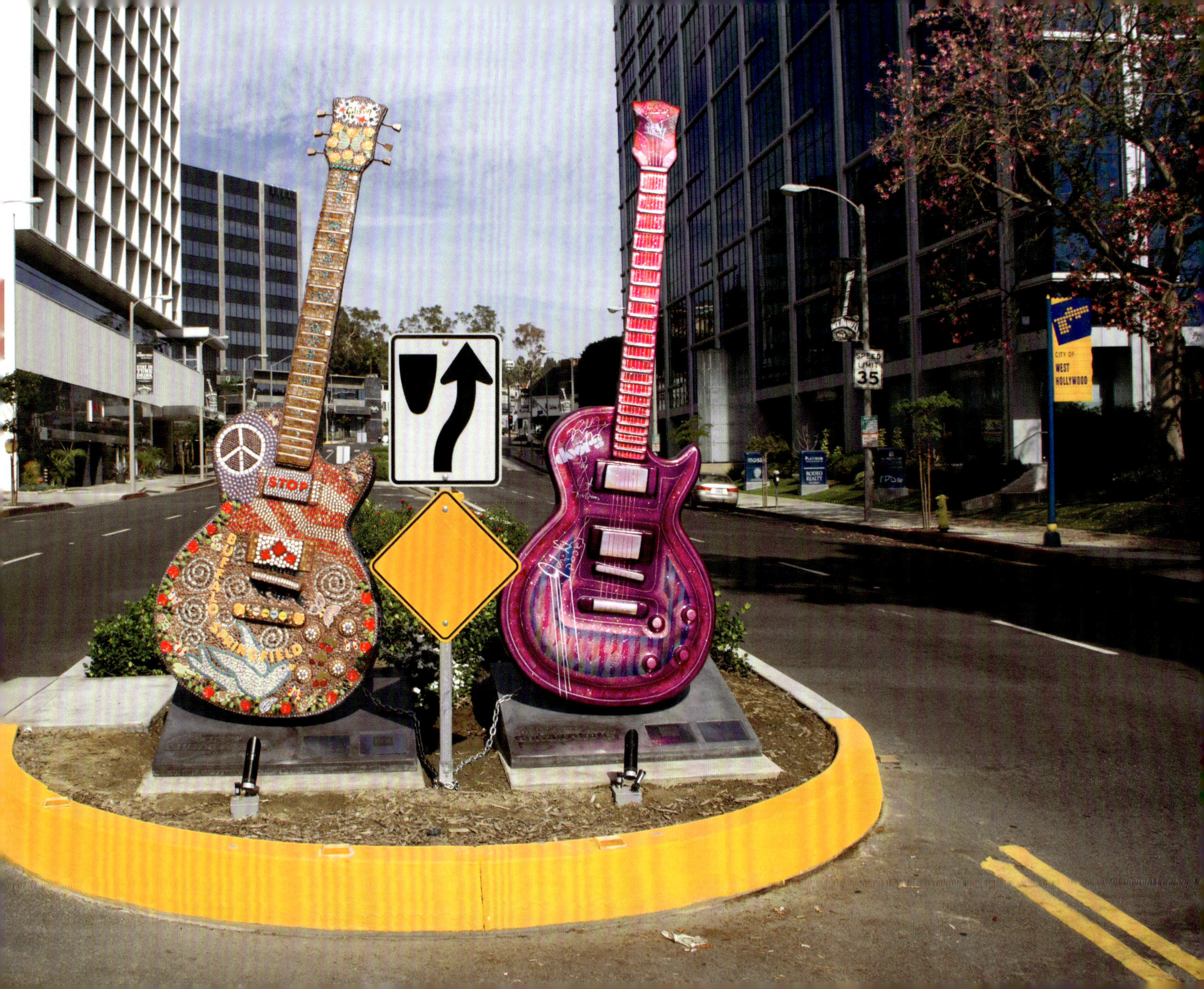
STOP
BUFFALO SPRINGFIELD
SPEED LIMIT 35
CITY OF WEST HOLLYWOOD

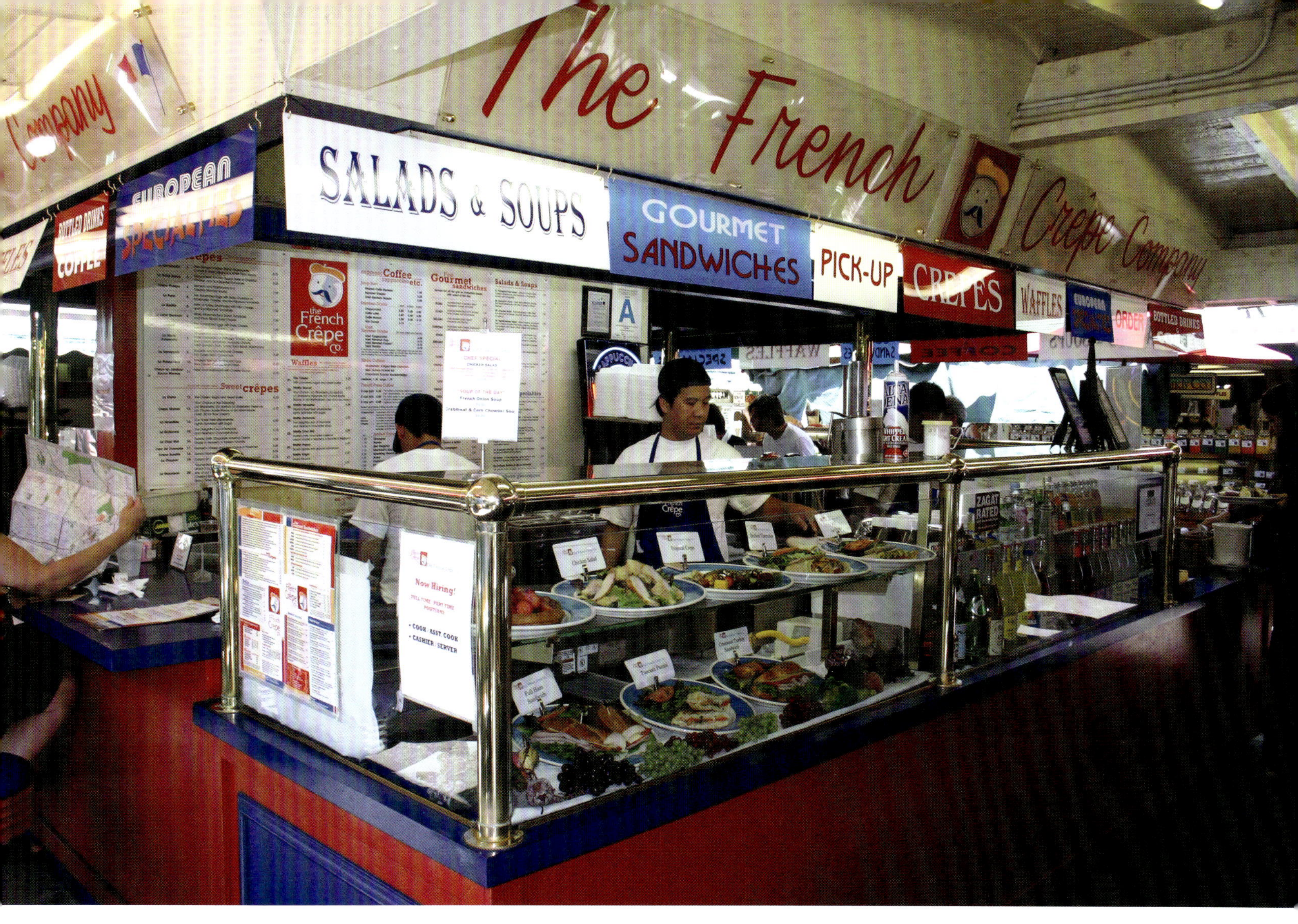

FRENCH CREPE STAND, Farmers Market, Los Angeles, California, 4/27/07

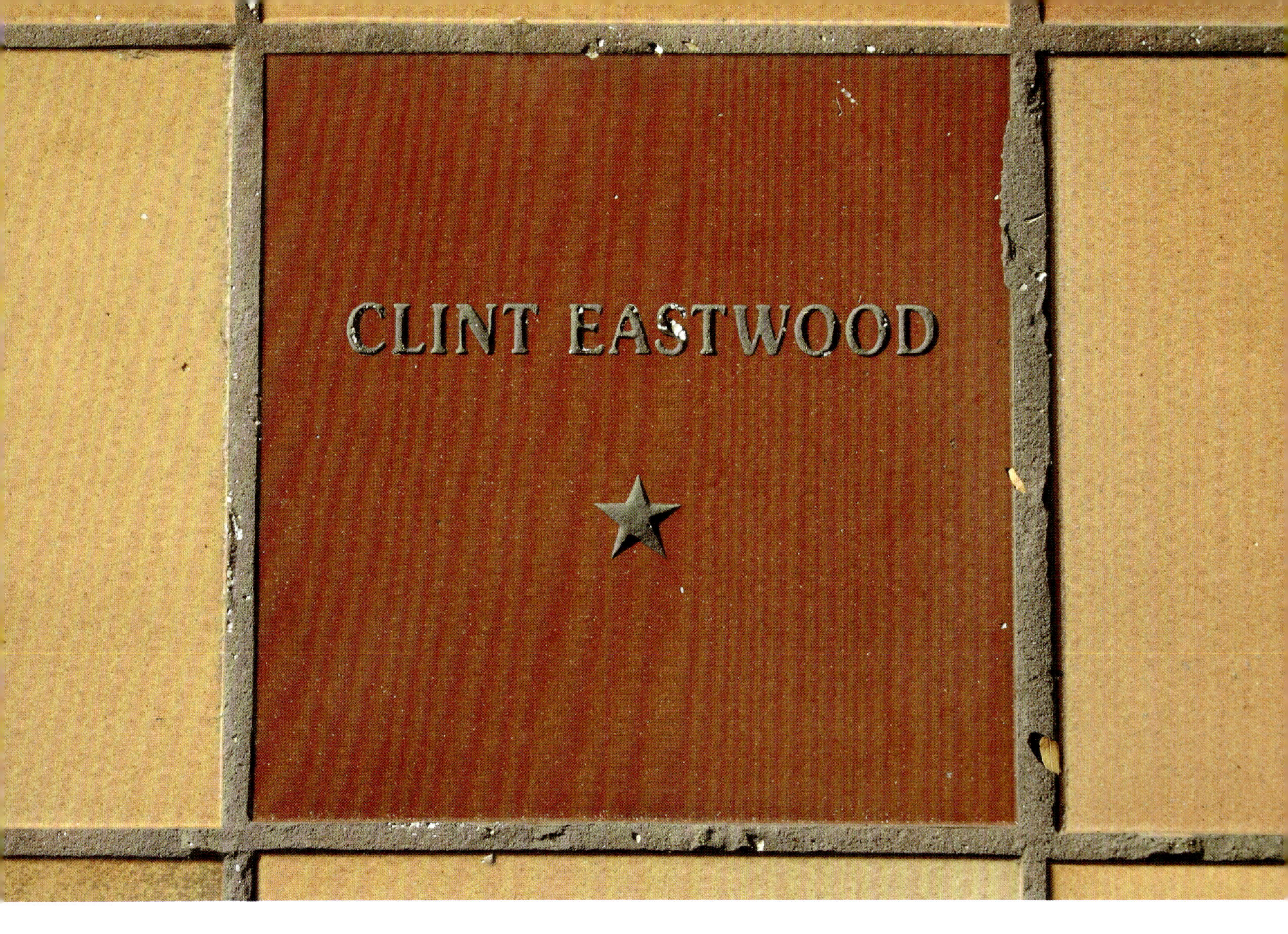

CLINT EASTWOOD TILE, Autry National Center, Los Angeles, California, 11/15/06

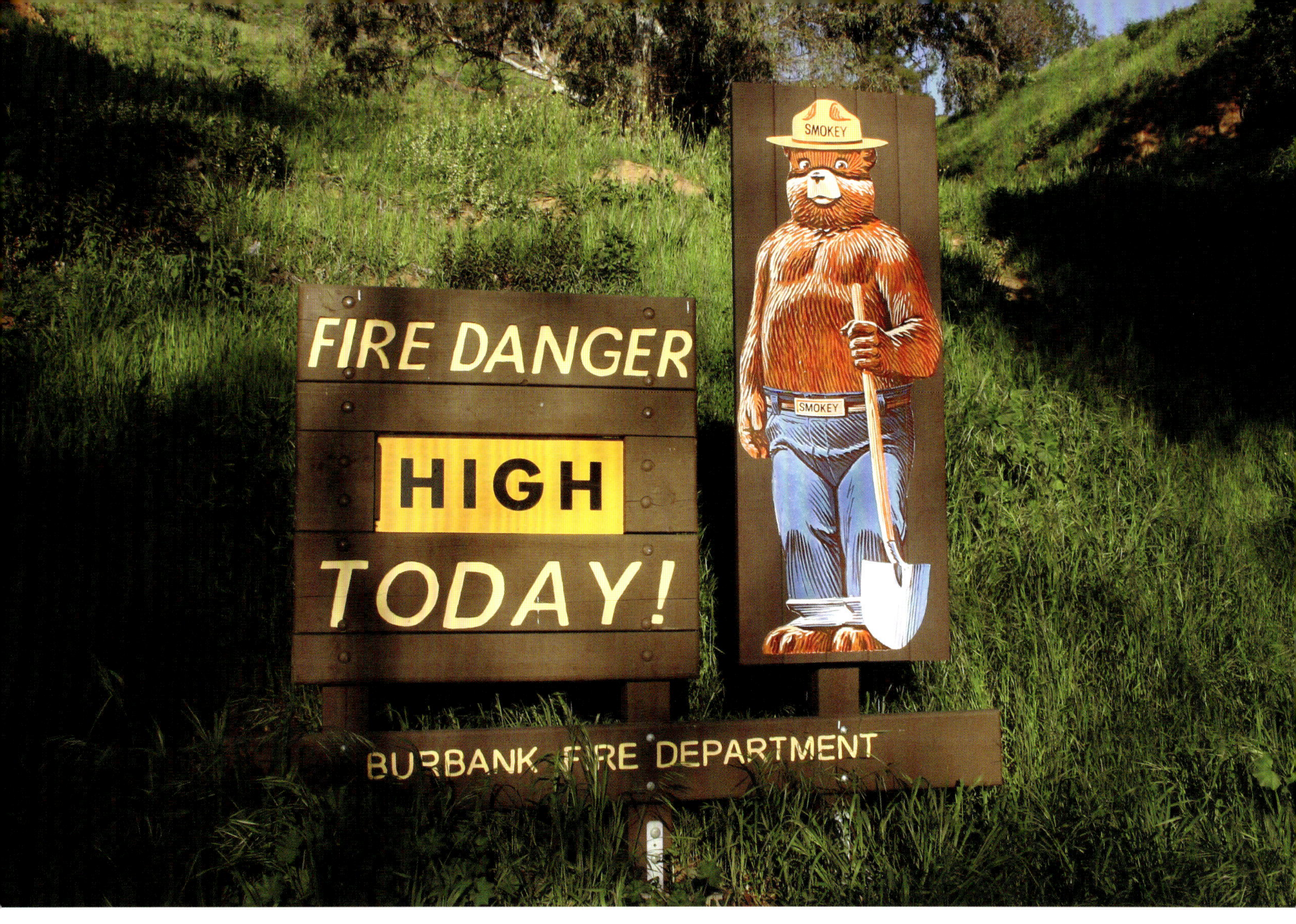

FIRE DANGER SIGN, Burbank, California, 2/26/08

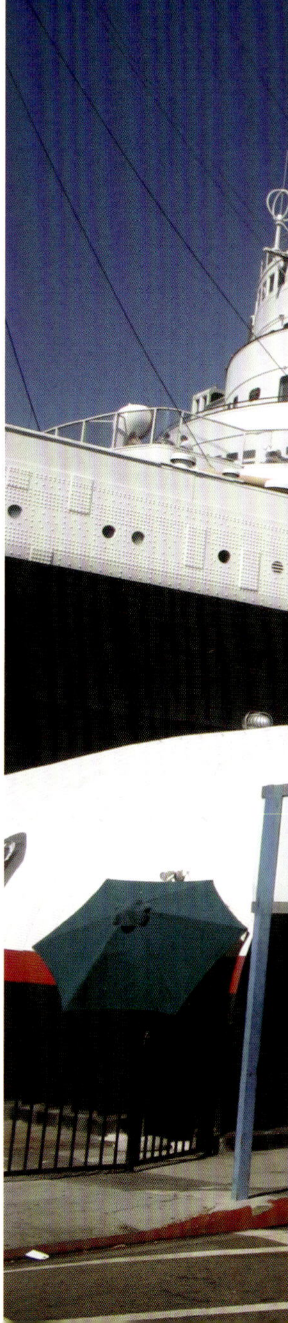

QUEEN MARY, Long Beach, California, 7/29/07

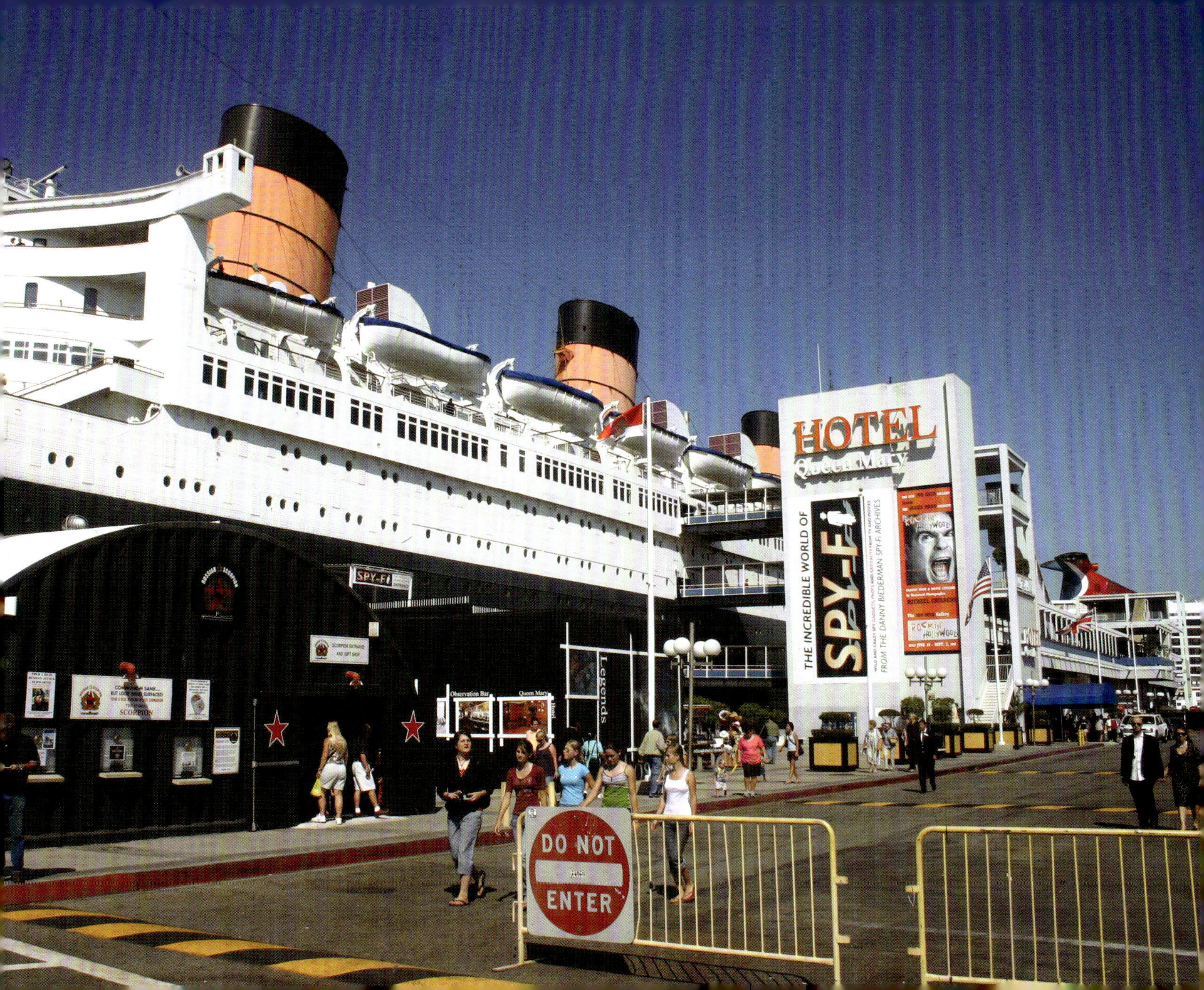
HOTEL
Queen Mary
THE INCREDIBLE WORLD OF
SPY-Fi
WILD AND CRAZY SPY GADGETS, PROPS AND ARTIFACTS FROM TV AND MOVIES
FROM THE DANNY BIEDERMAN SPY-Fi ARCHIVES
ROCKIN' HOLLYWOOD
SPY-Fi
Legends
Observation Bar
Queen Mary
SCORPION
DO NOT
ENTER

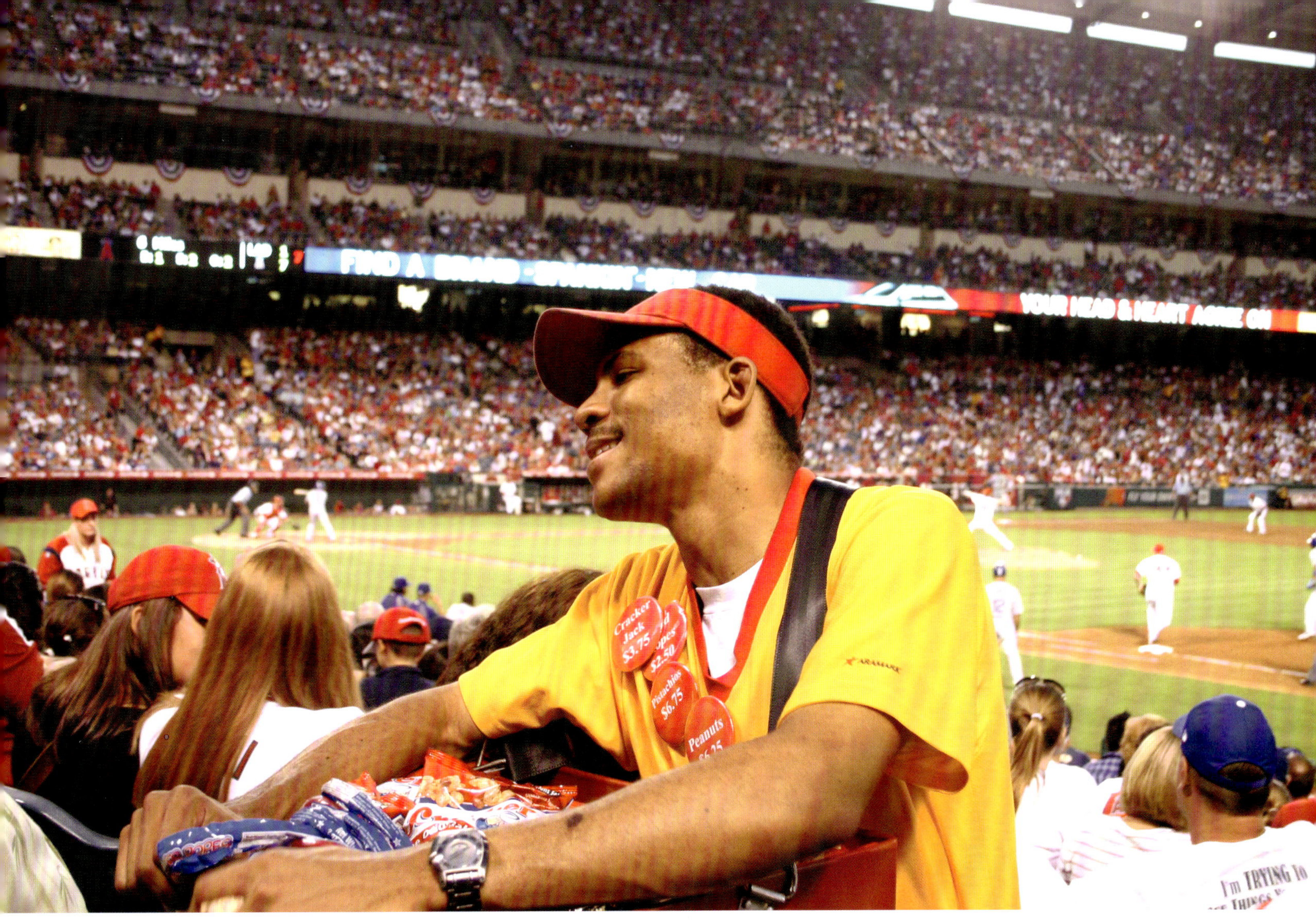

VENDOR AT ANGEL STADIUM, Anaheim, California, 7/2/11

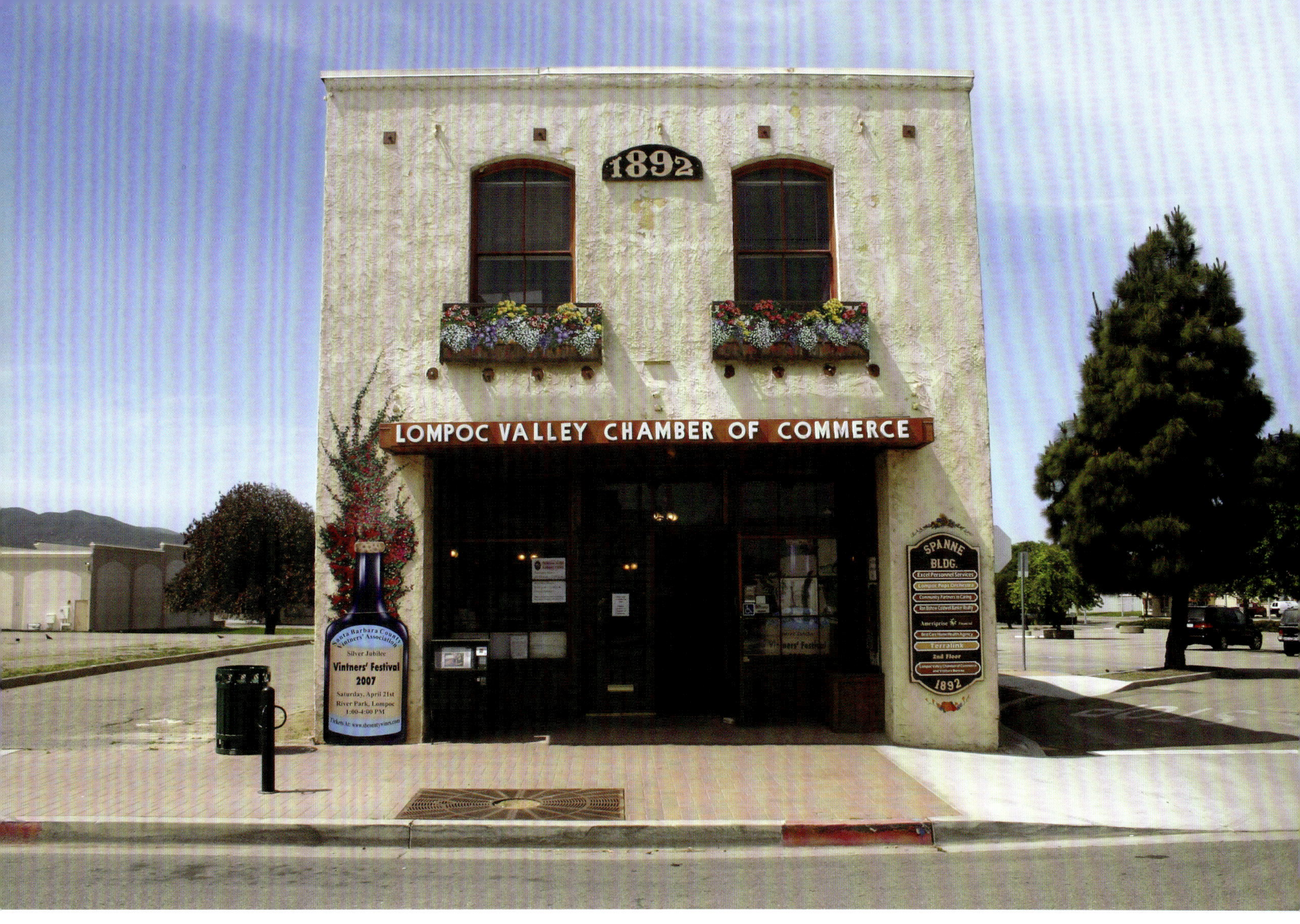

LOMPOC VALLEY CHAMBER OF COMMERCE, Lompoc, California, 4/2/07

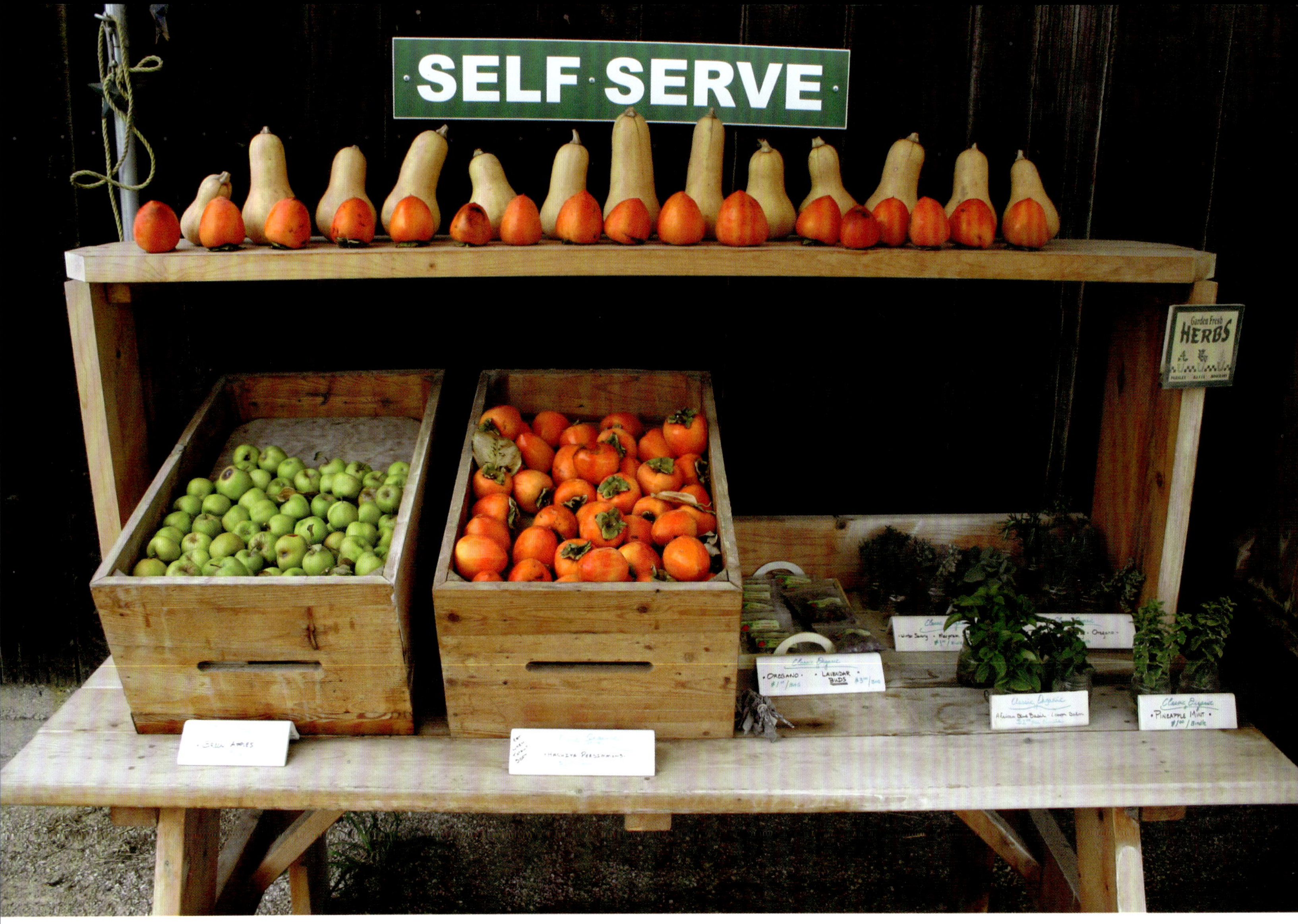

SELF-SERVE, Gaviota, California, 12/7/08

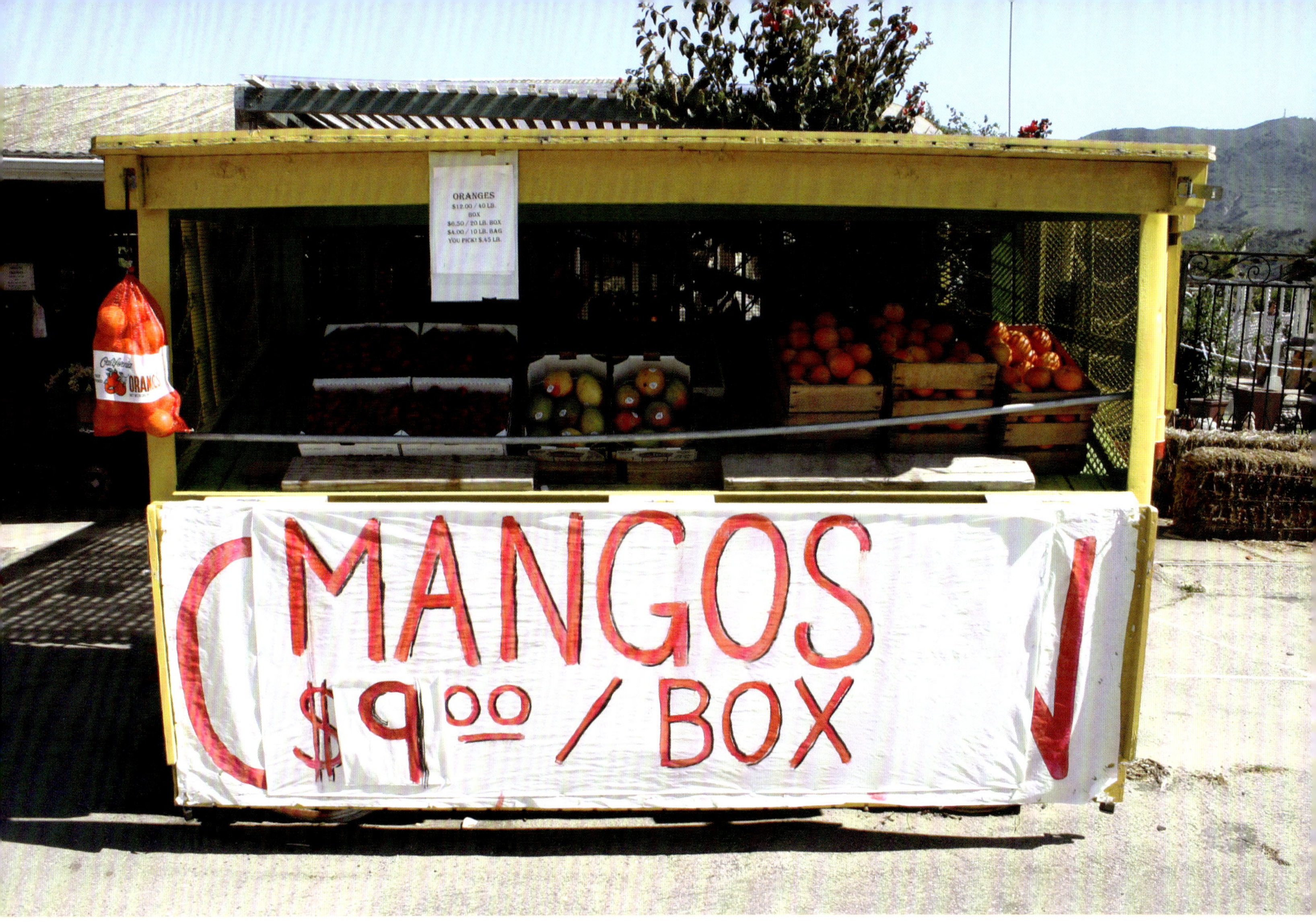

MANGOS, Santa Paula, California, 4/28/12

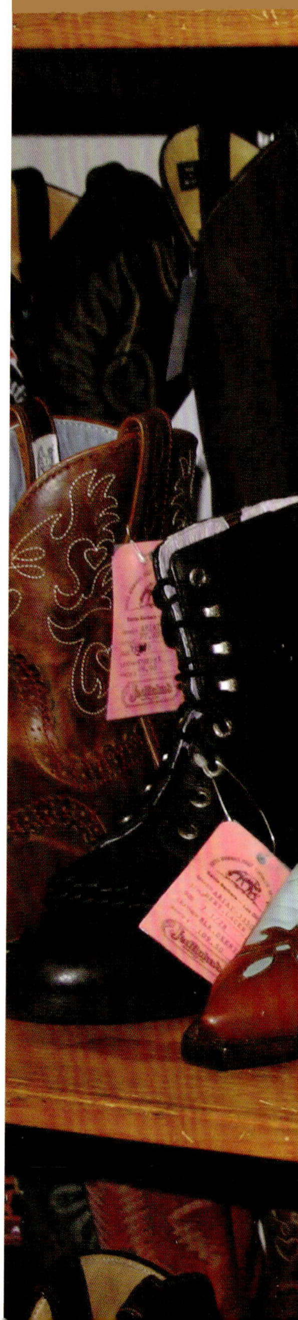

BOOTS, Jedlicka's, Los Olivos, California, 4/10/08

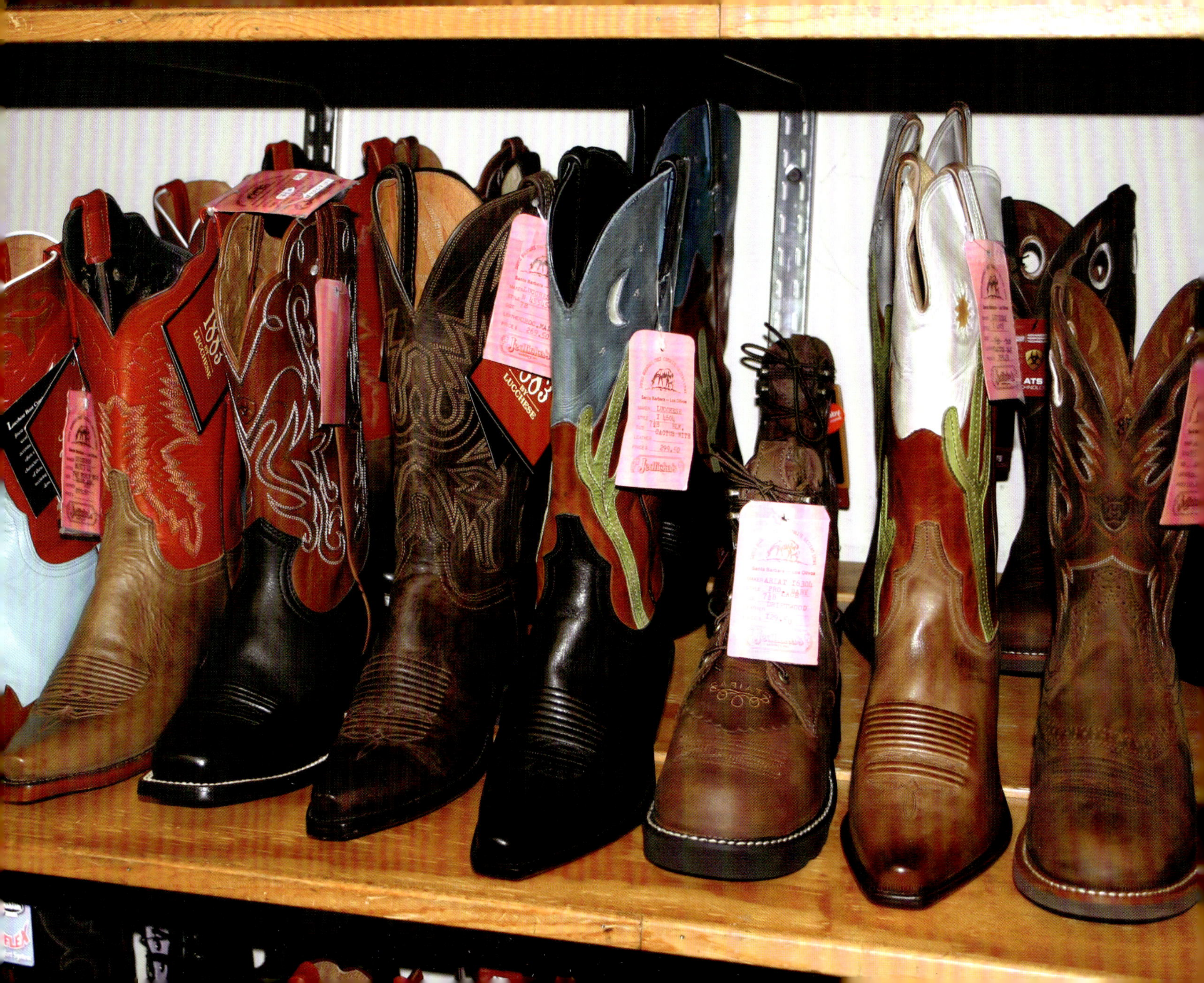
1883
BY
LUCCHESE
BY
LUCCHESE
FLEX
ATS

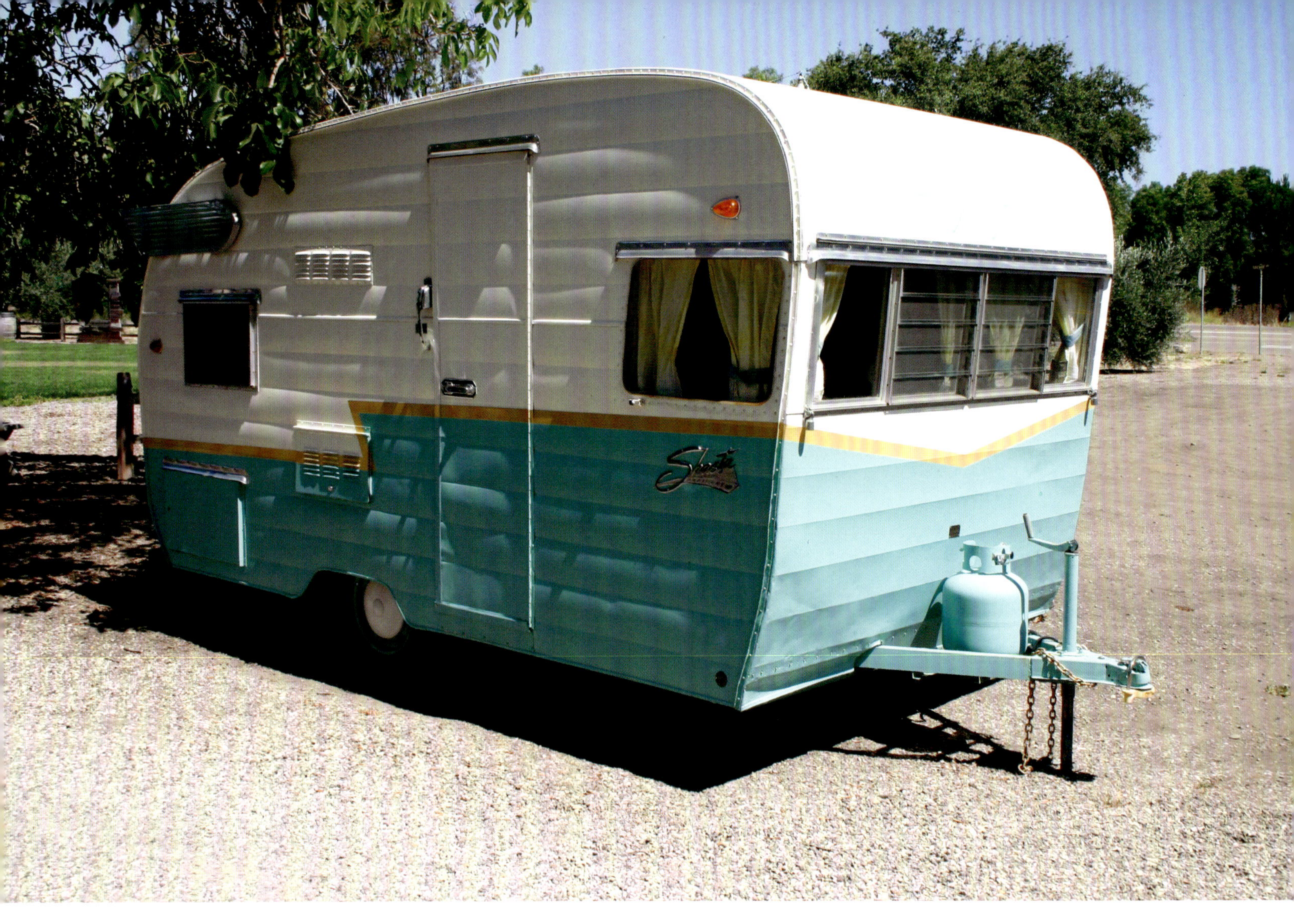

TURQUOISE TRAILER, Los Olivos, California, 7/21/11

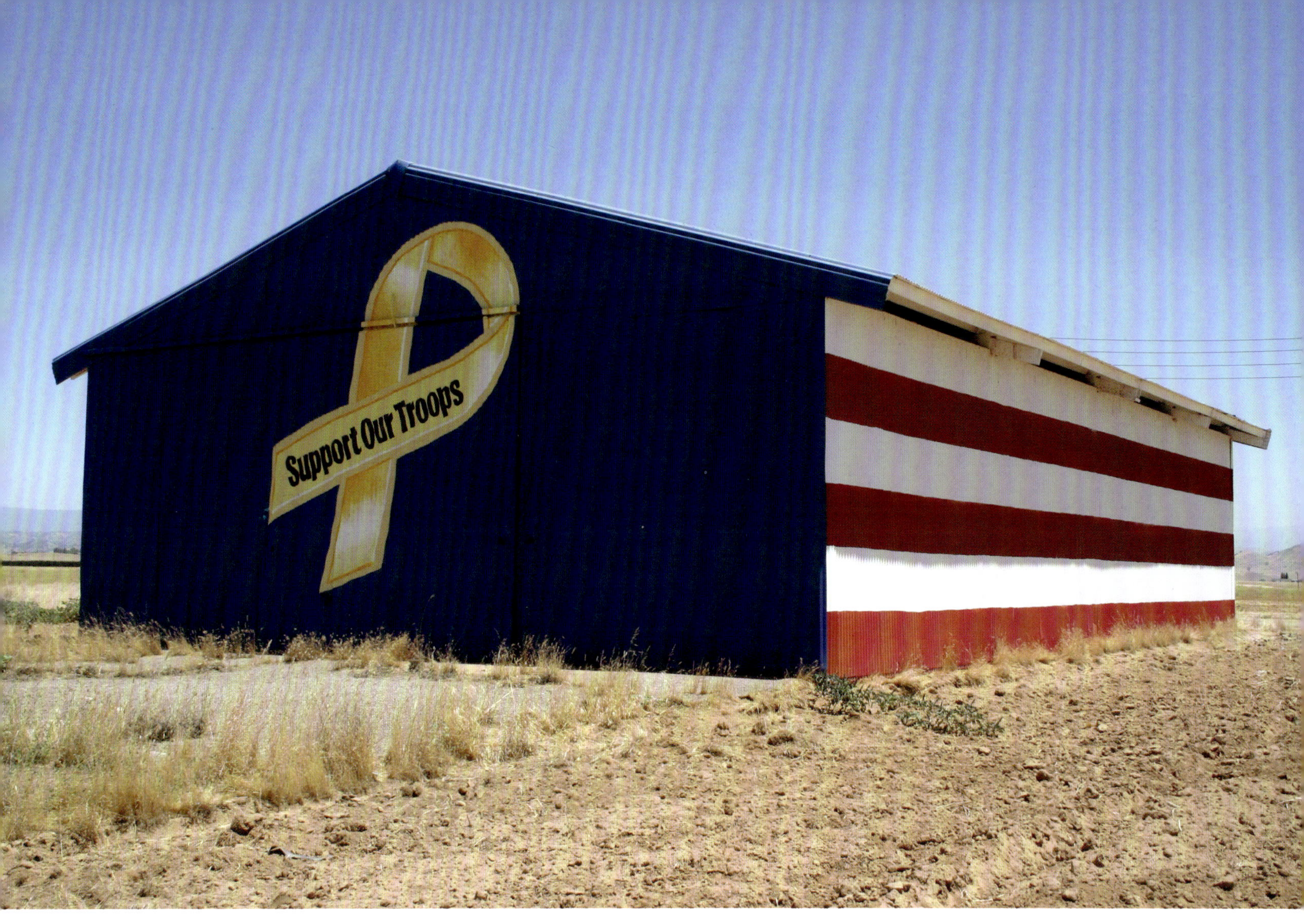

SUPPORT OUR TROOPS, Madera, California, 7/19/07

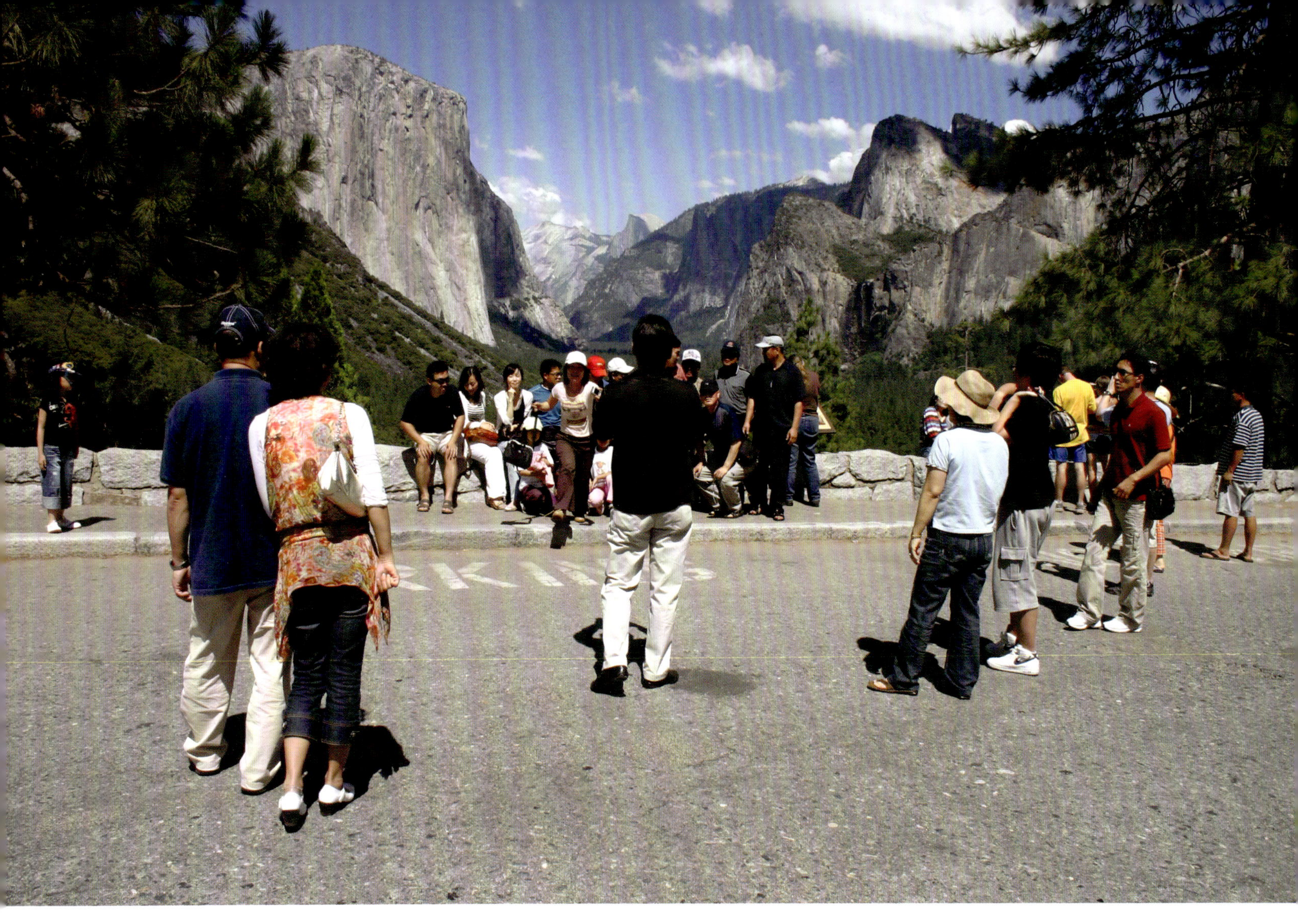

TAKE MY CAMERA, Tunnel View, Yosemite National Park, California, 7/18/07

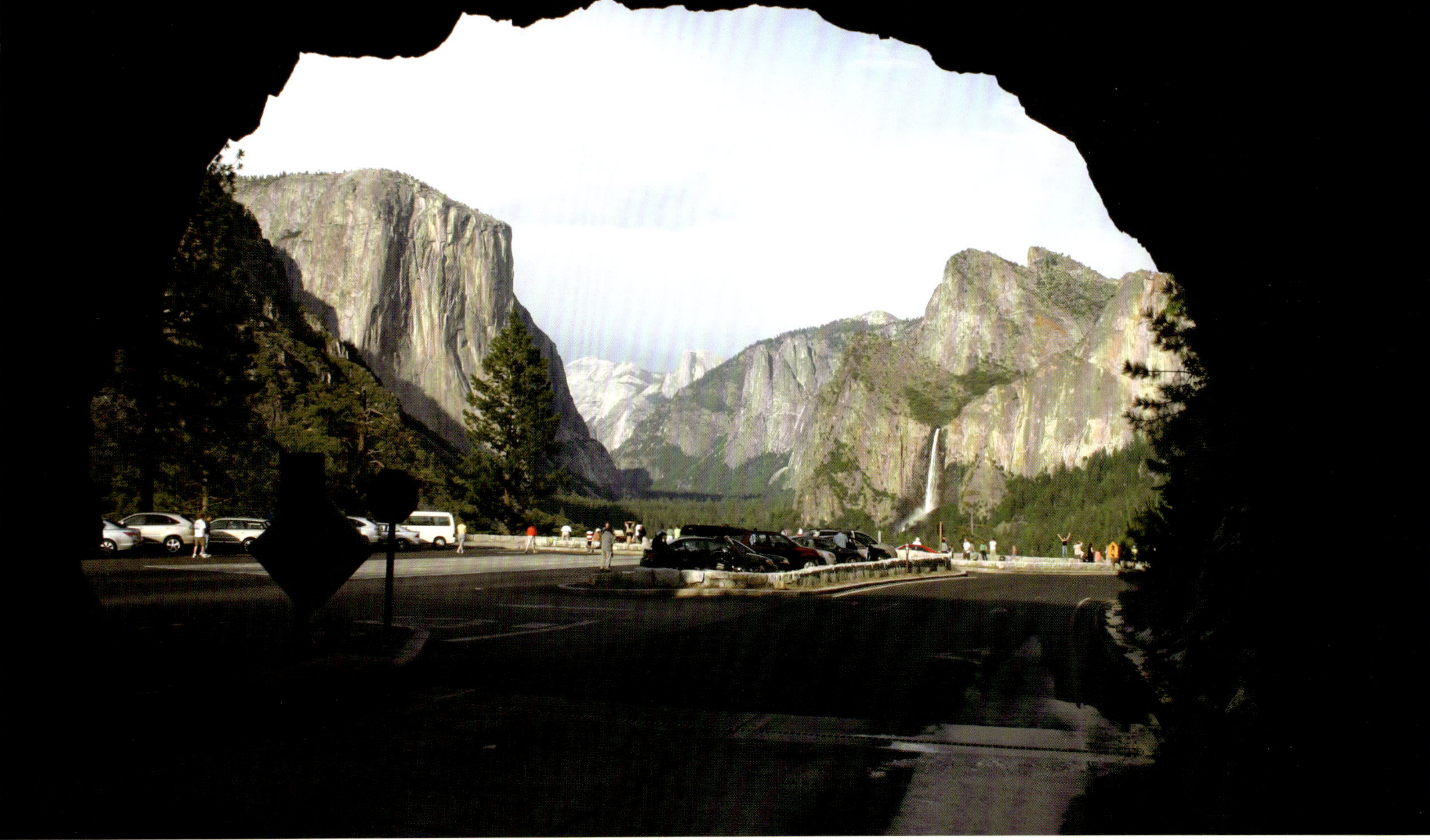

VIEW FROM WAWONA TUNNEL, Tunnel View, Yosemite National Park, California, 5/29/09

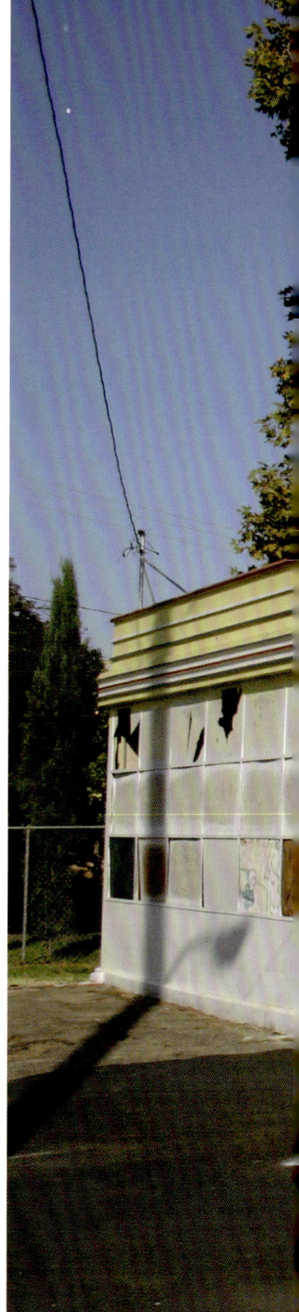

RICHFIELD GAS STATION, Lemon Cove, California, 9/20/08

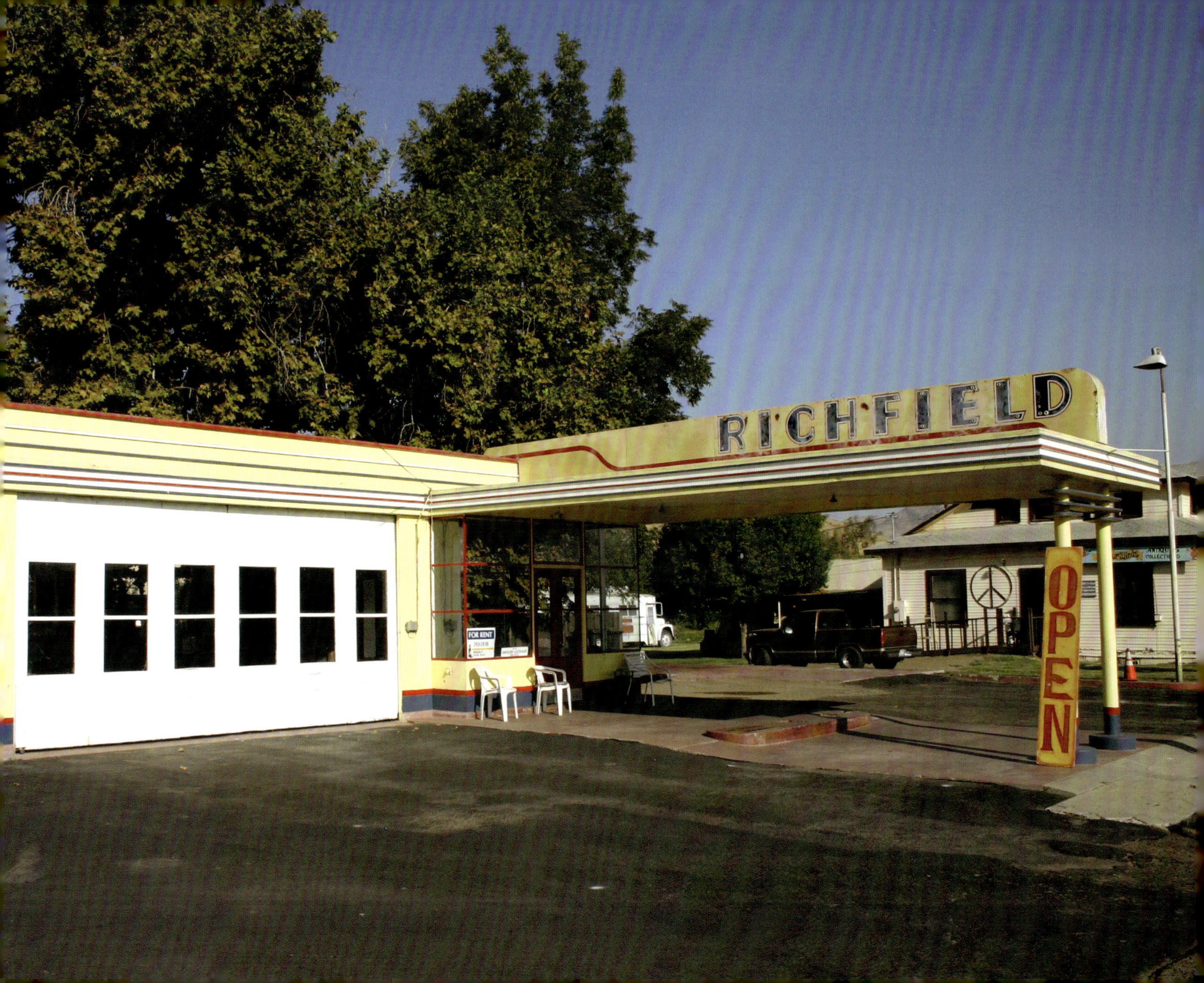
RICHFIELD
OPEN
FOR RENT

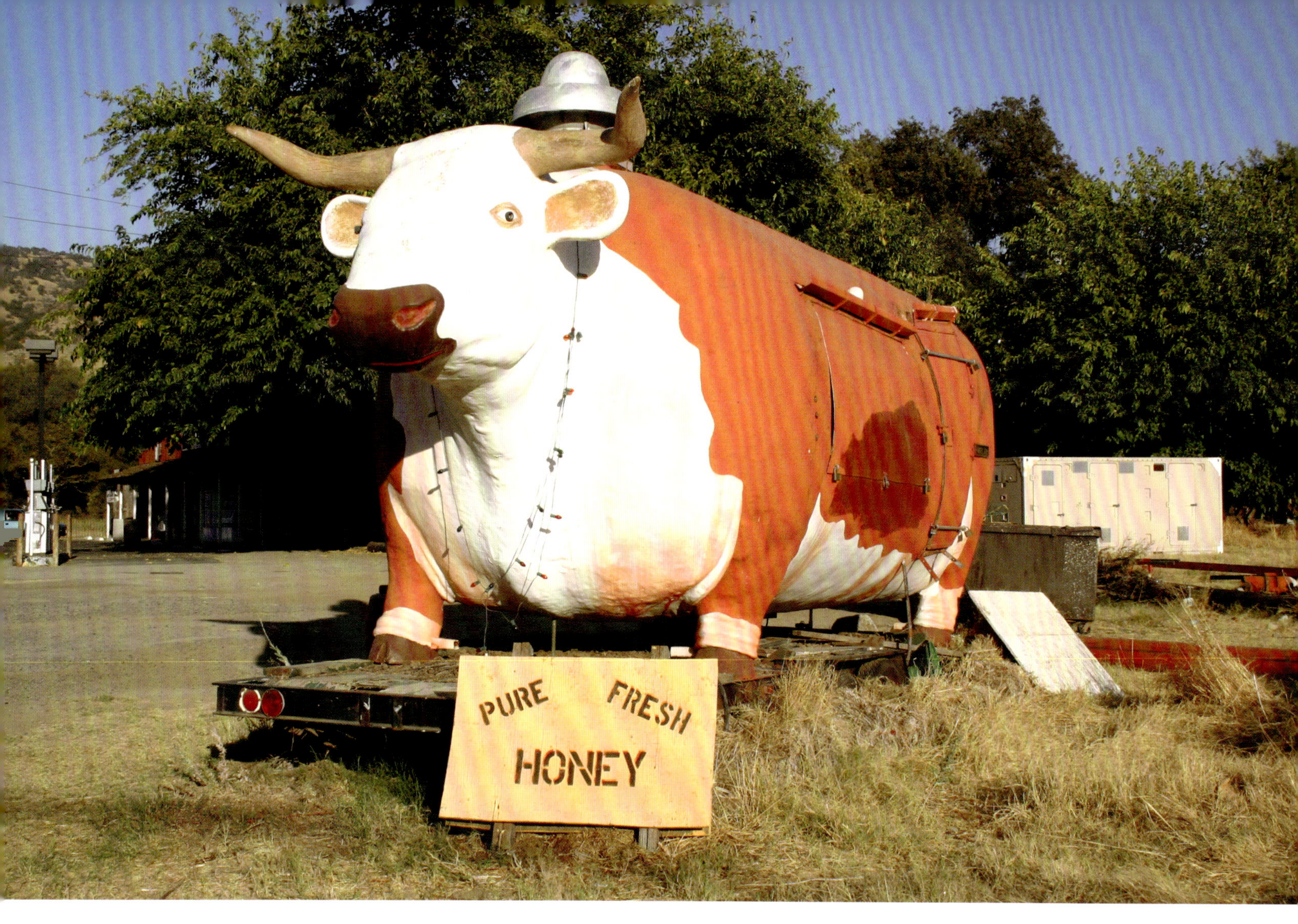

PURE FRESH HONEY, Three Rivers, California, 9/24/06

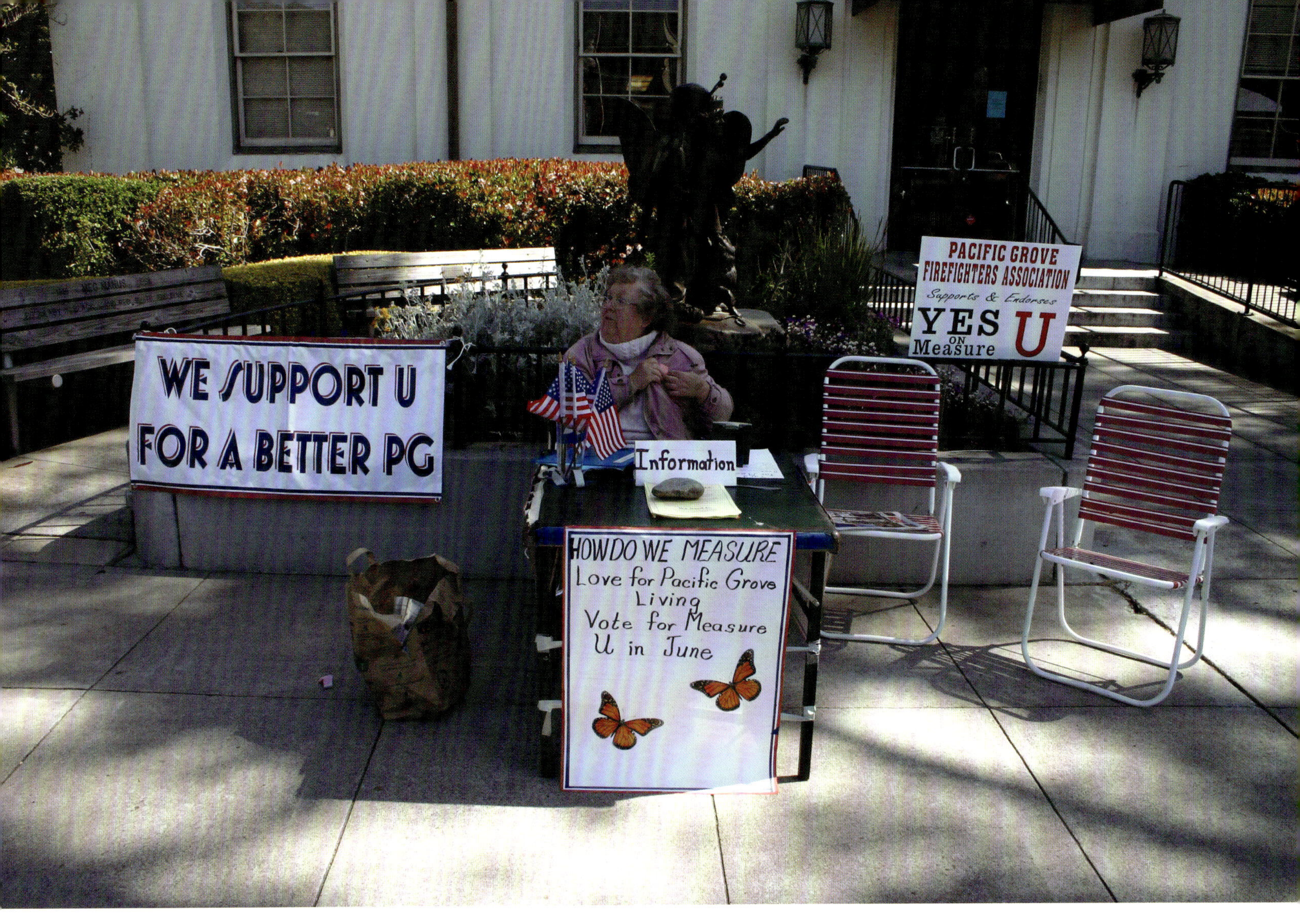

WE SUPPORT U, Pacific Grove, California, 5/1/08

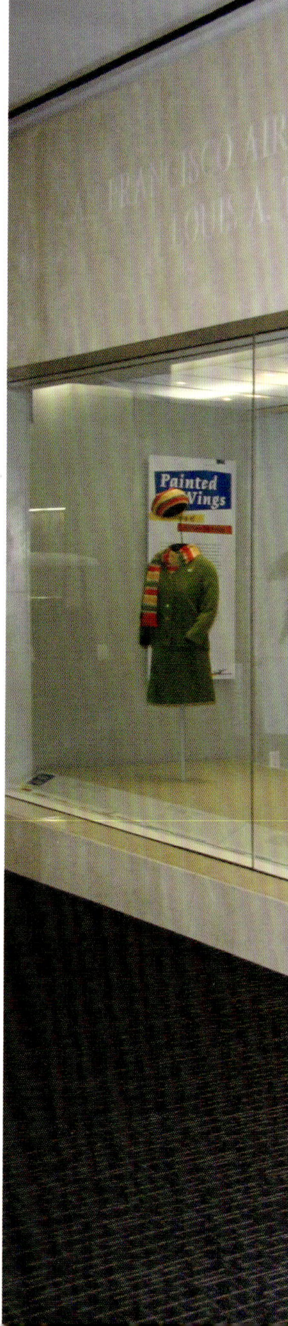

FLIGHT ATTENDANT UNIFORMS,

Louis A. Turpen Aviation Museum, San Francisco, California, 3/6/09

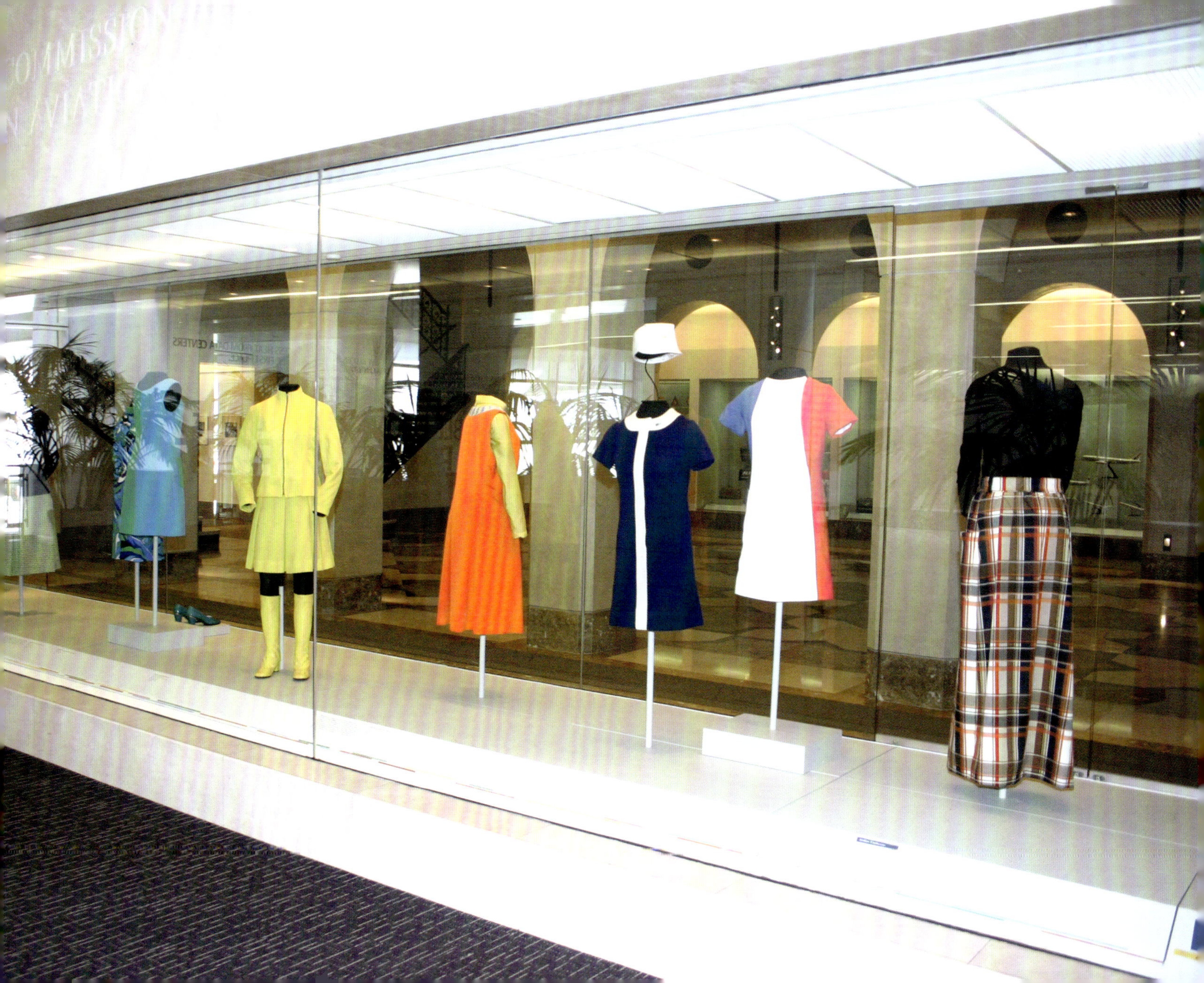

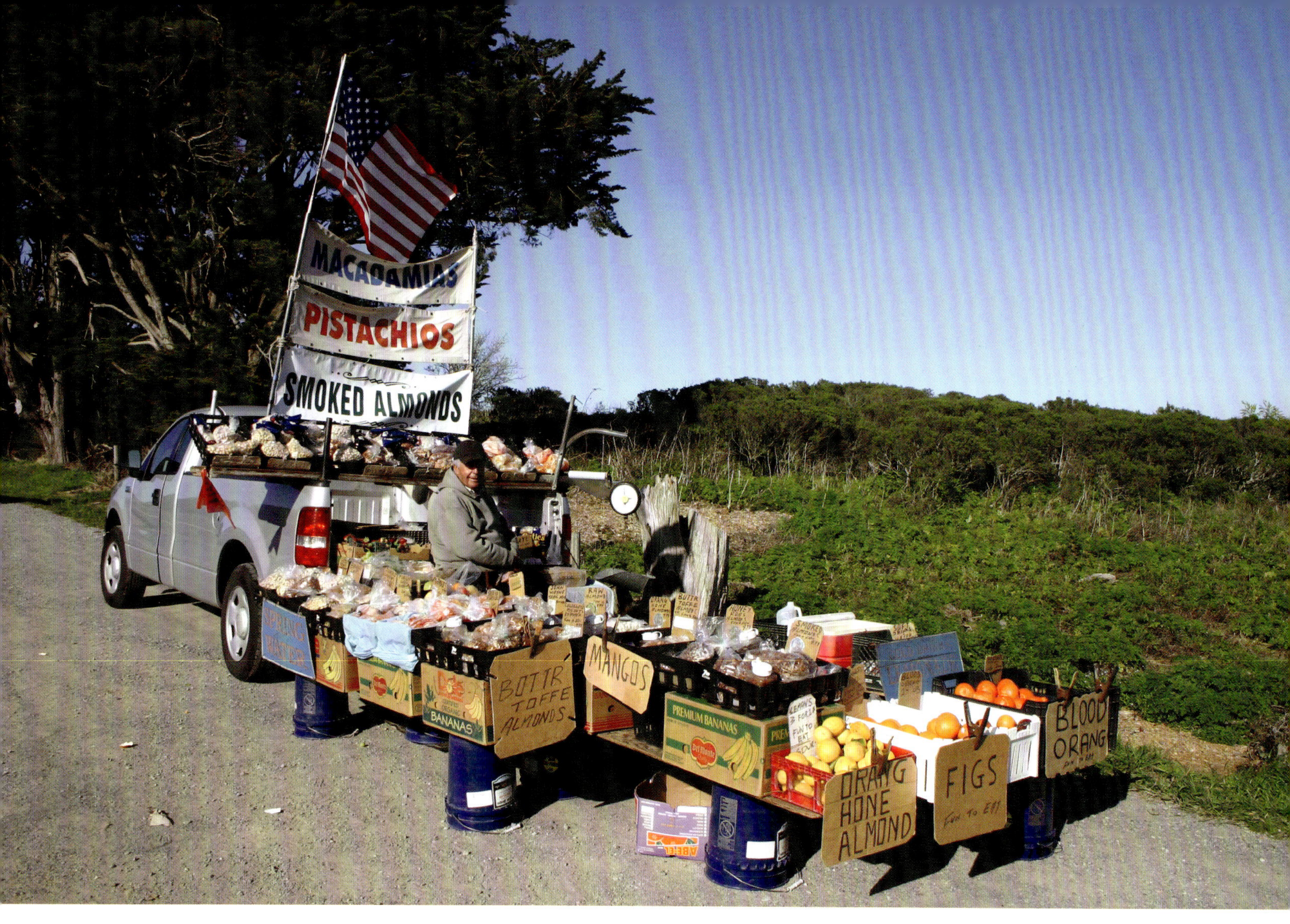

FRUIT AND NUT STAND, Muir Woods Road, Mount Tamalpais State Park, California, 3/8/09

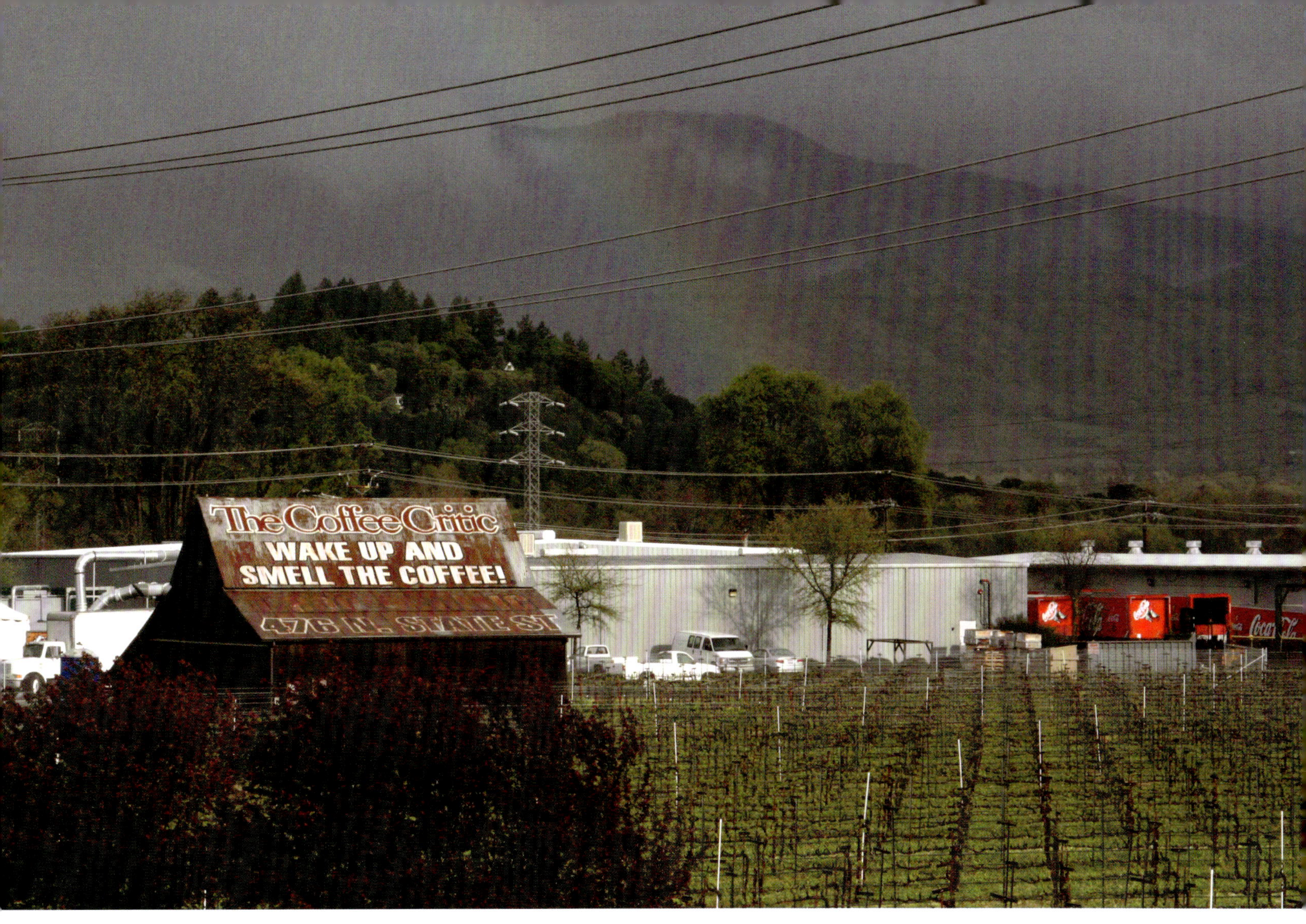

WAKE UP AND SMELL THE COFFEE, Ukiah, California, 3/19/05

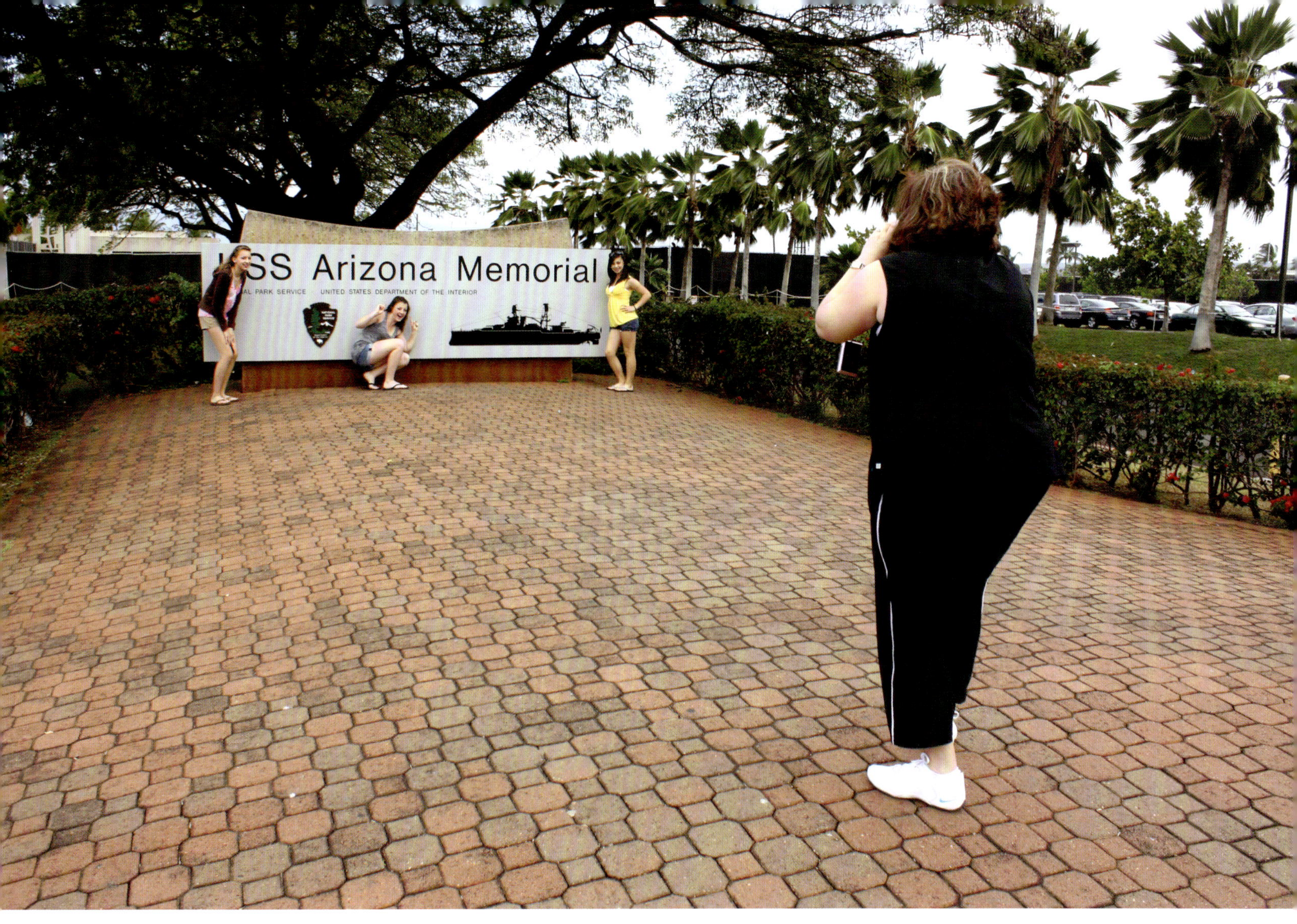

SMILE, USS Arizona Memorial, Pearl Harbor, Honolulu, Oahu, Hawaii, 4/5/09

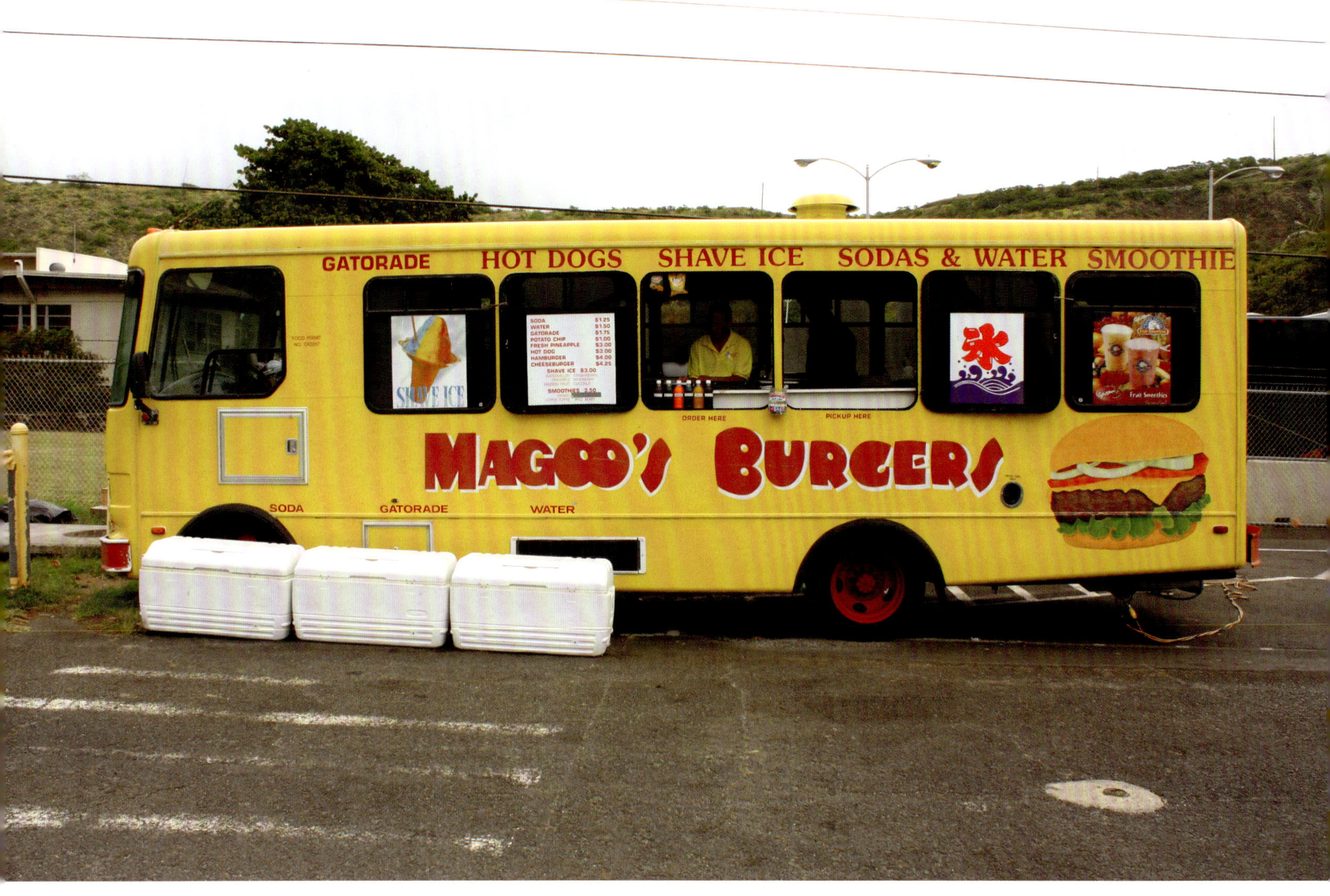

MAGOO'S BURGERS, Diamond Head State Monument, Honolulu, Oahu, Hawaii, 4/1/09

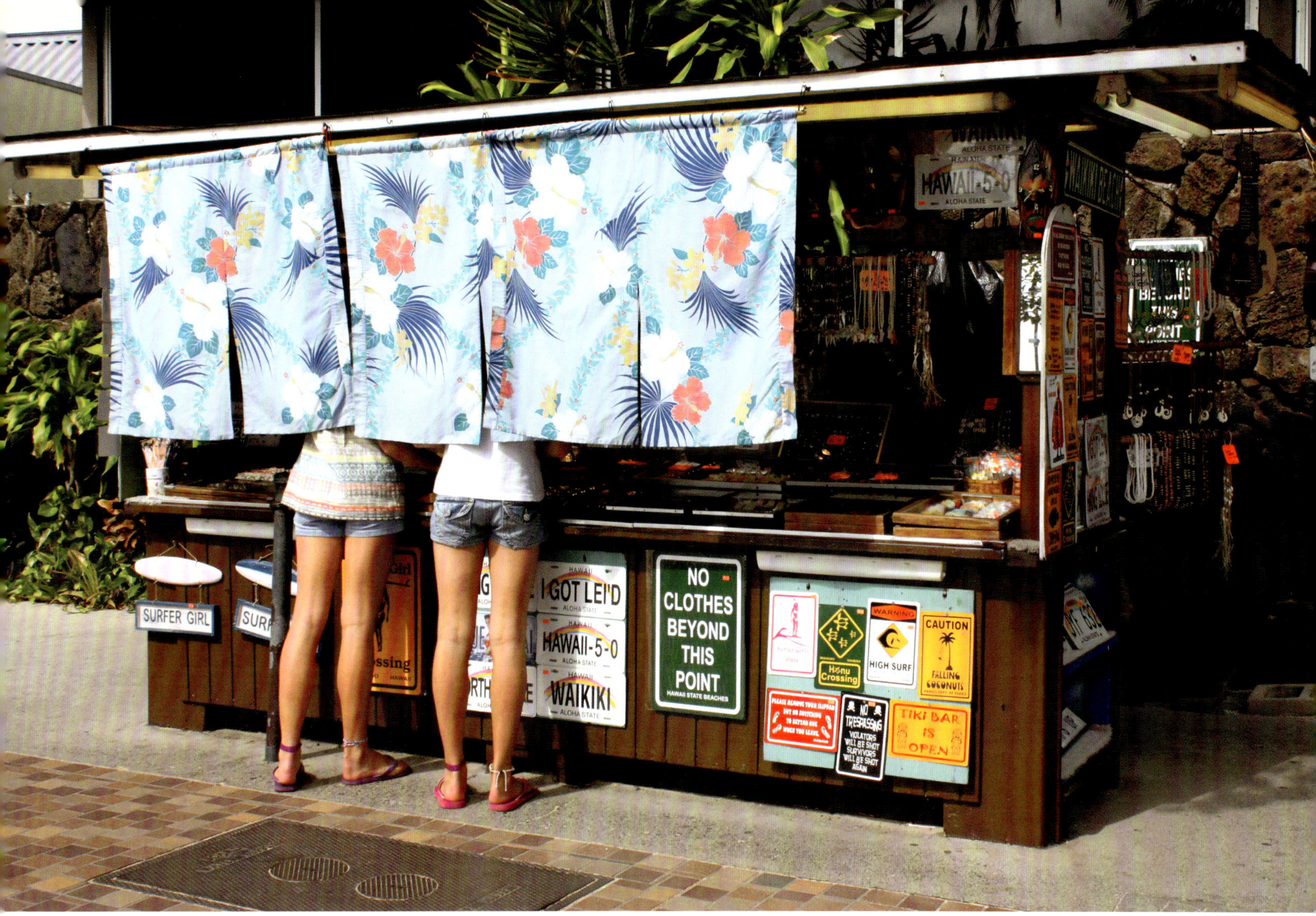

HIDING, Waikiki, Honolulu, Oahu, Hawaii, 4/5/09

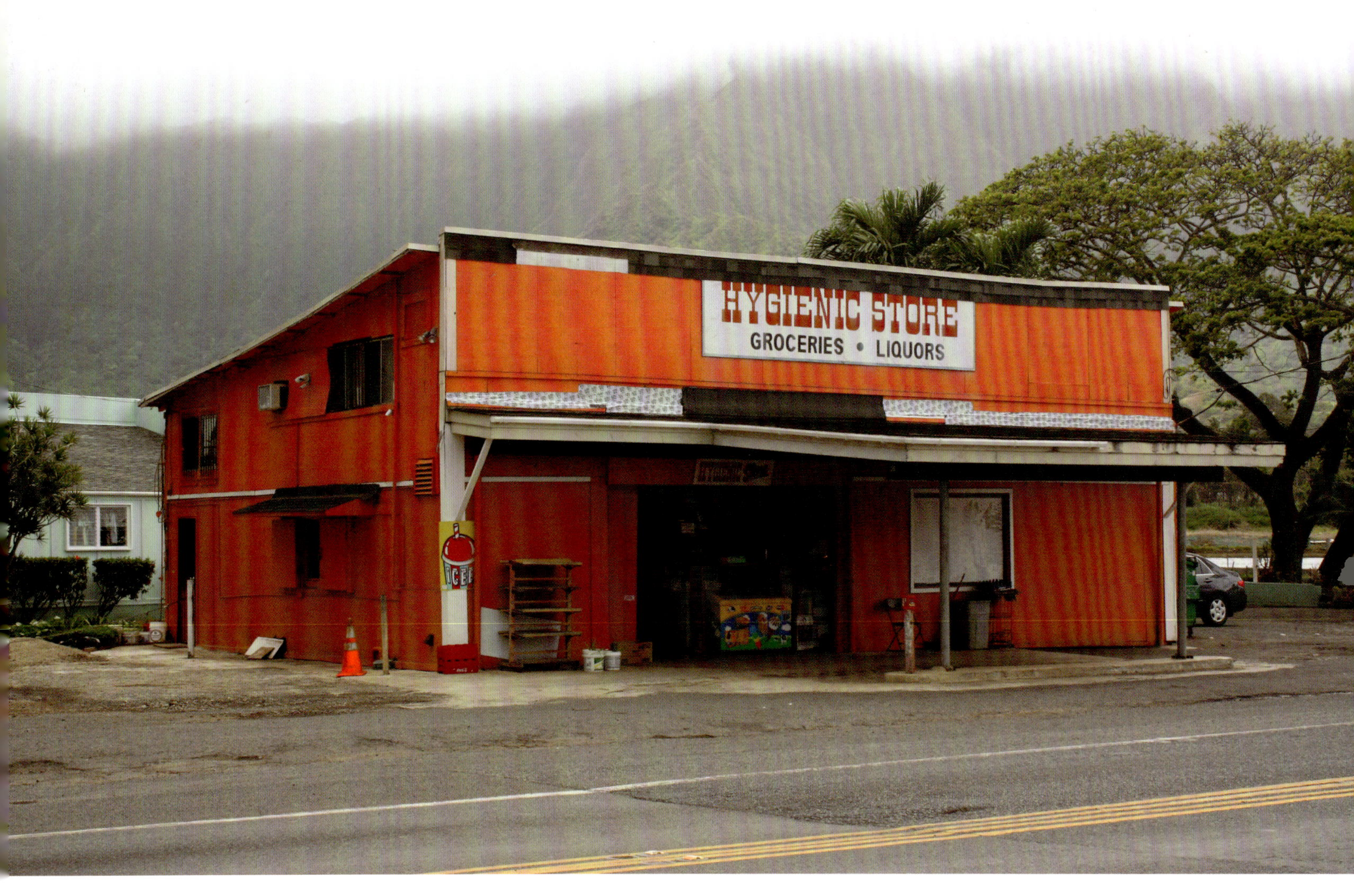

HYGIENIC STORE, Kahaluu, Oahu, Hawaii, 3/31/09

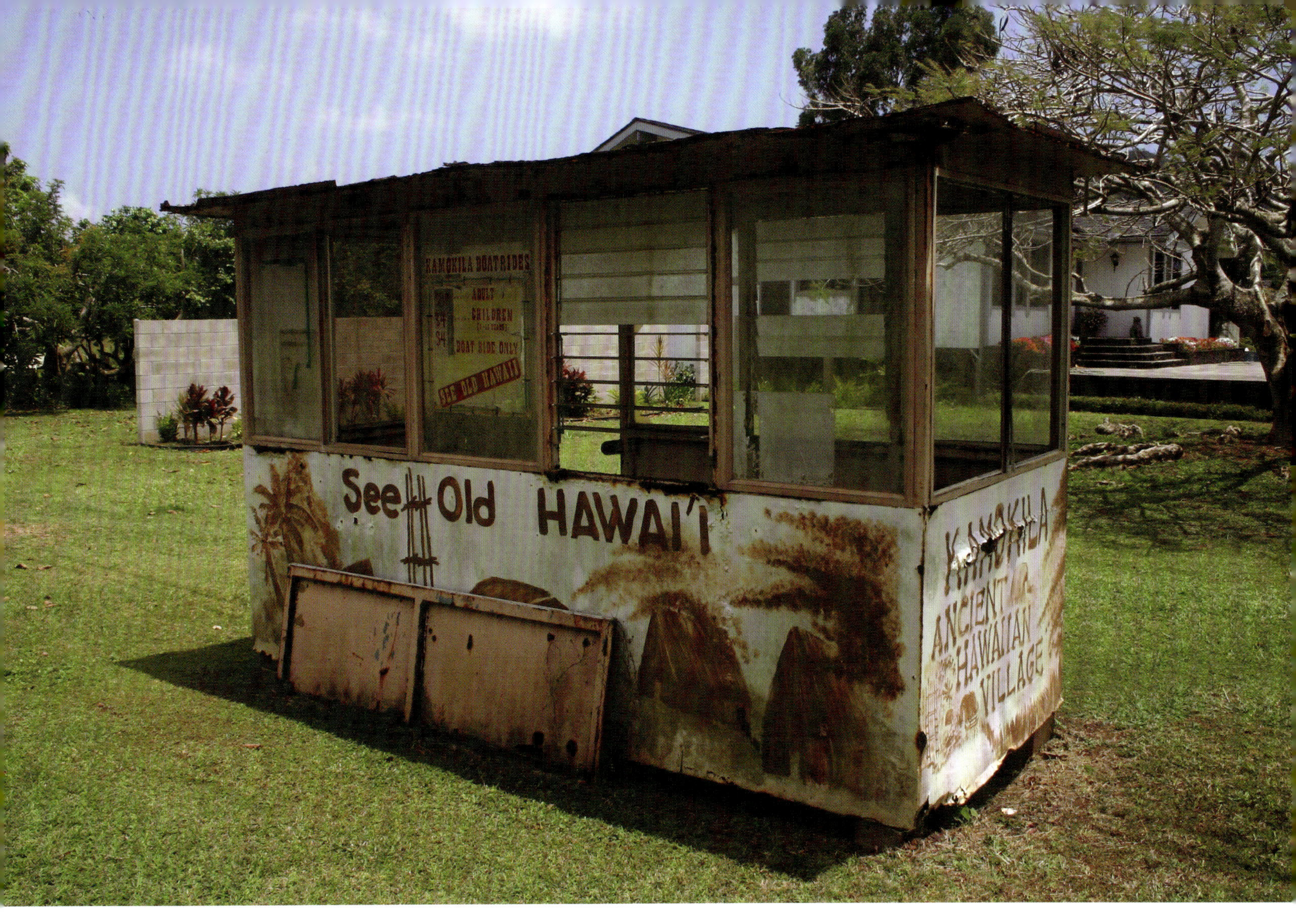

SEE OLD HAWAII, Kapaa, Kauai, Hawaii, 4/19/07

SURFBOARDS AND TRAFFIC CONE, Hanalei, Kauai, Hawaii, 4/17/07

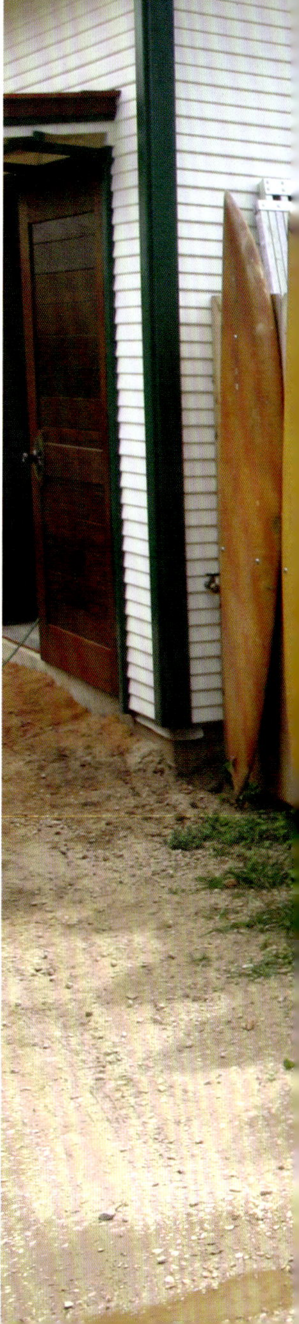

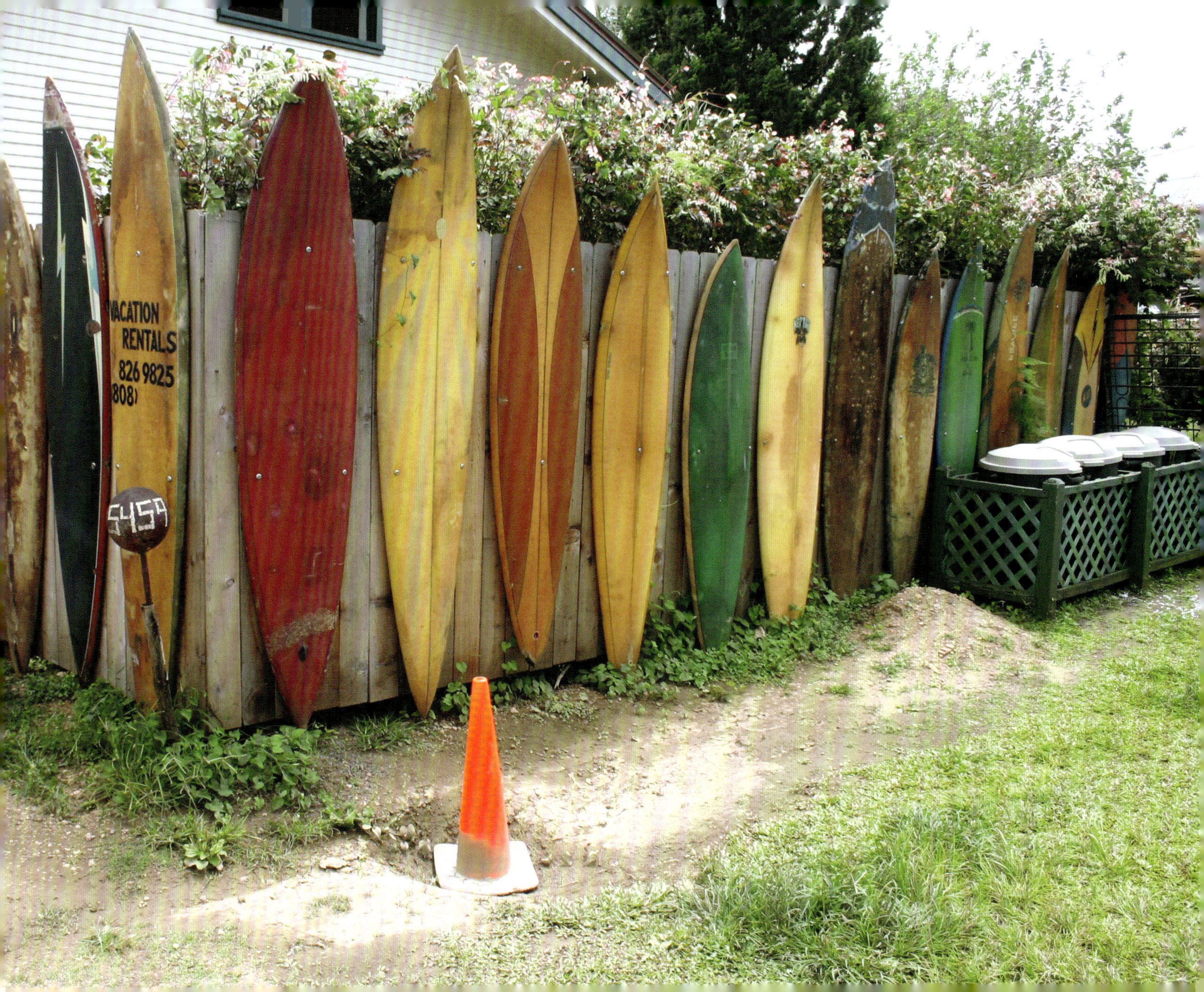
VACATION
RENTALS
826 9825
808)
5459

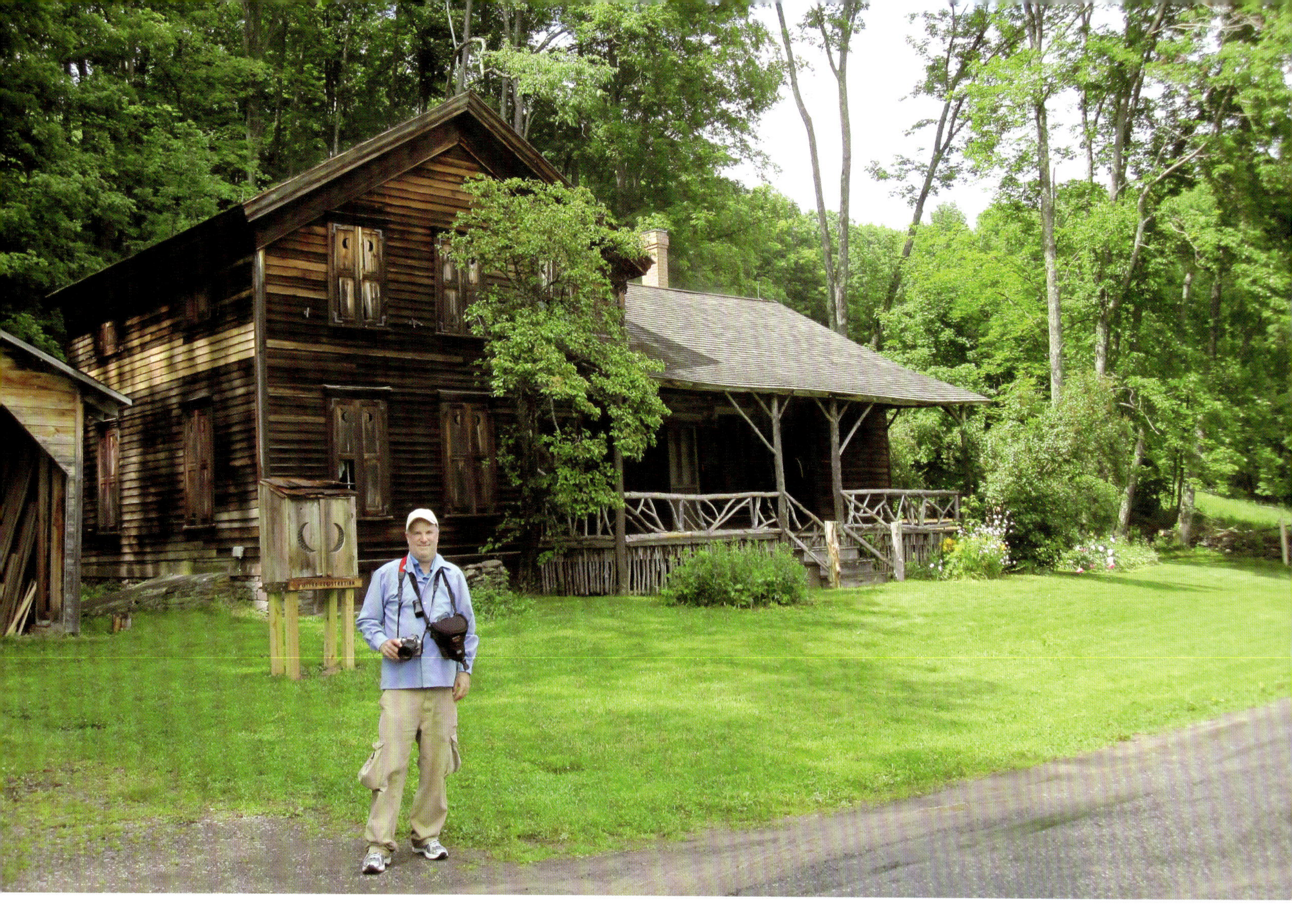

MATHEW TEKULSKY, Woodchuck Lodge, Roxbury, New York, 6/13/09.
Photograph courtesy of the author.

Afterword

★★★★

Although I modeled this book after Robert Frank's book *The Americans*, the history of American photography features masters of the form preceding Frank (who was born in Switzerland and who emigrated to the United States in his early twenties). Mathew Brady (after whom I was named, note the one "t" in Mathew) took photographs of the Civil War, and he also made portraits of Abraham Lincoln and Ulysses S. Grant. Early in the next century, Edward S. Curtis created his legendary collection of photographs of Native Americans, and Lewis Hine used his camera as an agent of social reform through his documentation of child laborers.

Perhaps the most important photographer of the twentieth century was Alfred Stieglitz, who was largely responsible for changing the public perception of the photograph as being not just a mechanical reproduction of reality but a work of art in and of itself. Stieglitz and his associate Edward Steichen took many cityscapes of New York City and Steichen, as director of photography at the Museum of Modern Art, created the legendary exhibition entitled *The Family of Man* in 1955, which celebrated the universality of the human experience. (The exhibition included seven of Robert Frank's photographs.)

During the twentieth century, photographers such as Paul Strand and Edward Weston captured shapes and forms in a new way, and Walker Evans and Dorothea Lange traveled the country during the Great Depression for the Farm Security Administration, documenting the lives of sharecroppers, migrant families, and other downtrodden people. Out West, Ansel Adams was breaking new ground with his photographs of the American landscape, including Yosemite National Park and other locations throughout the Sierra Nevada.

As the legacy of these pioneers of American photography worked its way into our culture, the prevalence of photographs as both an artistic and commercial medium expanded throughout all forms of media, from print to films and television and finally to the Internet. Today, everybody who owns a smartphone has a portable lens on the world, and because of social media, each of us has the ability to instantly publish a photographic record of the subjects that most interest us, from landscapes to street scenes to our families and pets.

Unlike film, a still photograph is not a temporal medium. As such, the same image can be viewed over and over again in real time. Because of this, many iconic photographs have become embedded in our communal awareness, such as the view of Earth from the moon, or the raising of the American flag on Iwo Jima. According to Ansel Adams, photographs are usually looked at, but they are seldom looked into. It is my hope that with this book, you will not only look at the photographs, but that you will look *into* them, and that by so doing, you will gain an appreciation and affection for life in America.

Appendix

★★★★

2 BARN WITH AMERICAN FLAG. On the day before Flag Day, I drove down Interstate 89 in Vermont and exited on State Route 107. About six miles past Bethel, along the White River, I spotted a barn with an American flag draped along its side.

17 THELMA & LOUISE. After driving from Bethel to Rutland, I saw this little restaurant as I entered town on U.S. Route 4. I loved the orange sign and the elegant charm of the white building that housed this eatery.

18 INTERNATIONAL HARVESTER TRUCK. As I continued along Route 4 west of Rutland, I drove through Fort Ann, just east of Lake George. Heading west on State Route 149, I noticed a rusty International Harvester truck sitting in an open field by the side of the road.

19 FORD FALCON. Just behind the International Harvester truck and to the left of the billboards, I saw a 1962 Ford Falcon station wagon. The "Garage Sale" sign in the front window is ironic.

21 PROUD TO BE AN AMERICAN. Continuing on my drive, I reached State Route 30 heading south toward Roxbury and nature writer John Burroughs' family home called Woodchuck Lodge. About twenty miles outside of Roxbury, in the hamlet of Fultonham, I spotted an inflatable Uncle Sam holding a banner that reads, "Proud To Be An American."

22 WOODCHUCK LODGE. Woodchuck Lodge was the summer retreat of naturalist and writer John Burroughs from 1911 to 1920, to which he would bring his son's young family. In this image, the banner "Faith Hope Charity" over the mantel is a key feature for me, as is Burroughs' desk, which his son made and features items that he used, such as a pair of eyeglasses, a letter opener, and a stone paperweight.

23 SLABSIDES. Writer and naturalist John Burroughs built the Slabsides cabin in 1895, a National Historic Landmark, and spent a great deal of time there writing, entertaining thousands of his readers, and studying the birds and animals in the area. The cabin looks much as it did when Burroughs was last there in the fall of 1920—sublime with the colorful autumn leaves and the sun reflecting off of the slab bark siding.

25 PATRIOTIC FENCE. Sometimes you don't need an American flag for a photograph to qualify as Americana. Here, a homeowner has added the colors of red and blue to his white picket fence.

26 TIME WARNER CENTER. In this photograph, we can see visitors entering the building; a line of yellow taxicabs; and the statue of Christopher Columbus atop a rostral column. The city beckons us in the background. We also have the words "Time Warner Center" above the entrance.

27 BUSKERS. On the other side of Columbus Circle from the Time Warner Center, I observed these enterprising musicians.

28 CENTRAL PARK SNACK STOP. Just outside the American Museum of Natural History, I noticed this food cart, which interested me because the vendor was nowhere to be seen.

29 IMAGINE MOSAIC. Central Park features a landscaped area called Strawberry Fields, in memory of John Lennon, who made New York City his adopted home. The *Imagine* mosaic shown here is visited by countless tourists, who sometimes stand or even lie down on the mosaic itself. I thought the deferential way that this woman was photographing the mosaic made a charming image.

30 BROADWAY AND 54TH STREET. Here, we have the Broadway street signage in the foreground; the *Sports Illustrated* bikini girl in the background; and, on the right, a banner that says, "Face your fears. Live your dreams." There is also an American flag in the background, on the right side of the image.

31 FOOD VENDOR WITH PIGEONS. This photograph has two American flags, one on the bus at left and a larger one above the food vendor who is feeding the pigeons. The woman on the mural on the right looks as if she were a real person, blending in with the other pedestrians.

32 ICE CREAM TRUCK. The decisive moment in this image is when the girl on the right glances back at me. She seems less annoyed than curious.

33 NATHAN'S. In this photograph, I was fortunate to have an interesting sky with its diverse clouds, adding texture to the image. The green, yellow, and red colors of the signage also contribute to the composition.

34 PETE'S CLAM STOP. There is an enormous amount of detail in this photograph. You can almost feel the wind that is blowing the flags around, and you can tell by the wet pavement that it has recently rained.

35 CHACHAS CHICKEN. With the famous Cylone roller coaster in the background, the Chachas Chicken stand provides an effective foreground that draws the viewer's eye into the image.

37 CONEY ISLAND TERMINAL. This New York City Subway station was built in 1919, and the view of this magnificent structure, with its American flag flying proudly, seems to harken back to a simpler, more innocent age, when Coney Island was the premiere summer resort destination for the New York metropolitan area.

38 NATIONAL ANTHEM. On this day, the New York Yankees were playing the Washington Nationals, and during the national anthem, an electronic American flag banner was displayed.

39 MARIANO RIVERA. The Yankees had a 5-3 lead going into the ninth inning, when the greatest relief pitcher of all time, Mariano Rivera, entered the game and proceeded to get a groundout, a strikeout, and another groundout, to record his fifteenth save of the season.

41 BARN. On my return to Vermont from New York, I took Interstate 91 through Hartford, Connecticut and Springfield, Massachusetts and on into the state of Vermont. When I exited the Interstate in the village of Bellows Falls, I saw this colorful barn, with an American flag flying beside it.

43 FOOD TRAILER. An hour and fifteen minutes after photographing the Bellow Falls barn, I was driving up U.S. Route 2 in Montpelier when I saw this food trailer.

44 LUV SHAK. The words "Luv Shak" are painted on the front of this structure, which was just down Lightening Ridge Road from my mother's summer home in Calais, where I was visiting at the time.

45 EAST MONTPELIER POST OFFICE. Less than a half hour after photographing the Luv Shak, I photographed former postmaster Jim Hudson entering the East Montpelier Post Office on U.S. Route 2.

47 MONTPELIER FROM CORSE STREET. Later that day, I photographed Montpelier from above. This image shows a small American city, complete with a church steeple and a Caterpillar steam shovel.

49 WOODSHED THEATRE. On my way home on the same day, I visited the Morse Farm Maple Sugarworks, where I photographed the Woodshed Theater, with its walls made out of sugar maple planks. Inside, you can sit on maple stump seats and watch a video about how maple syrup is made.

50 MARTIN COVERED BRIDGE WITH 1909 EMF MODEL 30. Two days later, I watched a series of antique cars driving on U.S. Route 2 in Marshfield, all of which were participating in the New England Brass & Gas Tour. Here, a 1909 EMF Model 30 is parked in front of the Martin Covered Bridge, which had been restored and placed in its original location spanning the Winooski River. The woman at right, dressed in a period costume and sporting a wide sun hat, adds a vintage feel to the photograph (see page 70).

51 DON'T BE GOOFY. Just up the road from the Martin Covered Bridge, I noticed this "Goofy" sign. I positioned myself behind the sign and took a number of photographs of the antique automobiles that were traveling south during the Brass & Gas Tour. Finally, I got a car just where I wanted it to be.

53 BARN. The following day, driving along Center Road toward Adamant, I passed this old barn. The cloud formations were so beautiful, and the date "1908" painted on the cupola adds a historic feeling to the image.

54 FOOD VENDOR. This enterprising man had set up a roadside stand on U.S. Route 2. I took some photographs of the food stand without the vendor, and then a few with the vendor behind the counter, but the image of the vendor reading the newspaper was the most interesting of all.

55 GOLF CLUBS. The next day, driving through East Montpelier, I saw these golf clubs for sale in the driveway of a private home.

57 FARMERS DINER. The day after that, I had breakfast at this diner in Quechee before visiting the Vermont Institute of Natural Science. The diner was housed in a Worcester Diner Car #787, built in 1946 by the Worcester Lunch Car Company.

58 RIVERBEND COUNTRY STORE. On the way home from Quechee, I finally got the photograph of the Riverbend Country Store that I had been waiting for, primarily because of the dark, foreboding clouds that rise up behind the building, contrasted with the afternoon sunlight on the south-facing side of the structure.

59 BRAGG FARM AND AMERICAN FLAG 76. I had to take a number of photographs before the wind blew this flag into place. The texture of the clouds adds a great deal to this image.

61 COCA-COLA TRUCK AND CITY HALL. This photograph was taken just before Independence Day, so hence the buntings on the fire station. But the subject of the image is not really the city hall or the fire station, but the Coca-Cola truck.

63 GIRLS ON BRIDGE. Montpelier has a number of old bridges that span the Winooski River. Here, we find two girls with their smartphones on the Langdon Street Bridge. Can you tell that it's summertime?

65 WOODPILE AND AMERICAN FLAG. Just down Lightening Ridge Road from my mother's summer home in Calais, I saw this woodshed with an American flag, sitting in a neighbor's front yard. Even though it was July, these folks had plenty of wood.

66 BLACKTHORNE FORGE. On a drive to Marshfield on U.S. Route 2, I stopped to photograph this old building, which had an interesting assortment of objects on its road-facing side, including a dragonfly, some old wagon wheels, and the signage.

67 PEACH ETIQUETTE. At the Adamant Co-op, the notice about the peaches makes a nice addition to the scene, especially the request to return the unused crate "as soon as possible."

69 BARN AND WILLYS JEEP STATION WAGON. This magnificent barn with an old Willys Jeep Station Wagon out front caught my eye one day as I drove up U.S. Route 2 in Marshfield. I'll bet that jeep has some stories to tell about the places it's been.

70 MARTIN COVERED BRIDGE. Just up the road from the barn, I saw the Martin Covered Bridge, which had been picked up and placed on blocks on the riverbank until it could be restored (see page 50).

71 NO WAR. When I took this photograph, the Iraq War was going on and a resident of Plainfield had decided to make a sign protesting that war.

72 I EAT FLESH. A graffiti artist made this statement on the Langdon Street Bridge, and I couldn't resist taking a photograph of the words.

73 SQUASH AND PUMPKIN DISPLAY. This photograph of a squash and pumpkin display at the Billings Farm & Museum was fittingly taken in October. The two people sitting on the bench in the background add an extra element to the image.

75 MOULTON PINK HOUSE. In the 1890s, Mormon homesteaders established a farming community in the Teton Valley of Wyoming. One of these settlers, John Moulton, arrived in 1907, and in 1934, he and his wife Alma built this house, the stucco exterior of which they painted pink.

77 CUNNINGHAM CABIN. Homesteader John Pierce Cunningham built this cabin in 1888, and he lived in it until 1895. The cabin, along with the Moulton house, is now part of the Grand Teton National Park, and you can see part of the Teton Range in the background.

78 BOY AND AMERICAN FLAGS. The Waves of Flags display at Pepperdine University is installed each year to commemor.ate the September 11 attacks of 2001. The flags remain standing for about two weeks. In this image, the challenge was to capture the running boy between the rows of flags and to make sure that he was not hidden by the tree.

79 JEWISH WAR VETERANS. The Jewish War Veterans of the United States of America is the oldest veterans organization in the country. On this Memorial Day at the Los Angeles National Cemetery, I photographed members of Jewish War Veterans Friendship Post 617 from Culver City.

80 JOHN MCCAIN, TRUE AMERICAN HERO. I took this photograph the day before the 2008 presidential election. John McCain lost his bid to become President of the United States, but that doesn't make him any less of a hero.

81 CHEVY NOVA. This image of a Chevy Nova, parked in front of a green hedge, is an homage to earlier Americana photographs.

83 ROLLER COASTER AT TWILIGHT. One evening at twilight on the Santa Monica Pier, I strolled around the amusement park and captured this moving roller coast at the top of the frame. It's a blur of fun on a summer evening.

84 HAPPY 4TH. It was well after the Fourth of July, but this front yard overlooking the Pacific Ocean still had its figures on display.

85 LIMOUSINE. Along with the palm trees, red building, and blue sky, this white limousine makes a compelling subject.

86 GOD BLESS THE GIPPER. The day after President Ronald Reagan passed away, I went down to the mortuary in Santa Monica where members of the public had placed American flags, signs, and even a jar of jelly beans on the grass.

87 IT'S MORNING IN AMERICA. A Toyota Tacoma pickup truck is parked in front of an abandoned Ford dealership, the interior of which is being emptied into the dumpster at left. On the exterior wall, President Ronald Reagan declares, "It's Morning in America."

89 BEVERLY HILLS HOTEL. This iconic pink building, framed by the palm trees, could only be the Beverly Hills Hotel.

91 GUITAR SCULPTURES. These guitar sculptures on Sunset Boulevard at the west end of the Sunset Strip were part of the 2012 Gibson GuitarTown on the Sunset Strip public art project. The guitar on the left, titled "There's Something Happening Here," is a tribute to Buffalo Springfield; and the guitar on the right, titled "Roadhouse Blues," is a tribute to the Doors.

93 FRENCH CREPE STAND. There is nothing better than having a crepe on the Champs-Élysées in Paris, but if you can't be in Paris, you can have a crepe at the Farmers Market in Los Angeles.

94 CLINT EASTWOOD TILE. On this day, I visited the Autry National Center to see the exhibition entitled "Yosemite: Art of an American Icon," and on the patio I spotted this Clint Eastwood tile.

95 FIRE DANGER SIGN. I have photographed many of these "Fire Danger" signs in the Los Angeles area, from Burbank to Malibu. This image serves as a reminder of how important fire prevention is in Southern California, even when the grass is green.

97 QUEEN MARY. I went to the Queen Mary to see an exhibition of photographs, and as I was leaving, I looked back and took my own photograph of the ocean liner.

99 VENDOR AT ANGEL STADIUM. The atmosphere at Angel Stadium is festive, and you can see this in the face of the vendor. In this image, Los Angeles Angels of Anaheim pitcher Jered Weaver delivers the ball to Los Angeles Dodger Aaron Miles. The Angels beat the Dodgers and their pitcher Clayton Kershaw by a score of 7-1.

101 LOMPOC VALLEY CHAMBER OF COMMERCE. This building, constructed in 1892, is one of Lompoc's oldest historical landmarks. The Vintners' Festival sign on the left side of the building is appropriate since Lompoc is located in Santa Barbara County, which is known for its wineries.

102 SELF-SERVE. On my way to Nojoqui Falls County Park, just north of Santa Barbara, I stopped at this roadside stand which featured organic produce and an honor system for paying.

103 MANGOS. Driving east on State Route 126 from the Pacific Coast, you pass by a number of roadside stands where you can purchase strawberries, oranges, and other fruits, including mangos.

105 BOOTS. This western wear outfitter was well-stocked with anything a horseman would need, including cowboy hats and belt buckles, but I liked the boots the best.

106 TURQUOISE TRAILER. Turquoise is one of my favorite colors, so when I saw this trailer, I had to stop and photograph it from all angles.

107 SUPPORT OUR TROOPS. I was driving north on State Route 41 on my way to Yosemite National Park when I saw this red, white, and blue painted barn on the right side of the road. Since it was morning and I was shooting into the sun, the results were terrible. A few days later, on my way home in the mid-afternoon, the light was perfect and I was able to capture this image.

108 TAKE MY CAMERA. The woman at the center of this photograph is giving her camera to the man in the black shirt so that he can take her picture with the group, but with her own camera. She sat back down, and he did just that.

109 VIEW FROM WAWONA TUNNEL. On this visit, I decided to walk back into the Wawona Tunnel and photograph the Yosemite Valley with the walls and roof of the tunnel framing the scene. The woman at right in the background has her arms held high as she is being photographed with Vernal Fall and the rest of the valley behind her.

111 RICHFIELD GAS STATION. After spending three days in Sequoia National Park, I left Three Rivers and drove on Sierra Drive around Kaweah Lake. At the intersection of Sierra Drive and Avenue 330 in Lemon Cove, I noticed this abandoned gas station.

112 PURE FRESH HONEY. On another visit to Three Rivers, I spotted this fiberglass bull in front of the general store. Mounted on a trailer, it had been used to sell barbecued food to visitors along the Kaweah River.

113 WE SUPPORT U. I saw this woman sitting at a table in Pacific Grove promoting the passage of Measure U, which would increase the local sales tax by one percent in order to pay for police officers, firefighters, and the fixing of potholes, among other things. The measure passed.

115 FLIGHT ATTENDANT UNIFORMS. These flight attendant uniforms were part of the *Painted Wings: A History of Airline Identity* exhibition which highlighted how airlines use identity to establish brand awareness and create perceptions of a unique passenger experience.

116 FRUIT AND NUT STAND. This vendor sold a variety of fruits and nuts, including almonds, cashews, and, as the sign says, macadamias and pistachios. Some oranges, lemons, and figs were also for sale.

117 WAKE UP AND SMELL THE COFFEE. I had driven north all day from Los Angeles, and it was late in the afternoon. As I approached my hotel on the side of U.S. Route 101, I spotted a rainbow arcing down in front of a hill. I also saw an advertisement for a local coffee shop, painted on the roof of a barn. Note the sun highlighting a fleet of Coca-Cola trucks at the local bottling plant.

119 SMILE. When you consider how many United States Navy officers and crewmen were killed aboard the USS Arizona at Pearl Harbor, it seems as if these girls could perhaps be in a bit more solemn mood.

120 MAGOO'S BURGERS. After hiking up to the summit of Diamond Head, I arrived back at the parking area at the base of the crater. Here, I took a photograph of this bus that had been converted into a hamburger stand.

121 HIDING. While walking down Kalakaua Avenue at Waikiki Beach, I glanced over and saw these four legs at a jewelry vendor along the sidewalk.

122 HYGIENIC STORE. Heading north on the Kamehameha Highway, I spotted this orange building on the left side of the road, with the fog wafting above the structure.

123 SEE OLD HAWAII. This old ticket booth sitting in a front lawn in a residential area on Kuamoo Road had been used at a nearby tourist attraction called Kamokila Ancient Hawaiian Village, which is located in the Wailua River Valley nearby.

125 SURFBOARDS AND TRAFFIC CONE. I was a block away from the beach at Hanalei Bay when I saw a row of surfboards attached to a wood fence. The orange traffic cone adds a nice touch to this photograph.

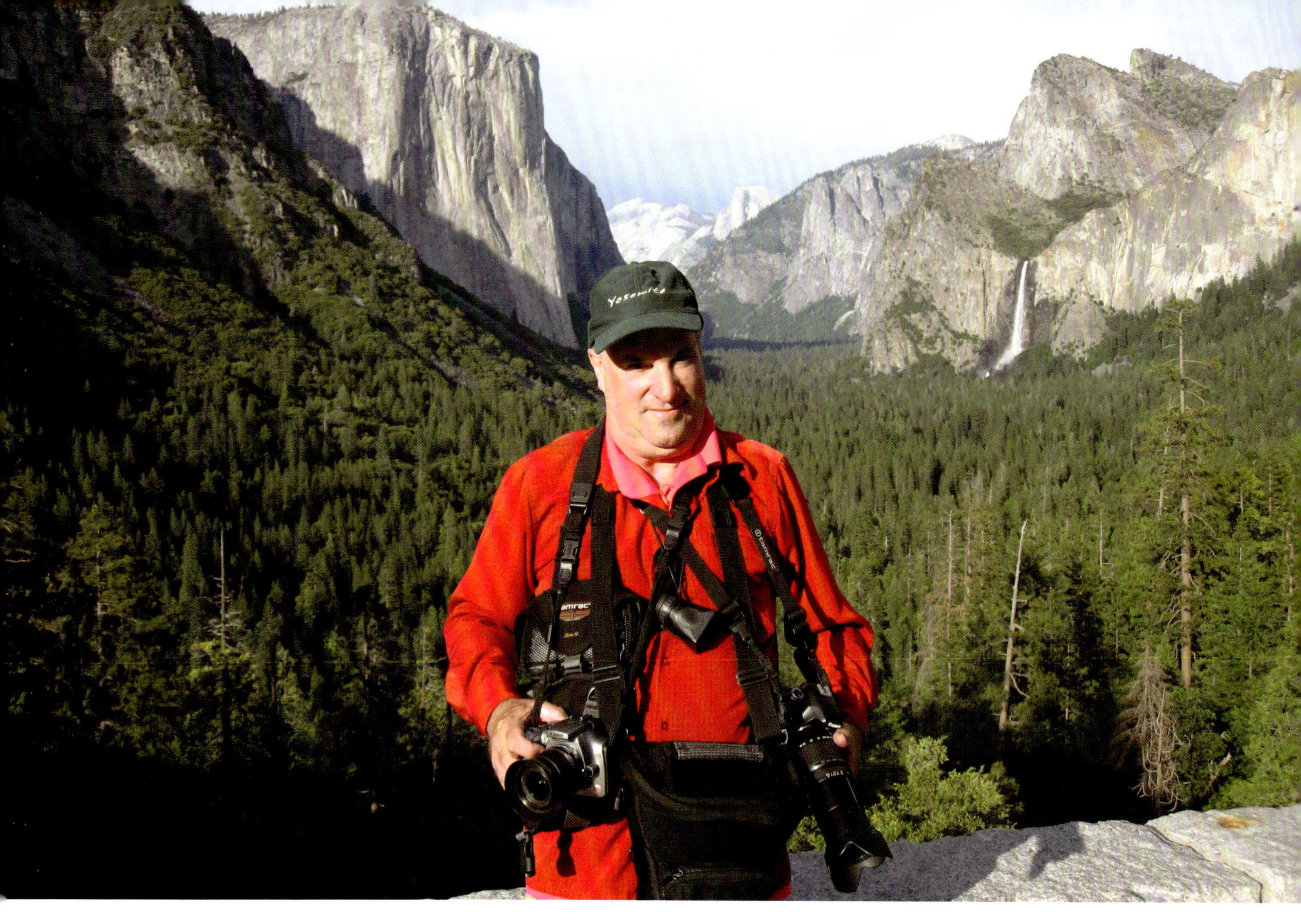

MATHEW TEKULSKY, Tunnel View, Yosemite National Park, 5/29/09.
Author photograph by Patience Fish Tekulsky.

About the Author

★★★★

Mathew Tekulsky is the author of *Galapagos Birds: A Photographic Voyage; Backyard Bird Photography;* and *The Art of Hummingbird Gardening,*, among other books. He is also the author of "The Birdman of Bel Air," a column on NationalGeographic.com that featured essays and photographs about his birding experiences. His bird photographs have been published in field guides such as the *National Geographic Field Guide to Birds: California* and the *Smithsonian Field Guide to the Birds of North America*. His bird photographs have also been exhibited in galleries and museums, including the Roger Tory Peterson Institute of Natural History.

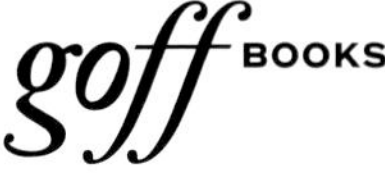

Published by Goff Books, an Imprint of ORO Editions.
Executive publisher: Gordon Goff.

www.goffbooks.com
info@goffbooks.com

Graphic Design: Rita Sowins / Sowins Design
Goff Books Project Coordinator: Kirby Anderson

10 9 8 7 6 5 4 3 2 1 First Edition

Library of Congress data available upon request. World Rights: available.

ISBN: 978-1-951541-57-6

Color separations and printing: ORO Group Ltd.
Printed in China.

International distribution: www.goffbooks.com/distribution

ORO Editions makes a continuous effort to minimize the overall carbon footprint of its publications. As part of this goal, ORO Editions, in association with Global ReLeaf, arranges to plant trees to replace those used in the manufacturing of the paper produced for its books. Global ReLeaf is an international campaign run by American Forests, one of the world's oldest nonprofit conservation organizations. Global ReLeaf is American Forests' education and action program that helps individuals, organizations, agencies, and corporations improve the local and global environment by planting and caring for trees.